China's Economic Diplomacy (2002-12)

Zhang Xiaotong, Wang Hongyu et al

Published by
ACA Publishing Ltd.
University House
11-13 Lower Grosvenor Place,
London SW1W 0EX, UK
Tel: +44 (0)20 7834 7676
Fax: +44 (0)20 7973 0076
E-mail: info@alaincharlesasia.com
Web:www.alaincharlesasia.com
Beijing Office
Tel: +86(0)10 8472 1250
Fax: +86(0)10 5885 0639
Authors:
Zhang Xiaotong, Executive Director of
Wuhan University Center of Economic Diplomacy
Wang Hongyu, Executive Director of the Centre for Economic Diplomacy
at the School of International Relations (SIR) at University
of International Business and Economics
Editors:
David Lammie, Martin Savery and Zhao Daxin
Publisher:
ACA Publishing in association with China National
Publications Import and Export (Group) Corporation (CNPIEC)
and Beijing T-Win Consulting Co Ltd

Published by ACA Publishing Ltd in April 2015

ALL RIGHTS RESERVED. NO PART OF THIS
PUBLICATION MAY BE REPRODUCED IN MATERIAL FORM,
BY ANY MEANS, WHETHER GRAPHIC,
ELECTRONIC, MECHANICAL OR OTHER, INCLUDING
PHOTOCOPYING OR INFORMATION STORAGE, IN
WHOLE OR IN PART, AND MAY NOT BE USED TO PREPARE
OTHER PUBLICATIONS WITHOUT WRITTEN
PERMISSION FROM THE PUBLISHER.

The greatest care has been taken to ensure accuracy but the
publisher can accept no responsibility for errors or omissions, or
for any liability occasioned by relying on its content.

ISBN 978-0-9927625-7-5

A catalogue record for China's Economic Diplomacy: The PRC's
Growing International Influence in the 21st Century is available from
the National Bibliographic Service of the British Library.

Contents

Foreword (Zhang Xiaotong)..5

Chapter 1 – A review – economic diplomacy of three generations of Communist leaders since the founding of the PRC (Zhou Yongsheng)

Section 1 Economic diplomacy in the era of Mao Zedong..................9

Section 2 Economic diplomacy in the era of Deng Xiaoping.............16

Section 3 Economic diplomacy in the era of Jiang Zemin..................23

Chapter 2 – The actors of China's economic diplomacy

Section 1 Main actors of China's economic diplomacy (Li Wei).........32

Section 2 New actors of China's economic diplomacy (Su Liang)......51

Chapter 3 – Economic diplomacy in different policy fields

Section 1 Financial diplomacy (Li Wei)..70

Section 2 Energy diplomacy (Wang Hongyu, Wu Junyi)....................90

Section 3 Oil diplomacy (Li Jing, Liu Xing).......................................102

Section 4 Environmental diplomacy (Wang Hongyu, Yan Zhanyu)...112

Section 5 Aid diplomacy (Wang Hongyu, Du Xiaona)......................121

Chapter 4 – China's economic diplomacy in international organisations

Section 1 WTO (Chai Xiaolin)..131

Section 2 IMF (Wang Hongyu, Yuan Miao).......................................141

Section 3 The World Bank (Wang Hongyu, Liu Danyang)................149

Chapter 5 – China's economic diplomacy towards major countries and regions

Section 1 China's economic diplomacy towards the US (Zhou Wenxing, Zhang Chengxin)..159

Section 2 China's economic diplomacy towards the EU (Wang Hongyu, Li Hongjia)....166

Section 3 China's economic diplomacy towards Japan (Ge Jianting)................180

Section 4 China's economic diplomacy towards BRICS (Wang Hongyu, Li Yiheng)......184

Section5 China's economic diplomacy towards Central Asia States (Marlen Belgibayev)..................193

Section 6 China's economic diplomacy towards Southeast Asia (Zhang Xiaotong, Tan Xiangning)..................201

Section 7 Caribbean-China economic relations (Annita Montoute)..................208

Chapter 6 – Prospects for China's economic diplomacy in the new century (Wang Hongyu)..................219

About the authors..................231

Foreword

A research agenda for China's economic diplomacy

By Zhang Xiaotong

Economic diplomacy can be traced back several thousand years. In China's Warring States Period (475-221BC), Su Qin, one of the most famous political strategists of the time, managed to persuade six warring states to forge an alliance against the most powerful state, Qin (秦), by offering gifts and financial incentives. In *The History of the Peloponnesian War*, Thucydides mentions a trade boycott imposed by Athens against Sparta's ally Megara. It was an act of economic diplomacy. In modern times, the first consuls of Spain, France, Britain and others, and even of the old city states of Geneva and Venice, were no more than trade delegates for their countries, paid and protected by the sovereigns of their day. They were economic diplomats in early times.

In contemporary times, there are more cases of economic diplomacy, as a result of rivalry between powers and the rise of regionalism and globalisation. The Marshall Plan after the Second World War was a large-scale operation of economic diplomacy, which revitalised Europe and strengthened the transatlantic relationship. The great integration adventure of the European Coal and Steel Community and later the European Community were perfect examples of economic diplomacy, using economic means for the purposes of political reconciliation and long-lasting peace in Europe, an unprecedented accomplishment in human history.

China is a great user of economic diplomacy. Economic means have been used for political and strategic purposes, or the other way round. As diplomacy is a synthesis of a leader's characteristics, bureaucratic organisation and a nation's comprehensive strength, economic diplomacy is no exception. China's economic diplomacy strategies varied under different leaderships from Mao Zedong to Deng Xiaoping, Jiang Zemin, Hu Jintao and Xi Jinping. China's economic diplomacy is a gold mine for academic research.

Economic diplomacy is not a secret garden for diplomats and policy-makers only. It is equally relevant in public affairs and events, in which everybody is a stakeholder; for example, it is prominent in anti-dumping cases, where thousands of jobs are at stake. But in reality, there is a dislocation between policy-makers' actions and scholarly research.

This book provides a panoramic view of China's economic diplomacy during President Hu Jintao's two terms (2002-12). It is aimed not only at scholars and professionals, but also at a general readership, since we believe that economic diplomacy touches on many interests. It has become a subject of general debate and not one that is the preserve of those in ivory towers or among political and intellectual elites. China also provides a case study in economic diplomacy in general and, in particular, economic diplomacy at a time when the global balance of economic influence is shifting. This book serves as a tour guide, leading you through the labyrinth of the interplay between economics, politics and diplomacy. But first, what is economic diplomacy?

Definition of economic diplomacy

The definition of economic diplomacy must be one of the most confusing concepts for students of international relations and diplomacy.

The key lies in how to define the word "economic" in "economic diplomacy". There are at least three broad definitions. The first sees economic diplomacy as centred on the use of economic instruments and negotiations to further economic objectives, such as a stable financial system, open trade, development, economic and/or sustainable growth and employment. Thus the business of economic diplomacy concerns policy areas such as international financial policy, trade, investment and policies related to these subjects such as on the environment.[1]

A second use of the term economic diplomacy might be the use of economic instruments in the pursuit of foreign policy objectives. Here, a central theme in policy and in the literature has been the use of economic sanctions.

Related to this use of economic instruments in the pursuit of wider political objectives is economic diplomacy in the form of "economic statecraft".[2] This term is more often used in American foreign policy parlance than in a European or a Chinese one. In China, the term "economic diplomacy" ("Jingji Waijiao, 经济外交") is much more commonly used than "economic statecraft". One of the reasons is that it is difficult to translate the word "statecraft". In American parlance, "statecraft" can be defined as the use of instruments at the disposal of central political

---

[1] Bayne and Woolcock, *The New Economic Diplomacy: Decision-making and Negotiation in International Economic Relations* (Surrey: Ashgate, 3rd edition, 2011), p. 1.
[2] Mastanduno, M. "Economic Statecraft" in Steve Smith, Amelia Hadfiled and Tim Dunne, eds., *"Foreign Policy: Theories, Actors, Cases"*, second edition, Oxford University Press, 2012, p. 204.

authorities to serve foreign policy objectives. In China, the translation for "statecraft" would be "Zhi Guoshu, 治国术", which basically means the art or science of governing a state. In China's context, "statecraft" serves more for domestic policy purposes than for foreign policy purposes.

Finally, some would include in economic diplomacy the activities of the state or state agents in search of business in the form of export contracts or attracting foreign investment. Others have sought to differentiate economic diplomacy in shaping the framework within which trade, investment and finance takes place, from this more micro commercial activity[3].

In this book, "economic diplomacy" refers to using economic means for foreign policy objectives, or using economic or diplomatic means for economic purposes. It is such a broad definition that it covers the American definition of economic statecraft and the traditional European or Chinese definition of economic diplomacy. In this volume "economic diplomacy" is seen not necessarily as serving only foreign policy objectives. It could equally serve economic purposes. There is no division between what has been traditionally defined as "high politics" and "low politics".

Economic diplomacy as defined in this volume goes beyond individual or one-off episodes in negotiation. It could equally refer to the formulation and execution of a strategy over a longer period of time. Taking the Marshall Plan as an example of economic diplomacy, it involved several years of strategy formulation and implementation as well as many rounds of negotiations back and forth between the US and Europe.

Uniqueness of China's economic diplomacy

Each country's experience of economic diplomacy is unique. China provides one of the world's most fertile grounds for research in economic diplomacy. First of all, it is equipped with both economic and political/strategic resources for conducting economic diplomacy. That is to say, as the world's second largest economy and an influential international actor, China has the potential to use either political/strategic or even military tools for economic purposes, or use economic tools for foreign policy objectives. Not many countries have such a luxury.

Second, China's economic and political/military strengths are imbalanced. In a global comparative perspective, China's power largely rests on its economic

---

[3] Bayne and Woolcock, *The New Economic Diplomacy: Decision-making and Negotiation in International Economic Relations* 2012

strength. Its military strength, though rising quickly, does not match its economic strength. In terms of political influence, China has not yet developed a global ambition. Keeping a low-profile in international affairs still dominated China's foreign policy thinking during Hu Jintao's time. Given such constraining factors, China's leaders and diplomats had to be masters of economic diplomacy, using economic resources for increasing political influence.

Third, China has a unique decision-making system, which is like a funnel open to many influences, ranging from China's political system to cultural traditions and history.

Last but not least, the overriding purpose of China's economic diplomacy during Hu Jintao's time was economic development, and this remains true today. Although China's economy is large, its GDP per capita is still low. The Chinese authorities believe that the top priority for China's foreign policy remains economic growth. This theme of China's statecraft has been largely consistent from 1978 when Deng Xiaoping refocused the country's attention on economic development through reform and opening up. This theme has yet to change.

Structure of the book

Chapter 1 provides a historical overview of the economic diplomacy designed and led by three generations of Chinese leaders – Mao Zedong, Deng Xiaoping and Jiang Zemin from 1949 to 2002, before President Hu Jintao came into office.

Chapter 2 identifies the main actors, including emerging ones such as local governments, companies, chambers of commerce and think tanks in China's economic diplomacy. It provides a unique insight into the policy- and decision-making processes.

Chapter 3 focuses on sectoral economic diplomacy, namely fiscal and financial diplomacy, energy diplomacy, oil diplomacy, environmental diplomacy and aid diplomacy.

Chapter 4 covers China's economic diplomacy in various international organisations such as the WTO, IMF and World Bank.

Chapter 5 covers China's economic diplomacy in various countries and regions.

Chapter 6, as the conclusion chapter, summarises the past 10 years of China's economic diplomacy and looks into the next decade.

Chapter 1

A review — economic diplomacy of three generations of Communist leaders since the founding of the PRC

Section 1 Economic diplomacy in the era of Mao Zedong

I. "Leaning to One Side" wins the assistance of the Soviet Union

After the founding of the New China, the country followed a political and diplomatic line characterised by "leaning to one side". Politically and diplomatically, China took the Soviet Union as its model and an ally in pressing ahead with the construction of a socialist society. The establishment of this policy caused controversy. At the time, China was faced with three choices: first, leaning to the Soviet Union and aligning with other socialist countries; second, siding with the US and aligning with capitalist countries; third, taking the "Third Way", being impartial to any side.

Leaning to the US side was hardly an easy matter for the Communist Party of China (CPC). For one thing, as Washington all along supported Chiang Kai-shek's Kuomintang regime, the CPC, while implementing its foreign policies, kept a wary eye on American policies. For another, though the US had high-level contacts with the CPC, it had no intention of propping it up. First, as the two sides completely differed from each other in ideology, the ideological confrontation was still there. Second, the US was not willing to have an active engagement with the CPC for fear that it might elevate the latter's status. Third, though the US was fed up with Chiang Kai-shek regime, the two sides still had deep bilateral relations, and backed one another. Fourth, no high-level communication channel was available between the CPC and the US though some people from the US State Department agreed to strengthen ties with the CPC, they were only low-ranking government officials taking a pragmatic attitude.

For the CPC, following the Third Way was no more than a romantic option because all countries that took the road were weak. This indicated that such a model was not sufficiently mature. Besides, taking this way meant giving up the existing Soviet model and exploring an unfamiliar road, which was unacceptable to Mao Zedong and other Chinese leaders.

Considering all this, it was inevitable that China would pursue its policy of "leaning to the Soviet Union". The reasons can be summarised as follows: (1) As the revolutionary cause of the Communist Party of China had long won the help and support of the Soviet Union, it had an inseparable relationship with the Communist Party of the Soviet Union (CPSU). (2) The CPC and the CPSU shared a smooth channel for communication and information transmission. (3) After the War of Resistance against Japan, China got help and support from the Soviet Union both in China taking control of its northeast region and in planning and preparing for the founding of the New China. (4) The CPSU had a clear and definite financial assistance scheme for China. This made China realise that, with assistance from the CPSU, it would develop the country into a rising socialist country.

On 21 June 1949, a CPC Central Committee delegation led by Liu Shaoqi paid a state visit to the Soviet Union. During the visit, China requested the Soviet Union to provide it with a US$300m loan along with the dispatch of Soviet experts on industries such as railways, electric power, iron and steel, coal mines, kerosene and military affairs to help China with its research programmes. The Soviet Union broadly consented to China's demands. This was the beginning of the Soviet Union's assistance to China in what became known as "156 aid projects".

On 16 December 1949, Mao Zedong led a CPC Central Committee delegation to visit the Soviet Union. This was not only Mao's first significant diplomatic move but also his first visit abroad. The visit aimed to form an alliance with the socialist Soviet Union, and to confirm loan and aid projects to China. The visit resulted in the signing of the *Agreement on Soviet Union Providing Loans to the People's Republic of China*. It stipulated that the Soviet Union provide China a loan of US$300m on favourable terms with an annual interest rate of 1% and that the money would be used to provide China with the first 50 large-scale projects of the 156 industrial projects, including coal and electric power plants, basic industrial projects such as steel, nonferrous metals and chemical engineering and national defence projects. In August 1952, Premier Zhou Enlai led a delegation to the Soviet Union, making detailed and exhaustive research on each project. This visit lasted eight months. On 15 May 1953 both sides signed the *Agreement on the Soviet Government's Assistance to the Chinese Government in Developing China's National Economy*. The aid projects prescribed in this agreement were the second batch of the 156 projects. The Soviet Union promised to help China build and rebuild 91 huge engineering projects from 1953 to 1959. The agreement also stipulated that 50 projects involving 141 enterprises signed in 1950 would come into operation from 1953 to 1959. In October 1954, President Khrushchev led a delegation to attend the celebration of the fifth anniversary of the founding of the People's Republic of China. Both sides signed an agreement stating that the Soviet government was to help the Chinese government build 15 new industrial enterprises which formed the third batch of the 156 projects. In March 1955, a new agreement was concluded between the two sides, including 16 construction projects covering military engineering, shipbuilding and raw materials. A verbal agreement was added, containing two more projects. By then, 174 aid projects were agreed upon. Finally, after repeated examination and adjustment, the 174 projects were reduced and fixed at 154. However, as both sides had previously announced a plan of 156 engineering projects, the whole scheme was still called "156 projects". These 156 projects formed a crucial part of China's first five-year plan (1953-57) for the development of the national economy.

As China was determined to form an alliance with the Soviet Union, the latter provided aid for the construction of the 154 projects, which laid a foundation for the industrial development of the New China. Without these projects, China's industry would not have undergone rapid progress. Thanks to its political and diplomatic policy of "leaning to one side" and forming a staunch political alliance with the Soviet Union, China won economic aid from the Soviet Union. It was also thanks to this approach that China laid a foundation for its industrial development and developed its national economy in a rapid and sound way. In a sense, "leaning to one side" was New China's first major strategy of economic diplomacy, namely, forming a political alliance with the Soviet Union in exchange for economic aid, which the New China badly needed.

II. Assisting developing countries in Asia, Africa and Latin America

After the founding of the New China, Mao Zedong and other leaders of the CPC brimmed with vigour and vitality, believing that communist societies would be realised across the whole world. Therefore, China, a socialist country, should try its best to carry forward the spirit of internationalism to support poverty-stricken and backward countries that were still plagued with untold sufferings. China secured great achievements during the early stages of its socialist construction, which laid the foundation for the country to aid other developing nations. In addition, during the reign of Mao Zedong, Mao himself and the CPC Central Committee enjoyed a lofty status among the Chinese people. As a result, decisions by the Central Committee and the personal opinions of Mao were more effective than law. For this reason, the policy of lending large-scale aid to foreign countries proposed by Mao Zedong, Zhou Enlai and other Chinese leaders did not meet with dissenting opinion. Before China's reform and opening up to the outside world, China rendered large-scale foreign aid that was beyond its national strength and level of economic and social development.

In February 1964, Premier Zhou Enlai paid a visit to 14 countries in Asia and

Africa. On 18 February 1964, he proposed eight principles for Chinese aid to foreign countries:

(1) the Chinese government always provides foreign aid on the principle of equality and mutual benefit;

(2) China strictly respects the sovereignty of aid recipient countries, with no strings or privileges attached;

(3) China provides aid by offering loans with zero or low interest, and if need be, it will alleviate the burden of recipient countries;

(4) China does not pursue the reliance of recipient countries as a result of its assistance programme, but instead aims to set them on the path of self-reliance and independent economic development;

(5) efforts should be made to achieve quick results and large profits with a small investment for construction projects with Chinese aid so that recipient countries may increase income and accumulate funds;

(6) China provides top-quality equipment, goods and materials and negotiates with reference to international market prices. Any products not up to the specifications and agreed quality will be returned or replaced;

(7) China ensures the aid recipient country masters the techniques that China provides;

(8) the experts China dispatches should enjoy the same respect as experts from the aid recipient countries.

These eight principles guided China's aid to foreign countries, African countries in particular, in the Mao Zedong era. China has for a long time adhered to these principles and never attached any political or other conditions for aid to Africa. This fully demonstrates China's sincerity in aiding poor and backward countries and the spirit of self-sacrifice that has won wide appreciation among aid recipient countries. China itself paid a heavy price in its economic development and personnel to support third-world countries and socialist countries.

(I) Aiding Vietnam

At the end of January 1950, Ho Chi Minh, President of Vietnam, left for Beijing and called on the Chinese government's help. Chinese Premier Zhou Enlai said on behalf of the CPC Central Committee (CCCPC) that China would offer a great amount of military supplies to help Vietnam fight against the army of French colonists. On 15 May that year, Vietnam requested that China supply it with rice. Mao Zedong formulated the principle that China would meet Vietnam's every need. From then on, country after country that was experiencing straitened circumstances began to ask China for help, and China complied. From 1950 to 1954, the Chinese government assisted Vietnam with Rmb1,670bn (old currency)[4]. On 13 March 1953, Zhou Enlai instructed Luo Guibo, the then Chinese liaison representative of the CCCPC to Vietnam, to send word to the Central Committee of the Vietnamese Labour Party: China would meet all Vietnam's demands for military supplies, to be delivered by the Logistics Department of the Military Commission of the CCCPC. In December 1953, China dispatched a military advisory team to help Vietnam in the Battle of Dien Bien Phu and provided material assistance including arms and ammunition, communication devices, provisions and medicine, which ultimately ensured victory in battle.

In May 1954, the Geneva Conference announced the end of the Vietnam-France War. In December 1954, the Chinese and Vietnamese governments signed protocols on China's assistance to Vietnam in economic and social development, including rehabilitating railways, highways, shipping, water conservation, restoring postal service and telecommunications. From then on, China's aid went up each year. By 1978, the various goods and materials sent as aid by China to Vietnam was worth approximately US$20bn. This aid had no strings attached and the vast majority of it was given gratis. A small part was in the form of interest-free loans. Apart from general economic aid to Vietnam, China rendered a tremendous amount of military aid. The military materials China supplied could be used to equip Vietnam's 2m-strong armed forces, and included various light and heavy weapons and other military supplies.

(II) Aiding North Korea

China's aid to North Korea dates back to ancient times. After the North Korean War broke out in 1950, China sent more than 1m volunteers to the Korean peninsula. During an arduous and bitter three-year war, China paid an enormous sacrifice in terms of casualties and military spending. Once the war was over, China continued to render assistance to North Korea, supplying it with various material aid. During the Mao Zedong era, the scale of assistance to North Korea was as large as that to Vietnam (US$20bn).

---

[4] "Old Currency" (旧币) was converted to "New Currency" in 1955, with the exchange rate of Rmb10,000 of Old Currency equivalent to Rmb1 of New Currency

(III) Aiding other countries and regions, including Africa

From 1950 to the end of 1964, China gave foreign assistance worth Rmb10.8bn, of which the largest portion occurred during the hard years between 1960 and 1964. In June 1956, China and Cambodia concluded a protocol on China aiding Cambodia in economic development and economic and technological assistance. The protocol stipulated that in 1956 and 1957, China would give Cambodia KHR800m (£8m) of goods and materials as non-reimbursable assistance. These materials were at the disposal of the Government of Cambodia, and the Chinese government did not play a supervisory role. This was in line with China's principle of rendering foreign aid with no special conditions. In October 1956, the governments of China and Nepal signed an agreement on economic assistance.

By the end of 1958, China had established diplomatic relations with many African countries. From then on, it began to give large-scale economic aid to African countries. By 1966, the amount of money spent to aid Africa amounted to US$423m. In early 1962, China committed Rmb6.9bn of foreign aid. Major recipient countries included Vietnam, North Korea, Mongolia and Albania. Other recipient countries included Cambodia, Pakistan, Nepal, Egypt, Mali, Syria and Somalia.

Under Mao, China's foreign aid fell into three main categories: non-reimbursable assistance, interest-free loans and concessional loans. Non-reimbursable assistance and interest-free loans were funded by national finance while concessional loans were given by The Import and Export Bank of China designated by the Chinese government. The main form of China's foreign aid was non-reimbursable assistance, which mostly comprised assisting recipient countries with food, crude oil, goods and materials, and in industrial and agricultural production, and industrial and engineering projects. China's aid played an important role in relieving their difficulties with economic development and natural disasters and in promoting industrial and agricultural production. Countries in Asia, Africa and Latin America fully backed China in its political struggle in the international arena. On 25 October 1971, for example, at the 26th General Assembly of the United Nations, those countries in Asia, Africa and Latin America that accepted Chinese aid supported China on a resolution, which was ultimately passed by an overwhelming majority, to restore all lawful rights of the PRC in the United Nations and to immediately expel representatives of the Kuomintang from the UN and all its affiliated agencies. This indicated that China's policy of foreign aid during the time of Mao Zedong brought about a striking effect in international politics.

III. Anti-America and anti-imperialism; not accepting aid from the West

Before and after the founding of the People's Republic of China, the US sounded out the CPC, attempting to establish relations with the new government of China. The US had a complicated opinion of the New China and at one time tried to draw the Chinese communist regime to its side by means of economic "aid". In June 1949, John Leighton Stuart, the then US ambassador to China, sent a message to Mao Zedong, saying the US may provide the new government of the CPC with US$5bn in loans on condition that New China took a stance of neutrality and should not lean to the Soviet Union's side. Owing to the fact that on 14 February 1950, China and the Soviet Union signed the Sino-Soviet Treaty of Friendship, Alliance and Mutual Assistance in which the Soviet Union promised to loan China US$300m. The US attempted to break the alliance between China and the Soviet Union. On 15 March 1950, Dean Acheson, Secretary of State, said in a speech on American policy to China that China should obtain loans not from the Soviet Union but from the US. However, the prerequisite was that China must maintain its previous relationship with the US. But owing to the fact that China had established the "leaning to one side" policy, Washington failed in its attempt to force apart the two socialist countries. With the outbreak of the Korean War on 25 June 1950, the US determined to support the Taiwan Kuomintang regime. Consequently, it began to impose an economic blockade against China. From then on, China, implemented a diplomatic policy to fight against Western developed countries on the one hand, and to do its best to remove their economic blockade against China on the other. Mao Zedong, Zhou Enlai and other Chinese leaders pointed out on many occasions: "We should do something to persuade the neutral states", and "We should contact countries like India and Japan to expand our camp". In 1974, Mao Zedong proposed the "Three Worlds" theory. According to Mao, China should become integrated with developing countries in Asia, Africa and Latin America, strive to win over developed countries of the "Second World" in an effort to isolate and fight against the two superpowers, the US and the Soviet Union.

On 27 January 1964, the Chinese and French governments released a joint communiqué and decided to establish diplomatic relations. This marked a key breakthrough in China's efforts to enhance relations with western European nations. On 13 March 1972, China and The UK established diplomatic relations at ambassadorial level. On 29 September 1972, China and Japan realised the normalisation of diplomatic ties. All these measures were of vital significance for China to break Western countries during the era of Mao Zedong. However, as China was isolated from the outside world, it was hard for the country to conduct normal economic and trade contacts with Western developed countries.

What's more, Western developed countries, generally following the stipulations of the Coordinating Committee for Export to Communist Countries, imposed a technological blockade against China. Though China longed to obtain industrial technology and equipment from Western countries, the restrictions made it very hard for China to get what it needed from the markets of developing countries. For this reason, the improvement of state-to-state relations between China and Western developed countries were of far greater significance politically than economically.

Section 2 Economic diplomacy in the era of Deng Xiaoping

Deng Xiaoping's theory on economic diplomacy can be summed up as opening up to the outside world with the aim of achieving the four modernisations and developing China's economy under a socialist system. It constitutes the core contents of Deng Xiaoping's thought on diplomacy, and has also been also the guiding principle and policy of the Chinese Communist Party and state since the reform and opening up.

Deng Xiaoping became the core of leadership of the CPC and the state around the Third Plenary Session of the Eleventh Central Committee of the Communist Party of China in 1978. From then on, his thought has directly guided the principles and policies of the country. Moreover, as China began to focus on economic development and proposed and implemented the policy of reform and opening up to the outside world, coupled with the great changes in the international and domestic situations, Deng Xiaoping thought on economic diplomacy has undergone continuous development and improvement. These are explained in the following paragraphs.

I. Preconditions, concrete contents and targets of China's economic diplomacy

1. Preconditions for China's economic diplomacy

Deng Xiaoping thought on economic diplomacy was not a product of a subjective act. Instead, it has been developed and improved under four preconditions. Or rather, it is based on four fundamental judgements in line with China's national conditions. First, China is still a poor and backward country; second, it is possible for China to have an environment of lasting peace and stability; third, China cannot develop itself in isolation of the world; fourth, China needs an environment of prolonged political stability at home. These four points are prerequisites for the country to pursue "economic diplomacy", which is to adopt the policy of reform and opening to the outside world.

First, China is still a poor and backward country. This was Deng Xiaoping's understanding of China's most basic condition which was based on facts. A very clear and simple fact as it seems today, in an era when China was flooded with ultra-leftist ideology, few people were realistic enough to recognise it.

Deng Xiaoping pointed out time and again that China was still poor and backward, coupled with a huge population, a low economic starting level and an inadequate per-capita share of natural resources. This was the basic condition of China. He often emphasised this fact in order to admonish some other leaders who felt a degree of satisfaction in what China had achieved. After all, China's poverty and backwardness could not be eliminated easily. Only by carrying out really solid work could the country eradicate poverty and backwardness. All this was the initial prerequisite for the development and improvement of Deng Xiaoping thought on economic diplomacy.

Second, it is possible for China to have an environment of lasting peace and stability. After the founding of the People's Republic, China entered the era of Mao Zedong in which political factors rose to prominence in the country's diplomatic activities. As the issue of war was taken as a top priority, economic diplomacy was considered insignificant. After the downfall of the Gang of Four, Deng Xiaoping and The Party Central Committee, gaining a better understanding of the issue of the Second World War, modified the old viewpoint that a new world war was inevitable and imminent, and made a judgement corresponding to reality. In 1987, Deng Xiaoping pointed out: "If the forces for world peace grow and Third World countries develop, a new world war can be avoided." With this judgement of the international situation, China was able to concentrate on developing its economy and foreign policy was subordinate to, and in the service of, the nation's overall economic construction. This was another prerequisite where Deng Xiaoping thought on economic diplomacy played an important role in his theory and became the core contents of his thought on foreign policy.

China cannot develop in global isolation. This third prerequisite sits between the above two. It may even be viewed as the inner core of Deng Xiaoping thought on economic diplomacy. Spurred by the functions of this "inner core", Deng Xiaoping thought on economic diplomacy has undergone continuous development and improvement since the implementation of the reform and opening-up. Deng Xiaoping thought on diplomacy not only aims to develop China's economy, but also anticipates that, once China's economy has grown stronger and more developed, the world will also need China. Thus it is clear that his thought on the economy and diplomacy is not unidirectional but bidirectional. It is not only in the interests of China, but also to the world at large.

Fourth, China needs an environment of prolonged political stability at home. As early as 1980, Deng Xiaoping said: "Without political stability and unity, it would be impossible for us to settle down to construction. This has been borne out by our experience in the past 20-plus years." Deng believed that, as China is a country that has been hit by war and unrest, it should learn from the historical lessons and hold dear all the more the goals of stability and unity. Without these things, "we could accomplish nothing", said Deng. He went on to say: "Our socialist construction can only be carried out under leadership, in an orderly way and in an environment of stability and unity. That's why I place much emphasis on the need for high ideals and strict discipline." He regarded "stability" at home as an issue of vital importance and discussed it in great detail and even elevated it to the "key" to China's modernisation, reform and opening up.

2. Specific contents of Deng Xiaoping thought on economic diplomacy

The contents of Deng Xiaoping thought on economic diplomacy are so rich and colourful that it is hard to make a comprehensive summary. However, its contents can be summarised as follows:

(1) We should learn from foreign countries everything useful, including science and technology, managerial methods and production experience; and introduce advanced technology, equipment, talent, intelligence and capital from abroad.

(2) We should establish economic cooperation with foreign countries, keep faith and follow international practices.

(3) We should introduce foreign capital; be open to borrowing foreign funds; the key is to focus on efficiency of fund utilisation.

(4) Efforts should be made to enhance the import and export trade and tap the international market in different ways; the key is to improve product quality.

(5) In special economic zones, the domestically-oriented economy should be transformed into an export-oriented economy. An export-oriented economy should be developed wherever conditions permit.

(6) In disputed territories, set aside the question of sovereignty and develop them jointly.

(7) China should take its place in the world in the field of high technology to strengthen its international standing.

3. Objects of economic diplomacy: Deng Xiaoping's thoughts on all-round opening up, exchanges and cooperation

The aims of Deng Xiaoping's economic diplomacy were all-directional, including developed capitalist countries, socialist countries such as the former Soviet Union and eastern European countries, and developing countries as well. Such multi-faceted diplomacy is gradually formed through the continuous implementation of the reform and opening-up policy. In a sense, it is a part of China's reform and opening-up policy.

From the late 1970s to the early 1980s, Deng Xiaoping talked of the general objectives of China's economic diplomacy. After the early 1980s, with ongoing proposals to establish a new international political and economic order, Deng pointed out on many occasions that it wasn't appropriate for developing countries to depend only on the settlement of the North-South problem and fix their hopes on developed countries. "We have to find new ways to increase South-South cooperation", he said, "to strengthen cooperation among Third World nations". In the mid-1980s, Deng developed his ideas of economic cooperation with other countries, which fell into three categories: (1) cooperating with "developed countries in the West", which are the main source of China's foreign investment and technological transfer; (2) cooperating with the Soviet Union and eastern European countries; (3) cooperating with developing countries. Deng also held discussions on the specific aims of economic cooperation, including cooperation with foreign governments and foreign enterprises. From a wider perspective, China should take the initiative to participate in South-South cooperation and North-South cooperation; from a narrower perspective, it should conduct multi-dimensional, multi-tier cooperation in science and technology, management and capital, or wholly foreign-owned enterprises in China.

II. Objectives, principles and guarantees of China's economic diplomacy

1. Objectives of economic diplomacy

Before the mid-to-late 1980s, Deng Xiaoping talked much about the general goal of realising the "four modernisations". With the developmental situation of reform and the deepening understanding of the modernisation drive, Deng began to realise that the term "four modernisations" could not express the goals China was pursuing. For the great goal of "socialist modernisation", what Deng talked of most was the three-step development strategy: by 1990, China will have doubled its gross national product (GNP); by the end of the 20th century, China will have quadrupled its GNP and secured a well-off livelihood for the people; by the mid-21st century, China's GNP will have approached or reached an internationally advanced level.

2. Principles of economic diplomacy

Principles of Deng Xiaoping's economic diplomacy may be summed up as follows:

(1) Opening to the outside world is a long-term and basic state policy. China should not cut itself off from the outside world.

(2) China should be independent and rely on its own efforts; it should seek outside help on the basis of self-reliance.

(3) We will import advanced technology and other items useful to the country. However, we will never learn from or import the capitalist system itself, nor anything repellent or decadent.

(4) We should also learn from foreign countries and draw on their experience, but do not copy mechanically. We should proceed from China's realities. We cannot afford to give up the advantages of our own system.

(5) Don't be afraid of cooperating with foreign countries; nor should we be afraid that they get money from us. We should keep the overall situation in mind.

(6) We should be bold in reform and opening to the outside world and in conducting experiments. We should carry out reform quickly and smoothly.

(7) We do not fear anyone, but we will not give offence to anyone either. We should act in accordance with the Five Principles of Peaceful Coexistence.

(8) We adopt the policy of reform and opening to the outside world, but cannot allow bourgeois liberalisation.

(9) We should keep our socialist banner firmly planted. We should observe calmly, hold our ground and never steal the show.

(10) While carrying out the opening-up policy, we should maintain vigilance against the "Right" but primarily against the "Left".

3. Guarantees of China's economic diplomacy

Deng Xiaoping made many comments on the guarantees of China's economic diplomacy. He held that it is a fundamental guarantee to concentrate on economic development and stick to the Four Cardinal Principles and the reform and opening-up policy proposed since the Third Plenary Session of the Eleventh Central Committee of the CPC, especially since the Thirteenth National Congress of the CPC. Moreover, he emphasised four aspects: the leadership of the Communist Party; developing the economy to improve people's livelihoods; firmly planting our socialist banner; the people's democratic dictatorship. All this is a warrant for success in China's policy of reform and opening to the outside world. In a sense, it is the guarantee for China's sustainable future development.

Deng Xiaoping thought on diplomacy, extensive and profound, covers many aspects including international strategy, diplomatic theory, diplomatic policy and the art of diplomacy, involving fields such as politics, the economy, military affairs and culture in international exchanges. Deng Xiaoping held a series of in-depth talks on developing economic cooperation and contact with foreign countries. We call it Deng Xiaoping Thought on Economic Diplomacy, which aims to achieve the four modernisations under China's socialist system, develop China's economy and make contributions to world peace and prosperity on the basis of China's economic strength.

III. Achievements in economic diplomacy in the Deng Xiaoping era

Since China implemented the reform and opening-up policy, Deng Xiaoping, China's most senior leader, made an enormous contribution to pushing forward China's economic diplomacy, and enabled China to secure great progress in economic diplomacy. Due to his foresight and wisdom, China has established normal economic and trade ties with developed countries, extensively tapped the market of developing countries, began attracting investment from overseas, all of which led to the rapid growth of the domestic economy.

1. Establishing normal economic and trade ties with developed countries

The US President Jimmy Carter sent Secretary of State Cyrus R. Vance and National Security Advisor Zbigniew Brzezinski in August 1977 and May 1978, respectively, to visit China and hold consultations on the normalisation of Sino-US relations. The two sides began negotiating on the establishment of diplomatic relations between China and the US. The Taiwan Question was the key element of negotiations. On 13 December 1978, Deng Xiaoping met with the negotiator of the US, Leonard Woodcock, directly exchanging views with him on the scheme of the joint Communiqué on the establishment of diplomatic relations between the two countries. Deng personally participated in the negotiations at a crucial moment and set the tone for the establishment of diplomatic relations. On 16 December 1978, China and the US issued the *Joint*

Communiqué on the Establishment of Sino-US Diplomatic Relations, announcing the mutual recognition of the two countries and formally established diplomatic relations on 1 January 1979.

In January 1979, after Deng Xiaoping headed the administration, he paid his first official visit to the US. When asked why he chose the US as his first visiting state, he said: "You might have found that all the countries that followed the US after the war have become rich. In contrast, those that set themselves against the US are still very poor." This indicates that when Deng was in charge of establishing diplomatic relations with the US, he had already foreseen the economic significance in promoting China's economic development by establishing diplomatic relations with the US.

Since the establishment of Sino-US diplomatic relations, bilateral economic ties have witnessed rapid development. According to official Chinese statistics, in 1979 Sino-US trade volume totalled US$2.45bn. In 2008, the figure reached US$333.74bn, a 130-fold increase in just three decades, with an average annual growth rate of 18.5%. According to US statistics, bilateral trade volume increased from US$2.37bn in 1979 to US$409.25bn in 2008, with an annual average growth rate of 19.4%. The US has gradually become China's largest foreign market and one of the biggest foreign investors in China, and has therefore played an important role in China's economic development.

On 12 August 1978, China and Japan signed the *Sino-Japanese Treaty of Peace and Friendship*, which laid a more solid foundation for good relations between the two countries. On the one hand, it brought about a broad prospect for bilateral exchanges in politics, economics, culture, and science and technology. It also had a positive influence on safeguarding peace and security in Asia and the Pacific region. Since 1979, China began accepting Japanese aid in economic development. China used Japanese yen loans to press ahead with the construction of infrastructure and industrial projects, which facilitated the rapid development of trade between China and Japan. In 1972, the trade volume between China and Japan was US$1bn. In 1978, the figure was US$5bn, rising to approximately US$90bn in 2001. In 2011, the trade volume between the two countries reached a historic high, amounting to US$344.9bn. Moreover, the amount of Japanese direct investment in China was also the highest in the world, with a cumulative total of more than US$90bn by 2012.

China has pushed forward economic and trade ties with developed countries such as Japan and the US since its implementation of the reform and opening-up policy, which also facilitated the establishment of normal economic and trade ties with EU member countries. After the mid-1980s, China had established and resumed economic and trade ties with all major Western developed countries, which not only created a sound external economic and trade environment, but also laid a sound policy foundation for China to introduce capital, technology and management techniques from Western countries.

2. Capitalising on the international market, improving the quality of exports and pursuing rapid growth of the national economy

Prior to reform and opening to the outside world, China had a closed economic system, with little economic or trade ties with foreign countries. In 1978, the value of China's foreign trade was only US$20bn. In 1980, its gross exports accounted only for 6% of GDP. Since China implemented the reform and opening-up policy, it has established economic exchange with the outside world in a comprehensive way. As a result, its gross volume of foreign trade has continuously increased and the proportion of its export trade volume in GDP has rapidly increased, to 9% in 1985, to 16.1% in 1990, to 23.1% in 2000 and to 36% in 2004. Its gross volume of import and export trade exceeded US$1,000bn in 2004, of which exports accounted for US$590bn. In 1978, China's gross export volume accounted for less than 1% of the global total, but this rose to 6.5% in 2004. In terms of foreign trade, China ranked 32th in 1978 in the world before rising to third place in 2003.

Moreover, the quality of China's export also improved. In 1980, industrial finished products made up just 49.7% of China's visible exports. The proportion rose to 74.4% in 1990; 89.8% in 2000; 92.1% in 2003 and 94.8% in 2010.

Economic diplomacy in the Deng Xiaoping era created an internal environment for China's rapid economic development since the implementation of the reform and opening-up policy. This enabled China to abandon ultra-left trends of thought and a closed environment and instead to establish normal ties with most countries and regions of the world. In particular, Deng Xiaoping made an important tour to south China between 18 January and 21 February1992, when he made a speech that outlined the developmental path of China's market economy. Deng's speech virtually affirmed the basic line of thought that socialist countries may engage in a market economy. It not only consolidated the achievements at institutional level in the exploration of reform and opening up, but also laid the foundation for China's deepening reform.

Section 3 Economic diplomacy in the era of Jiang Zemin

Following Deng Xiaoping's retirement, General Secretary and President Jiang Zemin held the reigns of the Chinese government. Jiang adhered to the line of reform and opening to the outside world designed by Deng. In the era of Jiang Zemin, China scored great achievements in economic diplomacy, opening up overseas markets, stabilising resource supply and improving the country's economic cooperation with foreign countries.

I. Deepening reform and opening up and further developing the market economy

During his reign, Jiang Zemin carried forward and developed the strategic thinking of Deng Xiaoping's reform and opening to the outside world. It was in this period that Deng's thinking of a socialist market economy was improved, systematised and theorised and the strategic thinking of developing a socialist market economy was eventually established. In Jiang's era, China broke the ideological shackle that socialism was tied to the planned economy, and admitted the basic function of the market in resource allocation and the macro adjustment of the national economy. Insignificant plans were discarded, to be replaced by major plans. Efforts were redoubled to create a socialist market economy so as to show clearly the direction to consolidate reform and opening up. As a result of this clarification of political orientation, the Chinese government continued to deepen reform and opening up on the one hand, while actively adjusting domestic policies and striving to become integrated with the world economic system on the other. China determined how quickly it would open up to the outside world and how it would be achieved. It demonstrated the spirit and aspiration of international coordination, and also maintained control over the tempo of reform and opening. Faced with an increasingly conspicuous trend of economic globalisation, China stuck to opening wider to the outside world, took the initiative to participate in international economic cooperation and competition, and took full advantage of various opportunities brought about by economic globalisation. However, it also remained clear-headed about the possibility of extraneous risks and took measures to safeguard the national economy. The most significant policy concerning China's integration with the world economy in this period was its efforts to join the World Trade Organisation (WTO).

In September 1982, on the premise of not damaging China's legal status as an original signatory state, China applied for the status of "observer" of the General Agreement on Tariffs and Trade (GATT). In November that year, China was admitted the status of "observer" and sent a delegation to sit in on the 38th contracting party conference of the parties of the GATT. From then on, the Chinese delegation attended all the conferences and special sessions of the GATT with observer status. In January 1984, the Chinese government was approved to sign the third international textile trade agreement of the GATT and became a full member of the GATT Textile Committee.

A Review

On 11 July 1986, the Chinese government presented an official note to the GATT General Secretary, pleading for the recovery of China's status as a signatory country of the GATT. The note elaborated the three principles for resuming China's contracting party status in the GATT. First, entering into the GATT by resuming its original founding member status instead of re-entry. Second, China takes tariff reduction or exemptions as promised terms but does not undertake specific import obligations. Third, China enjoys the corresponding treatment and assumes the obligations compatible with the level of China's economic and trade development in the capacity of a developing country. China cannot take on obligations beyond its economic and trade development level. From then on, China began its arduous and tortuous journey of rejoining the GATT.

In September 1986, China began to participate fully in the multilateral trade negotiations of the Uruguay Round of GATT.

In March 1987, the GATT Council established a China Working Party concerning China's status as a contracting party and began to review China's economic and trade system, asking all contracting parties to pose questions relating to China's foreign trade system. In October 1987, the China Working Party held its first meeting. By the 11th meeting in October 1992, the Working Party had essentially finished its deliberations over China's economic and trade system and initiated substantive negotiations concerning the contents of the protocol of China rejoining the GATT. In October 1993, China began bilateral negotiations on rejoining the GATT with contracting parties of GATT.

On 8 September 1999, President Jiang Zemin attended the Asia-Pacific Economic Cooperation (APEC) meetings in New Zealand and paid a visit to Australia, during which he reiterated China's three principles for its entry into the WTO, namely: (1) without China's participation, the WTO would be incomplete; (2) China must enter into the WTO in the capacity of a developing country; (3) for China entering into the WTO, its rights and obligations shall be balanced. On 11 September, President Jiang Zemin and the US President Bill Clinton, while attending the APEC leaders' meeting in Auckland, New Zealand, held a formal meeting. Talking about China's WTO entry, Jiang pointed out that it was not only the need of China's economic development and reform and opening to the outside world, but also the need of establishing a complete international trading system. China consistently took a positive attitude towards entry into the WTO, hoping that the negotiations would be conducted on the basis of equality and mutual benefit and an agreement could be concluded at an early date. With the common concern and joint efforts of the leaders of both China and the US, the two sides eventually signed on 15 November 1999 in Beijing the *Bilateral*

Agreement on China's Entry into the WTO between China and the United States. On 19 May 2000, China and the EU delegation signed a bilateral agreement in Beijing on China's entry into the WTO.

Reaching agreement on China's "entry into the WTO" with these countries and regions meant that China would open its market wider and conform to WTO stipulations on economic systems and laws and regulations, as a result of which China would become integrated with the international economic system and reduce its tariffs by a large margin.

II. Highlighting relations with great powers and contending but not breaking up

In this period, China attached great importance to developing relations with great powers and even put Sino-US relations as the top priority. In 2001, China entered into the WTO, manifesting its determination to opening to the outside world. From then on, the effect of China's rejuvenation became apparent. Against this background, the 16th National Party Congress was convened in Beijing from 8-14 November 2002, where the overall diplomatic strategy was stated clearly that "Great powers are the key, neighbouring countries are priorities, developing countries are the foundation and multilateral institutions are important platforms". China attached great importance to developing relations with Western developed countries, asserting that both sides should reinforce strategic dialogue, enhance mutual trust, deepen cooperation, put aside differences properly so as to develop long-term, healthy and steady bilateral relations.

Following an improvement in Sino-Soviet relations in the late 1980s, China and Russia established an excellent relationship. In 1992, both countries viewed each other as friendly. In 1994, China and Russia established their relations as a constructive and strategic partnership, before being elevated to strategic cooperative partnership in 1996. In 2001, the *Treaty of Good-Neighbourliness and Friendly Cooperation Between the* People's Republic of China *and the* Russian Federation *(FCT)* positioned Sino-Russia relations as a strategic partnership on the basis of equality and mutual trust, clarified the goal that the two sides would be "Good neighbours, good friends, good partners" and confirmed it in the form of treaty and law.

In this period, trade between China and Russia increased, from US$4.63bn in 1992, to US$5.46bn in 1995, US$8bn in 2000, US$10.67bn in 2001, US$15.76bn in 2003, US$21.23bn in 2004 and US$33.39bn in 2006. Furthermore, China's rapid progress in military equipment had much to do with its importation of military equipment and technology from Russia. Though bilateral trade grew rapidly, some deficiencies still existed and the relative importance of the trade relationship gradually decreased.

In the 1990s and the early 21st Century, China and the US experienced frequent political and economic friction. However, bilateral relations underwent great development, which had some something to do with China's adherence to the general principle and direction of Sino-US relations. In 2001, the September 11 terrorist attack occurred in the US. China responded with sympathy and support for American's anti-terrorism policies, which facilitated the maturity of Sino-US relations.

In this period, China strove to settle trade friction with the US to gain the latter's support for China's entry into the WTO. Politically, China made great efforts in promoting cooperation with the US, supporting Washington's policy of the global war on terrorism. In addition, China adhered to its hard-line stance on the Taiwan question and waged a stern and continuous struggle against the US and "Taiwan independence" forces. Sino-US trade and investment developed enormously. The volume of bilateral trade increased from US$17.49bn in 1992 to US$80.49bn in 2001, with an average annual growth rate of 18.5%. American direct investment in China increased from US$511m to US$4.358bnn in 2001, with an average annual growth of 31%. The speed of investment growth was higher than that of the preceding period.

For a long time, China adopted the policy of cooperating with the big powers of the EU. In the 1990s, China and Europe had intense friction in such fields as politics and human rights. In economic and trade issues, the EU adopted unfair trade policies against China through green barriers, technical barriers and for political reasons. Worse still, the EU had a tendency to discriminate against China after the "June Fourth" incident.

In 1992, as Sino-Europe relations were largely normalised, the two sides began an environmental dialogue. In 1994, China and Europe began a new bilateral political dialogue, which symbolised Sino-Europe relations entering into a strategic developmental stage. In 1995, the European Commission passed the strategic document entitled "A Long Term Policy for China-Europe Relations", laying great stress on developing political, economic and trade relations with China in a comprehensive way and initially establishing a policy framework on EU Strategy towards China. For its part, China strove to promote Sino-EU relations by enhancing its relations with European big powers including Germany and France. For those countries that were engaged in rebuking China, China reduced or cancelled governmental bulk orders. For those countries that took a more "positive" attitude, China encouraged this through government procurement and opening the Chinese market further.

In 1997, China and France established an all-round partnership. In 2001, the two countries started a strategic dialogue, the first of its kind between China and a great power. In 2004, the two sides decided to establish an all-round strategic partnership. In 1992, Sino-German relations gradually improved after the "June Fourth" incident, returning to the track of normal development. In 1993, the German government decided not to approve sales of submarines to Taiwan, thus furthering the development of bilateral relations. In July 1995, President Jiang Zemin paid a state visit to Germany. In November 1995, German Chancellor Helmut Kohl paid his fourth visit to China. Close bilateral political relations gave great impetus to the development of economic and trade relations. In May 2004, Premier Wen Jiabao paid a visit to Germany, during which the two countries issued a joint statement announcing that China and Germany would establish a partnership with global obligations within the framework of an overall strategic partnership between China and the EU. In 2001, China established a comprehensive partnership with the EU, ushering in a honeymoon period of Sino-Europe relations. China's policy of promoting cooperation with Europe proved to be effective. In 1975, China-EU trade volume totalled only US$2.4bn. In 2003, the figure climbed to US$125.2bn.

III. Pursuing a good-neighbourly policy and tapping the market of developing countries

"Neighbouring countries are priorities" was an important guiding principle of Chinese diplomacy under President Jiang Zemin's administration. In May 1991, in a speech delivered in Moscow, he said: "China has consistently stressed friendly, good-neighbourly relations with adjacent countries". On 1 July 1991, at the celebration of the 70th anniversary of the founding of the Communist Party of China, General Secretary Jiang Zemin stressed: "We will consistently adhere to the independent foreign policy of peace, improve and develop good relations with all countries, especially maintain and develop friendly, good-neighbourly relations with adjacent countries and strengthen solidarity and cooperation with developing countries." In December 1991, at the 46th session of the United Nations General Assembly, Qian Qichen, China's State Councillor and minister of foreign affairs, said: "To develop friendly, good-neighbourly relations with adjacent countries and create a peaceful and safe surrounding environment is an important part of China's independent foreign policy of peace." This indicated that the Chinese government explicitly declared the important diplomatic policy that China is fully aware of the importance of neighbouring countries and regions and that efforts should be made to improve its relations with neighbouring countries so as to create a sound external environment for the development of its national economy.

In 1992, Jiang Zemin said in his report for the 14th National Congress of the Chinese Communist Party: "work actively to open more markets abroad, facilitate diversification of foreign trade and develop an export-oriented economy", "work actively to expand Chinese enterprises' investment in foreign countries and transnational operation", "make more use of overseas resources and introduce advanced technology", which played an important role for China to tap the international market, realise a "diversification of foreign trade", "conduct transnational operations" and "open markets abroad". The Second Plenary Session of the 14th Central Committee explicitly proposed "carrying forward the strategy of international market diversification. While consolidating and expanding European, American and Japanese markets, we should endeavour to tap other overseas markets." All this played an important directive role in China's efforts to tap the markets of developing countries. Guided by this strategy, Chinese capital began expanding trade contacts and economic cooperation with developing countries, and direct investment there.

In establishing friendly exchanges with its neighbours, China attached great importance not only to leading powers such as Russia and Japan, but also to other countries such as South Korea, Pakistan, the five countries (Kazakhstan, Uzbekistan, Kyrgyzstan, Turkmenistan and Tajikistan) in central Asia, India and the ASEAN countries. On 24 August 1992, China and the Republic of Korea established diplomatic relations. Politically, leaders of the two nations paid mutual visits on many occasions. A solid and stable relationship of mutual trust between China and South Korea was gradually established. In November 1998, President Kim Dae-jung paid a state visit to China. As both sides have many common concerns in international multilateral activities, the two countries need and support each other, pushing forward the virtuous development of their political relations. On the economic front, mutually beneficial cooperation between the two countries continued to deepen. Economic and trade relations developed rapidly. The two sides became mutually important trade partners. The bilateral trade volume was only US$5.03bn. In 2001, it exceeded US$35.9bn billion before rising to US$63.2bn in 2003, with an average annual increase of more than 20%. This growth rate was much higher than 7%, the annual average growth rate of South Korea's entire foreign trade in the corresponding period. In 2005, trade between the two countries exceeded US$100bn for the first time, reaching US$111.99bn. In 2012, the figure exceeded US$200bn for the first time.

In 1989, the trade volume between China and Japan was US$14.663bn. In 2000, it rose to US$83.17bn, a 5.6-fold increase. During this period, China used

Japanese yen loans and funds to continue introducing complete sets of Japanese equipment on a large scale to elevate the production capacity of industrial and consumer goods, including household appliances and petrochemical engineering products. This facilitated steady growth both in trade between Japan and China and Japanese industrial investment in China. In addition, China, as Japan's second largest trade partner, played an important role in Japan's own economic development. After 2004, China became Japan's largest trade partner. Trade volume between the two countries grew dramatically, first exceeding US$200bn and later US$300bn. As a neighbouring state of China, Japan played a supportive role in China's economic development. For its part, Japan benefited considerably from its access to the ever-expanding market of China. The Chinese market played an indispensable role in maintaining the stability and growth of the Japanese economy.

China's economic cooperation in the 1990s and the early 21st century was a model in terms of economic diplomacy in this period for its surrounding countries and developing countries. The ASEAN was founded in 1967 with five founding member countries. This number has since doubled. ASEAN has become an increasingly important regional force in the international arena. China has striven to develop relations with ASEAN countries. Apart from promoting bilateral trade relations, China attaches great importance to strategic regional economic cooperation to improve economic cooperation of the two sides. Most of all, both sides, grasping the general strategic direction of constructing regional free trade areas, started to build the China-ASEAN Free Trade Area in 2001. This strategic move greatly promoted the development of bilateral relations. In 2002, trade volume between China and ASEAN stood at US$54.767bn. In 2007, bilateral trade volume amounted to US$200bn. In 2011, the figure exceeded US$300bn. These landmark achievements show the effect of the grand strategy of building up the free trade area.

The African continent contains many developing countries. In 1979, trade volume between China and Africa was only US$817m. After the 1990s, as Sino-Africa relations developed by leaps and bounds, cooperation between the two sides focused more on economic issues. In 1990, the trade volume between China and Africa rose to US$1.665bn. In the late 1990s, bilateral economic and trade relations witnessed rapid development. By 1999, total trade volume between China and Africa increased to US$6.49bn, an increase of 533 times within 50 years. Entering the 21st century, bilateral economic and trade relations have developed with each passing year. In 2000, the Sino-African trade volume exceeded US$10bn for the first time, after which it maintained a growth rate of more than 30% for eight years in a row. In 2003, the total volume of bilateral trade amounted to US$19bn. In 2008, the figure exceeded US$100bn for the first time. In 2012, the figure totalled US$198.4bn. In 2013, trade volume between the two sides was expected to exceed US$200bn. Since 2009, China has been Africa's largest trade partner. In 2000, with the successful convening of *Forum on China–Africa Cooperation* (FOCAC), the two sides began economic cooperation in a comprehensive manner. China began to import resources from Africa on a large scale, and also gradually intensified its efforts to invest in and aid the continent. Thanks to the efforts of both sides, Sino-Africa relations have seen steady development, deepening cooperation and larger cooperation scope.

To sum up, Chinese leaders from three generations have vigorously pushed forward China's industrialisation process and economic development by economic and diplomatic means. Under the ever-changing domestic and international environments, they elevated China's status in the international arena and improved the livelihood of the Chinese people. In particular, since the reform and opening to the outside world, Deng Xiaoping, with his strategic vision and pragmatism, led China to an era of leapfrogging economic development, greatly improving people's livelihood, enhancing comprehensive national strength and benefiting the broad masses of the people. During the term of Jiang Zemin, China, taking the road of socialism with Chinese characteristics pioneered by Deng Xiaoping, expanded and deepened the achievements of reform and opening up, and pressed ahead with the in-depth implementation of economic diplomacy. Following Jiang Zemin and Hu Jintao, Xi Jinping has broken new ground for the future, bringing China's economic development and comprehensive national strength to a new height and new stage through a round of comprehensive reforms. As a result, Chinese people's livelihoods are continuously improving. China has entered a new developmental era in which its national strength ranks second only to the US. Nevertheless, China's economic diplomacy is still a long and arduous task, which demands unremitting efforts.

Chapter 2

The actors of China's economic diplomacy

Section 1 Main actors of China's economic diplomacy

From 21 to 25 September 2009, the then Chinese president, Hu Jintao, attended the UN Climate Change Summit, the general debate at the 64th Session of the UN General Assembly, the United Nations Security Council Summit on Nuclear Non-Proliferation and Nuclear Disarmament and the Third G20 Leaders Summit on Finance at New York and Pittsburgh, America. The schedule was very tight. In addition to the five-day attendance at the four summits, President Hu conducted a series of bilateral interviews during the meeting intervals.

During this large-scale and complicated diplomatic activity, Hu was accompanied by a vast delegation composed of numerous high-ranking officials in charge of economic and financial affairs. Among them there were Wang Qishan, Vice-Premier of the State Council, Zhang Ping, Minister of National Department and Reform Commission (NDRC), Xie Xuren, Minister of Finance, Chen Deming, Minister of Commerce, Zhou Xiaochuan, Governor of the People's Bank of China, and Xie Zhenhua, Vice Minister of the National Development and Reform Commission (NDRC).

During the UN Climate Change Summit and the Second G20 Leaders Summit on Finance, these officials attended conferences at various levels, becoming major executives of diplomatic discussions and negotiations on China's economic affairs.

Apart from Ministry of Commerce, the NDRC, Ministry of Finance and People's Bank are ministries in charge of economic affairs. However, with economic globalisation, the domestic and international economies have become increasingly intertwined. As these economic institutions assume more functions that cover foreign economic issues, it is inevitable for them to have exchanges with corresponding institutions from foreign countries. While taking charge of domestic economic affairs, they represent the central government of China in specific fields and engage in ever-increasing international exchanges. The difference is that their international exchanges are more involved in economic affairs. Their activities at New York and Pittsburgh were, in essence, economic diplomacy. These economic ministers are the major executives of China's economic diplomacy.

Since its accession to the WTO in 2001, China has become more involved in the international economic system. Meanwhile, its national economy has developed rapidly, surpassing Italy, the UK, France and Germany in succession and overtaking Japan in 2010 as the world's second largest economy. China's foreign economic relations exert profound influence on the global economy. Against this backdrop, Chinese economic officials are more frequently invited to attend various conferences and discussions on the international economy. Their participation is an outstanding feature of the rejuvenation of China's economic diplomacy.

In the past 10-plus years, China's economic diplomacy has been rich and varied. It encompasses three levels: global, regional and bilateral. At the global level, China's economic diplomacy mainly deals with the country's relations with world economic institutions such as the WTO, the International Monetary Fund (IMF) and the World Bank, and sends delegations to attend various international conferences and negotiations held by these institutions. In addition, the Chinese government participates in discussions on global economic issues held by other institutional platforms, such as the previous dialogue between the G8 and developing countries, and a series of economic conferences of the current G20. At the regional level, China's economic diplomacy has focused on pushing forward economic cooperation and integration of East Asia and its surrounding area. This includes economic cooperation under the frameworks of APEC, the 10+3 summit (ASEAN plus China, Japan and South Korea) and the Shanghai Cooperation Organisation (SCO). At the bilateral level, China has been active in a host of economic diplomacy meetings, covering issues such as the Sino-US dispute on the renminbi exchange rate, energy negotiations with Russia, and trade negotiations with Europe.

In an era in which foreign economic relations are increasingly complex, economic departments of the central government conclude many economic cooperation agreements or establish various dispute settlement mechanisms through governmental exchanges to promote the sound development of foreign economic relations, which has been a common phenomenon on the international diplomatic stage. To have a good knowledge of the institutional structure of China's economic diplomacy - who is formulating the basic policy for economic diplomacy, and who is carrying it out - is a first step to understand China's economic diplomacy.

I. The overall policy of economic diplomacy of the State Council and China

In China's decision-making on political affairs, the Communist Party of China, the ruling party of the state, manages everything. Key principles, guidelines and policies concerning economic issues are formulated under the Party system. The annual plenary session of the Central Committee of Communist Party of China (CCCPC) and the Central Economic Working Conference are the major events where the country's key economic policies are decided.

Under China's political system, although the Party is responsible for planning overall economic issues, it is not responsible for the implementation of specific economic policies. With the evolution of China's political system in recent years, a stable political convention has taken shape; after an overall scheme has been drawn up at the Party's conferences (including the National Congress of the Chinese Communist Party, the Plenary Session of the Central Committee of the Communist Party of China and meetings of the Political Bureau), the premier of the State Council will take overall responsibility for economic and social issues. So far, a basic division of labour has taken shape that involves the Party's general secretary taking charge of political (including ideological), diplomatic and military issues, while the premier of the State Council is in charge of economic and social governance.

However, the premier of the State Council, as chief of the government, inevitably shares the responsibility of decision-making and implementation of China's diplomacy with the head of state (who is usually also general secretary of the CPC). Owing to the fact that the premier is mainly in charge of economic issues, he/she lays more emphasis on economic affairs. In this sense, the premier of the State Council is the key executive of China's economic diplomacy.

The premier gets involved in economic diplomacy mainly through scheduled or non-scheduled meetings of heads of government and mutual visits, as well as other forms. Since the 1990s, the Chinese government has attached increasingly high importance to multilateral diplomacy and the Chinese premier participates in several mechanisms of multilateral summit meetings. These mechanisms focus on discussing economic issues. For example, a regular meeting for premiers under the framework of the SCO is focused on discussing economic cooperation between member countries. As a result, the premier and head of state have distinct responsibilities. The 10+3 summit, for example, focuses on discussing regional economic cooperation in East Asia. Chinese premiers have used this platform to actively conduct economic diplomacy. In 2001, the then Chinese premier Zhu Rongji initiated the construction of the China-ASEAN Free Trade Area, which was a significant event of China's economic diplomacy.

Mechanisms of regular meetings attended by chiefs of the Chinese government

Name of mechanisms	Date of the first session
ASEAN-China, Japan and South Korea Summit Meeting	1997
Sino-EU Summit Meeting	1998
Regular Meeting Mechanism for Premiers of the SCO	2001
Summit Meeting of China, Japan and South Korea	2008

In addition to multilateral meetings, mutual visits are an important form of a Chinese premier's economic diplomacy. Although visits by the premier involve discussions on a variety of topics, economic affairs have always been the most important. In May 2013, the new Premier Li Keqiang paid his first visit abroad as head of the Chinese government, and his stated priority was to discuss economic issues and enhance economic cooperation with foreign countries. During his visit to Switzerland, the Chinese and Swiss governments signed cooperation documents on concluding negotiations on a free trade agreement. This was another key achievement of China's economic diplomacy. While visiting Germany, Li Keqiang actively appealed to the German government to oppose the EU's stand of trade protectionism against China's photovoltaic industry.

At the level of the State Council, apart from the premier, there are four vice-premiers and several state councillors (usually there are five councillors) who assist the premier in handling matters in a specific field. They also handle some diplomatic and external affairs in accordance with their respective functions.

Generally, the Chinese government appoints one of the vice-premiers or a state councillor to take charge of traditional diplomatic affairs, such as former vice-premier Qian Qichen, and state councillors Tang Jiaxuan and Dai Bingguo, all of whom have a background in diplomacy. Qian and Tang used to be foreign affairs ministers while Dai worked as minister of the International Liaison Department of the Central Committee of the CPC and administrative vice-minister of the Ministry of Foreign Affairs. Apart from handling diplomatic affairs, the state councillor or vice-premier is in charge of Hong Kong and Macau affairs and overseas Chinese affairs, which are closely related to diplomatic affairs. Sometimes, they are in charge of issues concerning Taiwan. Both the vice-premiers and the state councillors are important members of an inner-party steering group of diplomatic affairs of the CPC. Therefore, he/she is directly responsible, not to the premier of the State Council, but to the leader of the steering group of diplomatic affairs. As a matter of fact, the post of the foreign affairs leading group is taken by the general secretary of the Party who is also head of the state.

In addition to the traditional diplomatic decision-making system, a basic system pattern has taken shape in China in recent years where one of the vice-premiers is in charge of foreign economic issues. He/she and the state councillor or vice-premier who is in charge of traditional diplomatic affairs comprise the "two carriages" of China's grand diplomacy. The reason why the vice-premier is in charge of foreign economic issues is, according to the division of responsibilities in the State Council, because he/she is in charge of Ministry of Commerce (prior to the institutional reforms of the government in 2003, a large portion of the Ministry of Commerce was previously the Ministry of Foreign Trade and Economic Cooperation, otherwise known as Moftec).

Since the time of Wu Yi, the status of vice-premier in charge of foreign economic issues began to elevate. In the 1990s, Wu Yi worked as minister of the Ministry of Foreign Trade and Economic Cooperation in charge of issues concerning economic and trade relations with foreign countries and was a major sponsor and executor of China's entry into the WTO. Later, she acted as a state councillor in charge of foreign trade issues and as vice-premier of the State Council. While vice-premier, Wu Yi was directly in charge of economic diplomacy concerning the US, and in this role she became a bright star in economic diplomacy. While in office, she stood up to various diplomatic pressures from the US concerning the appreciation of the renminbi. To this end, she, together with the then US Secretary of the Treasury, Henry Paulson, initiated the China-US Strategic Economic Dialogue (SED) mechanism in 2006, which has been an important platform for economic diplomacy between China and the US. Later, it evolved into a large-scale strategic and economic dialogue mechanism during President Obama's term.

Wang Qishan, successor to Wu Yi, was also a key figure in China's economic diplomacy. Apart from taking charge of the Ministry of Commerce, Wang assumed responsibility for the People's Bank of China (PBC) while working as vice-premier. Therefore, economic diplomacy during his term of office highlighted finance and currency issues. China's economic diplomacy developed rapidly during Wang Qishan's term of office.

II. Ministry of Commerce and China's commercial diplomacy

Foreign trade is the most important aspect of foreign economic relations. Therefore, the Ministry of Commerce, which is in charge of domestic and foreign trade, is the most important department in the country's economic diplomacy. The Ministry of Commerce is also in charge of foreign aid, which adds to the weight of its duty in economic diplomacy.

The Ministry of Commerce, a very young government department, was founded in 2003. It was established by combining the then State Economic and Trade Commission in charge of domestic trade and Moftec in charge of foreign trade. Therefore, the main duties in the area of economic diplomacy of the Ministry of Commerce are reflected in the previous Moftec.

Nevertheless, in the early days of the People's Republic of China, the Administration of Trade of the Central People's Government was set up to take charge of foreign trade. With the rapid development of domestic and foreign trade, and in order to enhance foreign trade, lighten the workload of the Administration of Trade and do a better job in both domestic and foreign trade, the Administration of Trade was dismantled and the Ministry of Foreign Trade of the Central People's Government and the Ministry of Commerce of the Central People's Government were established in September 1952. From then on, these two ministries advanced along different tracks and foreign trade and domestic trade were under the leadership of different government departments. The Ministry of Foreign Trade was an administrative organ of the Chinese government in charge of the management of foreign trade between September 1952 and March 1982.

The main functions of the then Ministry of Foreign Trade included: 1. drawing up a plan for China's imports and exports and a plan for foreign exchange receipts and payments of foreign trade; and to organise and examine the implementation of these plans; 2. drawing up a communication plan for developing economies and trade and technical cooperation between China and relevant countries; negotiate on and sign agreements and protocols with relevant countries, and supervise their implementation; 3. drawing up and implementing basic laws and regulations on foreign trade management, as well as customs management rules and regulations and their implementation; 4.presiding over customs and steadily improving cargo supervision and political and economic security; 5. formulating operational procedures for imports, exports, shipments and packages of state-owned enterprises that engage in foreign trade; 6. signing and issuing licences for transit trade; 7. studying and drawing up a commodity inspection system; 8. before 1961, being in charge of Chinese foreign aid concerning complete sets of equipment; 9. before 1964, presiding over the China Council for the Promotion of International Trade.

As China's foreign economic relations became deeper and more complex since the policy of reform and opening to the outside world, foreign trade cannot cover all foreign economic relations. On 8 March 1982, the Ministry of Foreign Trade was officially dismantled and the Ministry of Foreign Economic Relations and Trade (Mofert) was established by combining the Ministry of Foreign Trade, the Ministry of Economic Relations with Foreign Countries, the State Commission for the Control of Import and Export Affairs and the Administrative Commission for Foreign Investment. It aimed to enhance unified management over foreign economic relations and trade.

The main duties of the newly-established Mofert included: carrying out policies and guidelines of the Party Central Committee and the State Council on developing foreign economic relations and trade; planning, managing and coordinating foreign trade activities of provinces, cities and autonomous regions; striving to develop foreign trade; excelling in the provision of economic and technical aid to developing countries; enhancing international multilateral and bilateral economic and technological cooperation; utilising foreign funds; organising import and export technology; undertaking contracted foreign projects and conducting labour service cooperation; making unified arrangements over inter-governmental comprehensive foreign trade activities.

In particular, Mofert explicitly increased the functions of foreign aid and management, and did not just focus on foreign trade.

The first minister of Mofert was Chen Muhua, who also held the post of state councillor. Later, she became governor of the PBC. She was an important participant in China's reform and opening up and reform of the economic system. The second minister was Zheng Tuobin and the third was Li Lanqing, who later worked as vice-premier of the State Council.

On 16 March 1993, the first session of the Eighth National People's Congress decided that the Ministry of Foreign Economic Relations and Trade (Mofert) was renamed Ministry of Foreign Trade and Economic Cooperation (Moftec). Though the word "cooperation" is added to the new name, it further strengthened Moftec's duties in economic diplomacy, including mapping out and implementing foreign and economic policies of countries (regions); organising conferences of bilateral mixed (joint) committees, holding economic and trade negotiations with foreign governments and signing relevant documents; giving guidance to the economic and commercial councillor's offices of Chinese embassies (consulates) abroad, and contacting foreign official commercial agencies in China; participating in international economic and trade activities on behalf of the Chinese government. Other duties include being in charge of multilateral foreign trade negotiations, international service trade negotiations, negotiations and signing of international treaties on the economy and trade, coordinating the views and opinions of relevant departments of the State Council in the course of negotiations; managing international negotiations on intellectual property; overseeing the domestic implementation of international treaties and agreements on the economy and trade; managing multilateral and bilateral aid given gratis to China and grant-in-aid; manage economic and technical cooperation in China conducted by the United Nations Development System and relevant international organisations; giving guidance to China's economic and trade representative offices in the UN and relevant international organisations.

Wu Yi, a famous Chinese economic diplomat, worked as minister of Moftec. During her tenure, the most important function of economic diplomacy assumed by the Ministry of Commerce was to take charge of economic and trade negotiations for China's entry into the WTO, central to which were the negotiations with the US. Later, Shi Guangsheng took over her duties in Moftec, while Wu was promoted to state councillor in charge of foreign trade. Later, Wu Yi retired from the post of vice-premier. She was a key figure in China's economic diplomacy for as long as 15 years.

China's accession to the WTO meant that its market became more integrated with global markets due to both adhering to the same trade rules. In March 2003, the first session of the 10th National People's Congress decided that,

The Actors of China's Economic Diplomacy

in accordance with State Council institutional reform plan and its *Circular of Institutional Structuring*, departments of the previous State Economic and Trade Commission in charge of trade and Moftec would be combined into Ministry of Commerce, thereby creating unified management over the domestic economy and foreign trade. As the Ministry of Commerce assumed all duties concerning foreign trade that were formerly performed by Moftec, and also took charge of domestic trade and market order, it was able to integrate domestic and foreign markets. Therefore, it has a solid authoritative foundation in economic diplomacy and maintains vigour and vitality.

Department-level institutions in charge of international affairs under the Ministry of Commerce

Major international institutions	Major international duties
General office (Secretariat of China International Trade Representative)	Edit and issue *Proclamation on China's Foreign Trade*; handle government affairs concerning the duties of international trade negotiators; establish Information Office of the Ministry of Commerce at the General Office; in charge of news propaganda and press briefings
Anti-monopoly Bureau	Investigate monopolistic behaviour in foreign trade according to law and take necessary measures to eliminate hazards; give guidance to antitrust defence of Chinese enterprises in foreign countries; take the lead in organising discussions and negotiations over competitive clauses of multilateral and bilateral agreements; conduct international exchanges and cooperation in multilateral and bilateral competition policies.
Department of Foreign Trade	Draw up reform scheme for foreign trade management system and development strategy for import and export trade; take the lead in working out foreign trade policies and coordinate with competent departments in drawing up policies on processing trade; take the lead in giving guidance to multilateral and bilateral negotiations or dialogue of key industries specialised in commodities; supervise the implementation and domestic management of bilateral agreements concerning commodity management.
Department of Foreign Investment Administration	Conduct macro-direction and comprehensive management over attracting foreign investment in China
Department of Foreign Assistance	Draw up and organise the implementation of policies and plans for China's foreign assistance and advance reform in foreign assistance modes; organise negotiations on foreign assistance and sign agreements, handle issues concerning inter-governmental aid; draw up plans for, and implement, foreign aid; supervise and examine the implementation of foreign aid projects.
Department of Outward Investment and Economic Cooperation	Organise and coordinate the implementation of the "going global" strategy; direct and manage external investment and economic cooperation, such as overseas investment, external processing trade and R&D, overseas resources cooperation, foreign contracted projects and foreign labour cooperation (including residents leaving China for employment).
Department of International Trade and Economic Affairs	Draw up and implement multilateral and regional economic and trade policies; deal with multilateral and regional economic and trade organisations according to division of labour; organise the implementation of the strategy on free trade zones; take the lead in organising negotiations with foreign parties on multilateral and regional economic and trade issues and free trade areas; represent China in economic and technological cooperation with international organisations including the UN; manage multilateral and bilateral non-reimbursable assistance and grant-in-aid provided to China (exclusive of grant-in-aid provided by foreign governments and international financial organisations under financial cooperation).

(continued)

Major international institutions	Major international duties
Department of WTO Affairs	Deal with the WTO on behalf of the Chinese government, in charge of various conferences, multilateral and bilateral negotiations under the WTO framework; assume the obligations of policy review, notification and consulting in trade and investment that China assumes in the WTO; in charge of trade disputes related to China together with Department of Treaty and Law, Department of Regions and other departments; have foreign-related consultations prior to resorting to the WTO's Dispute Settlement Mechanism (DSB); coordinate tasks after China's entry into the WTO; contact China's permanent delegation stationed in the WTO.
Department of Asian Affairs	Conduct economic and trade cooperation with Asian countries
Department of Western Asian and African Affairs	Conduct economic and trade cooperation with West Asian and African countries
Department of European Affairs	Conduct economic and trade cooperation with European countries
Department of American and Oceanian Affairs	Conduct economic and trade cooperation with Oceanic countries in America
Department of Foreign Affairs	Handle protocol matters in international economic affairs
Department of Fair Trade for Imports and Exports	Deal with business concerning fair trade and anti-dumping

The Ministry of Commerce gets involved in economic diplomacy via economic and trade negotiations, and also through various bilateral dialogue mechanisms in which the ministry takes the lead. One important example is the Joint Commission on Commerce and Trade (JCCT), which started in 1983 and is known as a "fire extinguisher" of trade friction between China and America. Since its establishment, it has played an important role in enhancing mutual understanding, pushing forward and strengthening mutually beneficial economic and trade cooperation, and safeguarding and promoting the stable development of bilateral economic and trade relations. At the end of 2003, Wen Jiabao, the then premier of China's State Council, paid a visit to the US during which leaders of both countries agreed to heighten the level of conferences of the JCCT. China's vice-premier acted as chairman of the Chinese side, while the post of chairman of the US side was shared by the US commerce secretary and the US Trade Representative (USTR). Conferences of the JCCT were upgraded to the highest-level economic and trade consultation mechanism between the two sides. As a consequence, the annual JCCT has become an important platform for Sino-US economic diplomacy.

III. Ministry of Finance and China's financial diplomacy

For a long time, the Ministry of Finance has been in charge of domestic economic issues, with responsibility for managing national treasury receipts and payments. The Ministry of Finance influences the domestic economy through collecting taxes and other revenues for government expenditure. In any country, the fiscal policy of the Ministry of Finance is used to exert financial macro-control of the market.

For some time, the minister of finance has not been the key figure in China's economic diplomacy due to the fact that trade has played a dominant role in China's external economic affairs. Rather, it is the Ministry of Commerce that is the key department in China's economic diplomacy. In China, economic diplomacy is often equated to commercial diplomacy.

However, with China's entry into the WTO, the focus of China's external economic relations has gradually shifted to finance. From this time, China also begins to play a role in global financial governance. On numerous international stages, we often see Chinese finance ministers attending financial conferences of the G7, G20, IMF and World Bank. Against the backdrop of financial globalisation, China's Ministry of Finance has gradually developed into a leading institution of economic diplomacy. Finance ministers have assumed more and more duties concerning economic diplomacy, though this process is somewhat passive.

In addition to some traditional economic duties, the Ministry of Finance has taken on a number of duties concerning economic diplomacy, such as, according to official statements, "organising international negotiations on external finance and debts and initialling relevant agreements", "joining in relevant international financial and economic organisations and conducting international exchanges and cooperation in finance and taxation on behalf of the Chinese government".

Specifically, the Ministry of Finance assumes the following duties concerning economic diplomacy:

First, attend global or regional dialogues between finance ministers. As the ministry of finance is the major macro-economic decision-maker in Western countries, it is viewed as the manager of the domestic economy. In the era of economic globalisation, domestic macroeconomic policy can have a huge spillover effect and influence other countries whose economies are mutually dependent. Therefore, Western developed countries have all along attached great importance to dialogue and communication between finance ministers so as to enhance coordination on macroeconomic policy. This is an important reason for the elevated status of finance ministers in the decision-making system of external contact. With the Chinese economy growing so rapidly, the country's finance minister is now routinely invited to attend global or regional financial dialogue mechanisms, such as the finance ministers' dialogue under the framework of the G20 and the finance ministers' dialogue under the framework of ASEAN plus China, Japan and South Korea.

Second, act as the representative of the Chinese government joining in global or regional international financial organisations. The Chinese government has become more involved in various global or regional international financial organisations, such as the World Bank, Asian Development Bank (ADB) and Inter-American Development Bank (IDB). These organisations have to deal with issues such as contributions and exercising the right of representation. China's Ministry of Finance acts as the contributor and exercises right of representation on behalf of the Chinese government. In this process, the Chinese finance minister is responsible for attending the annual meetings of these organisations and participating in various negotiations and discussions on relevant institutional reforms.

Third, participate in some financial and economic communication mechanisms specifically drawn up by both sides. In recent years, in order to enhance bilateral dialogue and exchanges on finance and the economy, the Ministry of Finance, together with corresponding departments of several other countries, has initiated a series of bilateral financial dialogue mechanisms, including the China-US Strategic and Economic Dialogue (S&ED, Economy) and the China-France Economic and Financial Dialogue. For this reason, China's Ministry of Commerce has assumed a great number of duties concerning bilateral economic diplomacy.

Unlike the Ministry of Commerce, there are no professional personnel or institutions in the Ministry of Finance that are in charge of external affairs. However, in recent years, a convention has taken shape that a vice-minister from the Ministry of Finance is in charge of international affairs

As the name suggests, the Ministry of Finance's Department of International Trade and Economic Affairs is in charge of international affairs.

Duties of Department of International Trade and Economic Affairs of the Ministry of Finance

Study and analyse international economic and financial issues and put forward relevant policy proposals
In charge of international multilateral and bilateral financial cooperation
In charge of loans and guarantees of the World Bank and the Asian Development Bank and of negotiations and discussions with foreign countries
Administer affairs of the Chinese Council at the World Bank and the Asian Development Bank
Participate in negotiations, lending and repayment of loads of the International Fund for Agricultural Development (IFAD);
Give suggestions on annual appropriation budget for foreign affairs of ministries and affiliated institutions; preside over the General Affairs Offices of Hong Kong Special Administration Region, Macao Special Administration Region and Taiwan under Ministry of Finance; organise and manage overseas investigation trips and training of administrative officials, Etc.

The second department directly involved in international affairs is the Department of External Economic Cooperation. If the Department of International Trade and Economic Affairs lays particular stress on international policy-making, the Department of External Economic Cooperation is focused on foreign contacts. It is the major participant and executor of China's financial diplomacy.

The Department of External Economic Cooperation assumes specific work concerning dialogue with foreign countries on finance and the economy assigned by the State Council; studies and gives suggestions on relevant policy proposals and dialogue schemes; assumes tasks such as coordination, liaison and negotiations; promotes all institutionalised bilateral cooperation, including the vice-premier-level mechanism for Sino-US Strategic and Economic Dialogue and the China-UK Economic and Financial Dialogue as well as eight other bilateral mechanisms.

Duties of the Department of External Economic Cooperation

Organise and comprehensively coordinate tasks for the Sino-US Strategic and Economic Dialogue and the China-UK Economic and Financial Dialogue
Organise Sino-US Joint Economic Committee and its deputies' conferences, and coordinate other subordinate conference mechanisms
Organize Sino-Europe Financial Dialogue and Sino-India Financial Dialogue; in charge of Sino-Japan Finance Ministers' Dialogue and Sino-Russia Finance Ministers' Dialogue
In charge of liaison, comprehensive organisational and coordinative work for institutionalised bilateral financial cooperation meetings such as Sino-Brazil Financial Dialogue and finance ministers' mutual visit mechanism and relevant activities.
Study and analyse relevant key financial and economic issues and put forward suggestions.

Bilateral dialogue mechanisms in the charge of Department of External Economic Cooperation

Name of mechanism	Starting time	Details	Main tasks
Sino-US Strategic and Economic Dialogue (Economy)	July 2009	Formerly known as the Sino-US Strategic Economic Dialogue starting from September 2006	Emphasis is given to discuss long-term economic issues of common concern and of strategic and overall importance without replacing, repeating or weakening other existing dialogue and cooperation mechanisms in other economic fields so as to push forward the health and stable development of Sino-US economic ties and overall bilateral relations. Ministries of finance of both sides are in charge of coordinating specific issues concerning the economic dialogue.
China-UK Economic and Financial Dialogue	2008	In January 2008, Premier Wen Jiabao and UK Prime Minister Gordon Brown established a vice-premier-level economic dialogue mechanism that was formerly known as vice-ministerial level Sino-UK Financial Dialogue	It is an effective platform for discussions on long-term issues of strategic and overall importance to enhance communication and coordination of both sides in macroeconomic policies and key international issues; it aims to promote bilateral economic and financial cooperation, consolidate and push forward Sino-UK economic ties and the development of strategic and collaborative partnership between the two countries.

(continued)

Name of mechanism	Starting time	Details	Main tasks
China-Europe Financial Dialogue Mechanism	February 2005	In February 2005, the Ministry of Finance and the EU Commission established a financial dialogue mechanism. The dialogue is an important platform for dialogue and communication between China and Europe on macroeconomic policies and financial cooperation. It is held once a year. So far, both sides have taken turns to hold five dialogues.	Enhance communication and coordination in macroeconomic policy; push forward bilateral pragmatic cooperation in the economy and finance to promote the development of Sino-Europe economic relations.
Sino-Russia Finance Ministers' Dialogue Mechanism	March 2006	On 21 March 2006, while Russian President Vladimir Putin visited China, the Chinese and Russian governments co-signed the *Memorandum of Understanding on Initiating Sino-Russia Finance Ministers' Dialogue Mechanism*, officially announcing the establishment of the Sino-Russia Finance Ministers Dialogue Mechanism. The two countries take turns to hold the ministerial-level dialogue once a year.	Topics for the dialogue include cooperation between China and Russia in macro-economic policy, fiscal policy, financial policy and international finance.
Sino-France Mutual Visit Mechanism			Both sides enhance communication in macroeconomic policy through regular mutual visits of finance ministers to promote mutual understanding on key international economic issues and enhance pragmatic and mutually beneficial cooperation in finance.
Sino-Germany Finance Ministers' Mutual Visit Mechanism		On 30 March 2011, Minister Xie Xuren and Finance Minister of Germany Wolfgang Schäuble co-signed the *Memorandum of Understanding on Financial Cooperation between China's Ministry of Finance and German Financial Ministry* to push forward bilateral and multilateral cooperation between ministries of finance of the two countries.	Both sides enhance coordination in macroeconomic policy through regular mutual visit mechanism of treasury secretaries to promote pragmatic financial and monetary cooperation and enrich economic cooperation between both sides.
Sino-Japan Treasure Secretary Dialogue	March 2006		Finance ministers of both countries exchange views on fiscal and economic policies and the developmental trend of regional and global economy

(continued)

The Actors of China's Economic Diplomacy

Name of mechanism	Starting time	Details	Main tasks
Financial Subcommittee of Finance under Sino-Brazil High-level Coordination and Cooperation Committee	March 2006	Formerly known as Sino-Brazil Fiscal Dialogue. In September 2009, China and Brazil established the Sino-Brazil Subcommittee of Finance under the Sino-Brazil High-level Coordination and Cooperation Committee to replace the Sino-Brazil Financial Dialogue Mechanism. Under the auspices of China's Ministry of Finance, the subcommittee is composed of the SDRC, PBC, China Banking Regulatory Commission (CBRC), China Securities Regulatory Commission (CSRC), China Insurance Regulatory Commission and other institutions (according to need, such as China Development Bank, Import-Export Bank, China Investment Bank). Its topics include: macroeconomic policy, issues concerning multilateral finance and economics, and currency. In principle, the two countries take turns to host the meeting once a year.	Both sides discuss and exchange views on the macroeconomic situation, fiscal policy and economic development strategy and international fiscal and financial cooperation.

In addition, the Department of Tariffs is established under the Ministry of Finance, involving many issues related to international trade.

Main duties of the Department of Tariffs

Study and propose rates of import and export duties
Assume daily routine work of the Tariff Commission of the State Council (TCSC)
Study and propose schemes for China's external tariff negotiations and discussions and participate in relevant negotiations and discussions; draw up clauses concerning import tariffs and tax in treaties signed between China and other countries, regions and international organisations and participate in negotiations and discussions.
Study and propose schemes for imposition of anti-dumping duties, anti-subsidy duties, safeguarding measures duties, retaliatory tariffs and others decided by other tariff measures; handle specific issues concerning administrative review of special tariffs.
Study and propose amendments to stipulations on import tax and stipulations on tonnage duties; study and propose policies on tariffs of border trade, processing trade, bonded areas and export processing zones, etc, and import tax. In charge of issues related to Ministry of Finance concerning the coordination and summary for China's obligations in its entry into the WTO. Give tariff guidance to local departments.

IV. People's Bank of China and monetary diplomacy

For a long time, the PBC did not play an important role in China's economic diplomacy. As its financial system used to be closed, China barely got involved in the international monetary and financial system. China didn't have a modern central banking system until recently. Besides, the central bank was merely a subsidiary body of the Ministry of Finance for a long time and even worked side by side with the ministry in the same building. Under an immature central banking system, the PBC was mainly in charge of foreign affairs concerning the IMF. Apart from this, it assumed no important diplomatic duties.

Under a unified planning system, the super-incumbent People's Bank was the basic means for the country to absorb, mobilise, gather and distribute credit capital. It assumed the function of managing the national treasury, while also having the function of a commercial bank. In 1993, the Chinese government began to modernise and improve its central banking system. According to the *Decision of the State Council on Reform of the Financial System*, the PBC intensified its duties in financial control, supervision and service, and transferred its policy-related and commercial bank businesses.

On 18 March 1995, the National People's Congress approved the Law of the People's Republic of China on the PBC, legally establishing the PBC as the central bank for the first time and ensuring that the central banking system was placed on a legal and regular track. This was a milestone in the institutional improvement of the central bank. In 1998, based on the spirit of the National Conference on Financial Work held by the CPC Central Committee, the management system of the PBC began to be reformed and provincial subsidiary banks were dismantled and inter-provincial branches were established. In 2005, with the PBC setting up its second headquarters in Shanghai, China began to gradually establish a central banking system featuring the modern market economic system. This provided an institutional foundation for the PBC to engage in international economic diplomacy.

Since China entered into the WTO in 2001, its economy has begun to become more integrated in the global economic system. Its financial system is now influenced by the global economic environment and its financial relations with foreign countries and regions have begun to influence the international financial system. China's huge foreign trade surplus has led to its accumulation of a huge US dollar reserve, which influences international capital movements and the international exchange rate system.

After the outbreak of East Asian financial crisis in 1997, the Chinese government decided not to depreciate the renminbi and conveyed this message to the international community through diplomatic visits. This may be viewed as an important symbol of the rejuvenation of China's central bank diplomacy. Later, China's central bank was involved in the dialogue mechanism for finance ministers of central banks under the framework of East Asia 10+3, and directly took part in the Chiang Mai Initiative that was later viewed as a watershed for East Asia economic cooperation.

The Actors of China's Economic Diplomacy

In 2003, under pressure from US Congress, the American government began to put pressure on China to appreciate the renminbi, a prelude to a chronic dispute on this issue between the two countries. As the PBC assumed direct responsibility for the exchange rate, it became the focus of pressure from the US side. PBC diplomacy on the exchange rate issue with the US helped to alleviate international pressure through communication, persuasion and internal reform. The dispute over the renminbi exchange rate between China and the US became the most important economic issue in the first 10 years of the 21st century, and this fact made the PBC an important actor that influences China's economic relations with foreign countries, and monetary relations in particular.

The dispute over the renminbi exchange rate between China and the US resulted in the rising status of the PBC in economic diplomacy circles. The outbreak of the US financial crisis in 2008 and the European debt crisis in 2010 consolidated its status. These two crises directly led to a more important role of financial and monetary issues in global governance and international cooperation, which made it urgent for the international community to exchange views over financial and monetary issues between central banks. As a result, central banks have played a notable role in the international arena.

Major dialogue and international conference mechanisms in which China's central bank participates

Name of mechanisms	Notes
Annual Meeting of Council of Caribbean Development Bank	On 22-23 May 2013, Li Dongrong, vice-governor of the PBC attended the 43rd annual meeting of the Council of Caribbean Development Bank at Saint Lucia. The Caribbean Development Bank is a sub-regional inter-governmental development financial institution founded in 1970 and headquartered in Barbados. It has 26 full members. China joined the Bank in 1997.
Meeting of Finance Ministers and governors of Central Banks of ASEAN plus China, Japan and the Republic of Korea (10+3)	On 3 May 2013, vice-minister of the Ministry of Finance Zhu Guangyao and governor of PBC Jin Qi led a delegation to attend Meeting of Finance Ministers and governors of Central Banks of (10+3) in Delhi, India.
Executives' Meeting of East Asia and Pacific Central Banks (EMEAP)	On 15-17 July 2012, Governor of the PBC Zhou Xiaochuan led a delegation to attend the 17th executive meeting of the EMEAP in Japan.
Ministerial-level Conference of International Monetary and Financial Committee (IMFC) of IMF	On 20 April 2013, the 27th session of the ministerial meeting of IMFC of IMF was convened in Washington, the US; Governor of the PBC Zhou Xiaochuan and vice-governor Yi Gang attended the conference.
Meeting of Finance Ministers and Central Bank Governors of Brazil, Russia, India, China and South Africa (BRICS)	On 26 March 2013, on the eve of the fifth meeting of leaders, finance ministers and central bank governors had a meeting in Durban, South Africa. Governor of the PBC Zhou Xiaochuan and minister of finance of China Lou Jiwei led a delegation to attend the meeting.

(continued)

	Name of mechanisms	Notes
Multilateral	South-East Asian Central Banks [SEACEN] Organisation Governors & Council Meeting	On 22-23 November 2012, vice-governor of PBC Yi Gang led a delegation to attend the 48th governors meetings and the 32nd council meeting of SEACEN at Ulaanbaatar, Mongolia.
	Central Bank Governors Meeting between China, Japan and South Korea	On 1 August 2012, the fourth Central Bank Governors Meeting between China, Japan and South Korea was held in Dalian, China. Governor of the PBC Zhou Xiaochuan hosted the meeting. Governor of Bank of Japan Masaaki Shirakawa and Governor of Bank of Korea Kim Choong-soo also attended.
	Annual Council Meeting of African Development Bank Group	From 31 May to 1 June 2012, vice-governor of the PBC Yi Gang led a delegation to attend the Annual Council Meeting of African Development Bank Group in Arusha, Tanzania.
	Finance Ministers and Central Bank Governors Meeting of SCO	On 17 May 2012, SCO Second session of Finance Ministers and Central Bank Governors Meeting was held in Beijing. Minister of Finance Xie Xuren and Governor of the PBC Zhou Xiaochuan co-hosted the meeting.
	Financial Stability Board (FSB)	On 10 January 2012, the tenth plenary session of the FSB was convened in Basel, Switzerland. Governor of the PBC Zhou Xiaochuan and vice-president of China Banking Regulatory Commission (CBRC) Wang Zhaoxing and representatives of the Ministry of Finance attended the meeting.
	The 27th session annual Council Meeting of the Eastern and Southern African Trade and Development Bank	The 27th Council Meeting of PTA was held in Mauritius on 20 December 2011. Governor assistant of the PBC Li Dongrong led a delegation to attend the meeting. PTA Bank is the largest sub-regional development bank in Southeast Asia. It has 20 members. China is the only extra-regional member country.
	The Central Bank Governors' Club of Central Asia, Black Sea Region and Balkan Countries	Peoples' Bank of China officially joined The Central Bank Governors' Club of Central Asia, Black Sea Region and Balkan Countries on 9 April 2011. Governor assistant Li Dongrong led a delegation to attend the signing ceremony of China's official entry into the organisation on behalf of the PBC and attended the 25th executive meeting in Istanbul, Turkey.
	Finance Ministers and Central Bank Governors Meeting of G20	
Bilateral	Sub-committee on Financial Cooperation of Kazakhstan-China Cooperation Committee	From 30-31 May 2013, the eighth session of the Sub-committee on financial cooperation was convened in Guilin, Guangxi Zhuang autonomous region, and both sides agreed that the ninth session would be held in Kazakhstan in 2014
	Sub-committee on Financial Cooperation of China-Russia Prime Ministers' Regular Meeting Committee	The 13th session of Sub-committee on Financial Cooperation of China-Russia Prime Ministers' Regular Meeting Committee was held in Kunming, Yunnan province from 20-21 June 2012. The meeting was co-hosted by Jin Qi, Chinese chairman of the sub-committee and assistant governor of the PBC and Victor Nikolaevich Melnikov, Russian Chairman of the sub-committee, vice-governor of Central Bank of Russia.

(continued)

Name of mechanisms	Notes
Sino-German Financial Stability Forum	The agreement that China and Germany establish a mechanism of financial stability forum was written into the Sino-German Joint Communiqué during the first round of governmental discussions between China and Germany in June 2011. On 11 July 2011, the PBC and Deutsche Bundesbank held the first Sino-German Financial Stability Forum in Frankfurt, Germany. Vice-governor of PBC Yi Gang and member of the board of directors of Deutsche Bundesbank Andreas Dobre made speeches at the meeting.

As governor of the PBC, Zhou Xiaochuan has had a huge amount of financial exchange reserves at his disposal. He became a star on the stage of international financial and monetary diplomacy. Zhou ranked 15th in Forbes' list of the World's Most Powerful People in 2011. Within the central bank, Yi Gang, vice-governor and director general of the Foreign Exchange Administration, and Jin Qi, governor assistant, are in charge of international affairs. Jin Qi used to act as head of the Department of International Trade and Economic Affairs and vice-executive director of China at the IMF.

The Department of International Trade and Economic Affairs under the PBC is in charge of issues concerning the PBC's official communication and business contact with financial organisations such as the International Finance Corporation, financial organisations of Hong Kong and Macau special administrative regions, and Taiwan as well as central banks of foreign countries and the European Central Bank. It also gives guidance to the overseas institutions of the PBC. Under the Department of International Trade and Economic Affairs, there are several units that are in charge of the IMF and Bank for International Settlement affairs, regional financial cooperation, multilateral development banks and cooperation with central banks. The establishment of these division-level institutions is indicative of the function of economic diplomacy of central banks.

V. National Development and Reform Commission and climate and energy diplomacy

The National Development and Reform Commission (NDRC) plays an important role in China's economic decision-making system. This is due to its origin under the previous Planning Commission. It is also known as the "minor State Council". The NDRC's duties include: drafting and organising the implementation of strategy of national economic and social development, long- and medium-term plans and annual plans; planning for and coordinating social and economic development; studying and analysing the domestic and foreign economic situation and putting forward goals and policies for national economic development, regulation and control over general price levels and optimising key economic structures.

The NDRC has an important duty in economic diplomacy in organising the drafting of key strategies, and planning policies for coping with climate change. It also takes the lead, together with other departments, in organising and participating in international negotiations on climate change, and dealing with issues concerning China's implementation of the United Nations Framework Convention on Climate Change.

The NDRC established the Department of Climate Change, which is in charge of organising, studying and putting forward suggestions on the general policy and schemes for China's participation in international negotiations on climate change. It also takes the lead in drawing up and organising the implementation of counter-proposals for specific negotiations, and works jointly with other parties to take the lead in organising and participating in international negotiations and international conferences.

The Department of Foreign Affairs acts as a window in economic cooperation and exchanges with foreign countries in the NDRC. Its main tasks include: actively expanding the fields and scope of the NDRC's cooperation with foreign countries; striving to promote the establishment of bilateral and multilateral cooperation mechanisms with foreign governments, international organisations and institutions; enhancing exchanges and cooperation with famous transnational companies in energy, automobiles, high-technology, communications, aviation, chemical engineering, finance, etc; taking the initiative to coordinate and promote China's "going global" strategy. In addition, the department is responsible for selecting diplomats for the department of economic affairs of Chinese embassies and consulates abroad and organising them to analyse, investigate and survey the economic situation, macroeconomic policy and important topics of the countries of their residence. Currently, Xie Zhenhua, vice-director of the NDRC, is in charge of participating in international negations on climate change and environmental issues on behalf of the Chinese government.

The National Energy Administration, a vice-ministerial-level department under the NDRC, is the major executing agency of China's external energy policy and diplomacy. It is responsible for: taking the lead in conducting international cooperation in energy; negotiating and signing agreements with foreign energy departments and international energy organisations; coordinating energy development and utilisation in foreign countries; examining or approving key overseas energy investment projects (coal, petroleum, natural gas, electric power, natural uranium, etc) in accordance with the regulations. The Department of International Affairs under the NEA is in charge of international energy cooperation.

Duties of National Energy Administration

Take the lead in international energy cooperation
Organise negotiations with competent departments of foreign countries and international energy organisations.
Study the developmental situation of international energy; work out energy opening-up strategy, developmental planning, annual plans and policies.
Coordinate the development and utilisation of energy of foreign countries; work with relevant departments to put forward the layout for overseas investment projects and examination reports for key projects such as coal, coal fuel, electric power, natural uranium and oil refining; participate in related work regarding overseas investment projects in petroleum, natural gas, etc.
Participate in formulating policies on finance and taxation, environmental protection and tackling climate change concerning international energy cooperation.
In charge of office work of external affairs; coordinate with international energy agencies.

The National Energy Administration has become involved in a series of international mechanisms on energy cooperation on behalf of the Chinese government. These mechanisms are an important platform for China's energy diplomacy.

The vice-director of the NDRC's Academy of Macroeconomic Research acts as the dean. It is the major advisory body and policy research institution of the NDRC. Under the academy, there is the Foreign Economic Research Institute, which specialises in studying key economic issues with foreign countries.

In addition to these institutions and departments, the Ministry of Foreign Affairs, as the core department in charge of traditional diplomacy, is involved in economic diplomacy In 2012, the Ministry of Foreign Affairs established a special Department of International Economic Affairs to enhance research on key international economic issues.

To sum up, through decades of institutional evolution, especially against the backdrop of China integrating with the global economic system, a sound institutional structure of economic diplomacy has gradually taken shape in the country. This institutional structure ensures that China can conduct vigorous economic diplomacy in the international arena in a way that serves national interests.

Section 2 New actors of China's economic diplomacy

The National People's Congress (NPC) is the highest organ of state power in

China. The Chinese People's Political Consultative Conference (CPPCC) is the principal organ for all political parties, groups and ethnic groups, and the general public to participate in, deliberate and administer state affairs and exercise democratic supervision. These two major organs, with special functions of legislative oversight and participating in the deliberation and administration of state affairs, play an important role in economic diplomacy. It carries out this role through specialised commissions. Moreover, local governments, enterprise institutes such as commercial associations and think tanks, and the media have begun to play an important part in China's economic diplomacy.

I. National People's Congress

The NPC's Foreign Affairs Committee is a special committee established within the NPC. Its main duties include examining and submitting relevant bills, examining administrative laws and regulations, decisions or orders that contravene the Constitution or statutes as well as investigation and survey, and also submitting a request for approval of bills for concluding treaties and important agreements with foreign countries and presenting a considered report to the Standing Committee of the NPC.

As an internal committee of the NPC in charge of foreign affairs, the Foreign Affairs Committee plays an important role in economic diplomacy, which is fully reflected in its work such as an intensive and comprehensive investigation on relevant policies and treaties, coordinating with relevant departments of foreign affairs and providing subsidiary communication channels. In terms of specific action, it is responsible for establishing a mechanism of regular communication with the parliaments of other countries.

The mechanism of regular communication meetings established by the NPC's Foreign Affairs Committee on the basis of the NPC and parliaments of many countries is an important case of the Foreign Affairs Committee's direct participation in diplomatic issues, of which economic diplomacy, an essential part, is often mentioned in the dialogue of parliamentary exchanges.

On 25 September 2006, Baleka Mbete, president of the National Assembly of South Africa and Wu Bangguo, the then Chairman of the Standing Committee of the NPC, signed a Memorandum of Understanding on establishing regular communication mechanism between China's National People's Congress and the National Assembly of South Africa.

In October 2011, Nomaindia Mfeketo, vice-chairman of the National Assembly of South Africa and Chairman of the South Africa side of the regular communication mechanism between China and South Africa led a delegation to China and attended the first session of the regular communication mechanism between the NPC of the People's Republic of China and the National Assembly of South Africa. In March 2012, the vice-chairman of the Standing Committee of the NPC and the chairman of the Chinese side of the regular communication mechanism between the NPC of the PRC and the National Assembly of South Africa led a delegation to South Africa and attended the second session of regular communication mechanism between the two sides.

Economic diplomacy is prominent in the two dialogues between China and South Africa.

In the first dialogue, both sides discussed bilateral relations, bilateral parliamentary exchanges, coping with climate change and environmental protection. The dialogue involved the prospect for cooperation and opportunities, signalling that enterprises of China and South Africa would cooperate in these fields. In this dialogue, the South Africa side expressed hope that legislatures of both countries could push forward the implementation of the *Beijing Declaration* and key cooperation projects. It also hoped China could provide loans on favourable terms and cooperate in mineral products and resources. The China side made active responses in these areas. After the meeting, progress on a number of projects was quickened.

The second dialogue was devoted to discussing training young people and job expansion, poverty eradication, state-owned enterprises and infrastructure construction. As a matter of fact, discussions were mainly focused on economic diplomacy. Thanks to a wide range of interest and enthusiasm about these topics, the dialogue lasted four hours instead of the scheduled two hours and a half. Pragmatic issues were discussed. The South Africa side hoped the Chinese side could give support to and invest in the former's infrastructure construction projects, such as railways, roads, waterways and electric power, support South Africa (in cooperation with eight other African countries) in competing for a radio telescope project. South Africa appealed to China's NPC to offer help and coordinate with relevant Chinese departments or local governments to assist South Africa in setting up entrepreneurship training institutions and it proposed to create a mechanism for a parliamentary forum of the BRICS countries.

In 2007, while Wu Bangguo, the then Chairman of the NPC's Standing Committee, paid a visit to Egypt, Ahmed Fathi Surour, Speaker of People's Assembly of The Arab Republic of Egypt, formally signed a memorandum of understanding on establishing a regular exchange mechanism between The National People's Congress (NPC) of the PRC and the People's Assembly of Arab Republic of Egypt.

In October 2007, Surour led a delegation to China and attended the first meeting of the Sino-Egypt Regular Exchange Mechanism. In November 2008, Isma'il Tiliwaldi, Chairman of the Chinese side and vice chairman of the NPC Standing Committee, headed a delegation to Egypt. Both sides held the second meeting of the Regular Exchange Mechanism. In December 2009, Zainab Radwan, Deputy-Speaker of Egypt's People's Assembly led a delegation to visit China and attended the third meeting of the Regular Exchange Mechanism. In March 2010, Wang Zhaoguo, vice-chairman of the NPC Standing Committee headed a delegation to visit Egypt and held the fourth meeting of the Regular Exchange Mechanism. The topics for discussion at the first meeting of the Regular Exchange Mechanism were bilateral relations, parliamentary exchanges, planning and operation of the bilateral exchange mechanism. The topics for the second meeting were economic and trade cooperation, the financial crisis and international and regional hot topics. Topics for the third meeting included climate change, energy and environmental protection, the international financial crisis and Sino-Egypt economic and trade cooperation, cultural and civilisation diversity, and the situation in the Middle East. Topics for the fourth meeting included the trade imbalance, tourism cooperation and the Middle East peace process.

The discussion topics for the regular exchange mechanisms between parliaments of China and South Africa and between the parliaments of China and Egypt have focused on economic issues. Almost every dialogue involved fixed topics on economic diplomacy, such as economic and trade cooperation, financial crises and energy economic cooperation. After the dialogue, according to NPC rules, the Foreign Affairs Committee and other special committees will quicken the implementation of dialogue achievements through proposals, supervision and other means.

Apart from the Foreign Affairs Committee, the NPC has several other committees involved in issues regarding economic diplomacy and their duties are reflected in legislation and supervision over the implementation. These committees include the Financial and Economic Affairs Committee, the Environmental Protection and Resources Conservation Committee, and the Overseas Chinese Affairs Committee.

The Financial and Economic Affairs Committee is in charge of research and legislative proposals in finance and the economy, which is an integral part of economic diplomacy. Economic diplomacy serves the development of the domestic economy. It participates in international and regional financial cooperation in a constructive manner by enhancing communication and policy coordination of all sides to promote the steady and rapid growth of the domestic economy.

Based on this, the Financial and Economic Affairs Committee of the NPC gets involved in investigations and the study of economic diplomacy. For example, in April 2010, a delegation of the Financial and Economic Affairs Committee visited Vietnam and had a working conference with the financial budget committee of the Vietnamese National Assembly. Both sides exchanged views on policy responses to the international financial crisis, as well as on climate change, energy conservation and emission reduction and environmental protection.

The Environmental Protection and Resources Conservation Committee (EPRCC), which is in charge of research and legislation in environment and resource conservation, also gets involved in economic diplomacy. Environmental diplomacy between the parliaments of two sides and the enhancement of bilateral environmental cooperation are an essential part of its work agenda.

The EPRCC's functions in economic diplomacy are: actively conducting exchanges in environmental and resource legislation and law enforcement with special committees of parliaments of foreign countries; keeping contact with international organisations and institutions such as the UN Environment Program (UNEP) and the Global Environmental Fund (GEF); making energetic efforts to win subsidies from the World Bank and the Asian Development Bank (ADB) and conducting legislative investigation and surveys, and training in law.

Delegations of the EPRCC regularly attend the Asia Pacific Conference on Environment and Development and other international conferences on environmental protection, such as the World Summit on Sustainable Development, the UN Convention to Combat Desertification, and International Conference on Mountainous Regions. NPC members investigate and study aspects such as legislative experience in environmental protection, especially cleaner production law, law for the assessment of environmental impacts, air and water pollution control, the disposal of solid waste, and developing a circular economy.

These tasks only enhance the international community's understanding of China's efforts in environmental protection, and they also push forward legislation in China in a more scientific way so as to promote domestic economic development and exchanges in environmental protection and economic development with foreign countries. For this reason, they have become an important vehicle of economic diplomacy.

To some extent, the Overseas Chinese Affairs Committee assumes functions of economic diplomacy. It is mainly in charge of legislation, investigation and study of overseas Chinese affairs. In real life, overseas Chinese affairs have much to do with the economic and investment environment and protection for foreign services, which can find expression in economic diplomacy.

The Overseas Chinese Affairs Committee often participates in activities of parliamentary diplomacy organised by the NPC and the NPC Standing Committee. For example, it visits the countries of overseas nationals to find out and investigate the conditions in safeguarding their legitimate rights, seeking their opinions on China's democracy and legal construction, especially legal construction in affairs of overseas nationals, strengthening ties with parliaments and competent government departments of their countries of residence to create a sound condition for them to seek a better livelihood and development. The economy plays an important role in all these activities.

In addition to these special committees, there are many other committees within the NPC, such as the Law Committee and the Agriculture and Rural Affairs Committee, whose duties are involved in economic diplomacy.

II. Chinese People's Political Consultative Conference

The Chinese People's Political Consultative Conference (CPPCC) is also involved in economic diplomacy and actively seeks to play an important role in this field.

In recent years, the Foreign Affairs Committee of the CPPCC has brought its features and advantages into full play. Based on investigation, study and inspection, and taking the promotion of public diplomacy as the principal line and highlighting the expansion of friendly exchanges with foreign countries, the Foreign Affairs Committee has assumed the functions of political consultation, democratic supervision, administrating and discussing state affairs, and actively exploring new fields, approaches and ways of fulfilling its duties.

As the CPPCC is composed of 34 sectors and gathers political and social elites throughout China, members of the CPPCC have more opportunities to visit foreign countries. According to Zhao Qizheng, previous director of the Foreign Affairs Committee of the CPPCC, the status of members of the CPPCC as "both a government official and an ordinary person" is more easily acceptable to foreigners. Therefore, the CPPCC plays a special role in economic diplomacy.

In the field of economic diplomacy, the Foreign Affairs Committee of the CPPCC has conducted various investigations and studies in recent years and submitted a series of proposals and suggestions, which have influenced the decision-making of the government.

In 2010, members of the CPPCC submitted an *Investigation Report on the Public Diplomacy in the "Going Global" of Chinese Enterprises*, to which state leaders gave important written instructions. Moreover, international exchanges organised by the CPPCC have enriched the organisational form of China's economic diplomacy. In 2012, a CPPCC member delegation left for the UK to attend The London Book Fair and attended forums on "Public Diplomacy and Cross-Cultural Communication" and "Sino-UK Soft Power Creative Industry" held by the House of Commons. They delivered a keynote speech, offering advice on cultural industry exchanges between China and the UK, which proved to be very effective. Suggestions and opinions contained in the speech received the active response of Chinese government departments and enterprises.

III. A comparison: features of the NPC and the CPPCC's participation in economic diplomacy

The main features of the NPC and the CPPCC in terms of their participation in economic diplomacy may be summarised as follows:

First, both are indirectly involved in economic diplomacy. As neither of them is a government agency, deputies to the People's Congress and members of the CPPCC regulate activities of economic diplomacy through legislation or legislation proposals, and promote the development of economic diplomacy through supervision and suggestions.

Second, the two institutions can communicate with economic and diplomatic counterparts in diversified ways. As deputies to the People's Congress and members of the CPPCC come from all walks of life, their handling of economic and diplomatic affairs provide sufficient experience for economic diplomacy.

Moreover, as the two are neither decision-makers nor executing agencies, they can explore new thinking and new ways to develop China's economic diplomacy.

IV. Local government

According to traditional concepts and definitions, the actors of diplomacy should be national states. However, with the continuous progress of globalisation, actors of various forms have appeared on the diplomatic stage. Though they differ from traditional national states in behavioural patterns, they play a very important role. What's more, with the deepening of global economic integration and greater interdependence, diplomacy has surpassed the traditional understanding featuring politics and security as its main contents. Instead, it has "broken through" the boundary, which finds expression in all fields, and economics in particular.

Different from traditional diplomacy, local governments can play a role in economic diplomacy, creating new opportunities and growth points through cooperation and exchange with foreign cities and provinces. Under the guidance of China's reform and opening-up policy and the strategy of "going global", several governments have entered into a new era of economic diplomacy and have played an essential part of China's external economic diplomacy.

By what means do local governments play their part in economic diplomacy?

First, under the general framework of the national policy of economic diplomacy, local governments may take advantage of this trend and take effective measures to promote the development of the local economy and growth of foreign trade.

In Yiwu, Zhejiang province, the local government, responding to the reform and opening-up policy and the "going global" strategy, by proposing the idea of "constructing Yiwu as a distribution centre for the global market". On this basis, it has built Yiwu International Trade and Commercial Center. Its watchword "buy global and sell global" attracts people from all over the world to Yiwu to conduct commodity transactions. Guided by this strategy, the city of Yiwu has promulgated more convenient measures for international manufacturers to go through formalities such as ordering and customs clearance so as to facilitate the development of the local economy.

Like Yiwu, many Chinese cities have taken various measures and made good use of local advantages to attract foreign capital and develop the local economy. They have also adopted favourable policies targeted at foreign countries to promote economic growth.

In 2012, South Korea's Samsung invested in a chip project in Xi'an, Shaanxi province. The project is likely to create employment opportunities and stimulate the local economy. During project negotiations, senior leaders from Shaanxi and the city government participated in negotiations and showed off the city's advantages. Through their unremitting efforts, Xi'an won the favour of Samsung. In order to attract the project, Xi'an offered Samsung favourable investment conditions, and also applied for supporting facilities such as a comprehensive bonded area. This case demonstrates that local governments can creatively conduct diplomatic activities and handle foreign affairs by bringing their own subjective initiative into full play in economic diplomacy.

Second, local governments strive to enhance international exchanges and increase opportunities for bilateral investment to push forward the development of economic diplomacy by establishing sister cities and provinces.

The "Sister Cities International" refers to a partnership established between different countries, cities or local governments so as to promote understanding and seek opportunities for cooperation through communication. The first pair of sister cities international was a partnership set up between Keighley in West Yorkshire, the UK, and Poix-du-Nord in France after the World War I. In China, there are two pairs of sister cities internationally, namely, Tianjin and Yokohama, Japan and Shanghai and Osaka, Japan established in 1973.

Economic exchange is an important component in the cooperation of sister cities international. Take the southern Chinese city of Guangzhou as an example. Guangzhou has established partnership sister cities with many economically developed cities in Europe and America, such as Lyons and Los Angeles and targets them for inward investment and high-tech industry exchange. In these sister city agreements, Guangzhou, Lyons, Los Angeles and others acknowledge the importance of economic cooperation. Furthermore, Guangzhou has set up two-way partnerships with cities such as Frankfurt and Sydney to implement the strategy of Chinese capital "going global" and brining in foreign capital so that both sides can use the other's resources in a rational manner. Guangzhou has also built up partnerships with cities of developing countries such as Ho Chi Minh City in Vietnam. Guangzhou takes advantages of the resources of these cities to tap new markets and seek more investment opportunities. These activities of economic diplomacy benefit both sides and help upgrade Guangzhou's degree of internationalisation.

Haidian District People's Government of Beijing, relying on its advantages of a high-tech industry and a high standard of education, has become sister cities with nine cities or regions in Asia, Europe and North America. In the course of economic diplomacy, Haidian cooperates with regions whose industrial structure is similar to that of its own, such as Nerima, Tokyo, whose animation industry is very developed, and San Jose, California, which is home to Silicon Valley. Haidian district exchanges economic interaction missions and enterprise delegations with these regions to enhance cooperation and communication in economy, trade, cultural creativity and high- and new-technology.

Third, while engaging in international cooperation and economic diplomacy, the local government is able to promote the development of quasi-international organisations that are similar to international city organisations and international industrial organisations through multilateral cooperation at sub-national level. It can also push forward globalisation, integration and urbanisation.

International organisations composed of these sub-national actors are voluntarily established by the local governments of the countries. Local governments may exchange practical experience in local management and development within these organisations and learn from others' strong points to offset weaknesses of their own. These organisations also provide a platform of multilateral exchange for local governments to get more involved in economic diplomacy. Besides, it not only makes a region better known to the outside world, but also publicises the image and investment environment of the region.

International organisations composed of local governments include United Cities and Local Governments (UCLG), the United Nations Human Settlements Programme (UN-HABITAT), and the Asia-Pacific City Summit (APCS). Chinese cities including Shanghai, Guangzhou and Tianjin, along with Hunan province, are members of the UCLG, in which many Chinese local governments, with the coordination of The Chinese People's Association for Friendship with Foreign Countries, participate in a great variety of forum activities on economic cooperation to facilitate economic diplomacy.

By various means, Chinese local governments can play a role in economic diplomacy that the central government cannot, especially in the fields of promoting local economic development and trade. This type of cooperation helps to deepen exchange and consolidate economic ties.

Nevertheless, activities of economic diplomacy have posed challenges to local governments in China, the greatest of which is that most of them do not have sufficient ability in economic diplomacy. This is manifested in the shortage of talent in foreign economic and trade cooperation and in an insufficiency of international behavioural competence. Some local governments have tried to propel bodies such as scientific research institutions, non-governmental organisations and enterprises to engage in economic diplomacy, which has achieved good results.

V. Enterprises, chambers of commerce and industrial associations

On the one hand, economic diplomacy refers to diplomatic activities oriented to state and sub-state actors. On the other hand, it aims to push forward trade and economic exchange. In this sense, economic diplomacy depends largely on various front-line actors in economic activities, namely, enterprises, and commercial and industrial associations. In modern diplomacy, no one can afford to ignore the influence and functions of these associations and large-scale transnational enterprises.

Trade relations between enterprises are not diplomatic behaviour but traditional economic and trade relations. However, with the development of international trade and globalisation, trade between enterprises has become more frequent, surpassing the frequency of diplomatic relations between countries. Relations between enterprises and relations between enterprises and commercial associations are, in the final analysis, still economic activities whose fundamental goal is to pursue economic benefit. Only when enterprise behaviour has a connection with the government can it be regarded as a behaviour of economic diplomacy.

Diplomacy in the early days was the behaviour of economic diplomacy, with merchants and enterprises as the basic unit. With the expansion of economic strength, modern cities and countries gradually took shape and so emerged diplomatic relations between nations.

With the implementation of the reform and opening-up policy, China has entered a new era. The Chinese economy has become the second largest in the world in terms of overall size, behind only the US. Enterprises and commercial associations are playing a dominant role in activities of economic diplomacy and assuming functions that the government cannot. What's more, large transnational enterprises have settled down in China and have connections with Chinese governments at all levels, pushing forward the internationalisation process of Chinese economic governance.

Enterprises and commercial associations, playing a new role in China's economic diplomacy, have two layers of meaning. First, they are carrying out the "going global" strategy and participating in international interaction as the actors of economic diplomacy. Second, large transnational enterprises have established operations in China and conduct activities of economic diplomacy oriented to the Chinese government.

Chinese enterprises, especially those following the "going global" strategy, are an important constituent part of China's foreign economic policy, and they are a crucial element of economic diplomacy. Chinese enterprises that are "going global" have contacts with governments of other countries, thus becoming a special link of China's economic diplomacy.

Chinese investment can be found in 178 countries across the world, covering many fields such as agriculture, industry, services and new- and high-technology industries. China's stock of foreign investment approaches US$400bn, making it the world's fifth largest outward foreign direct investor. The number of Chinese overseas workers has also increased sharply. Contract workers of various kinds through the Foreign Labour Service Cooperation amount to 812,000.

Gill Bates, a famous China expert and an American scholar at Stockholm International Peace Research Institute (SIPRI), and James Reilly, Dalian Office of American Friends Service Committee (AFSC), have looked at Chinese investment in Africa as an example. They point out that, in the course of large Chinese state-owned enterprises going global, China is faced with the "principal-agent problem". By this they are referring to increasing tensions and contradictory relations that have resulted from the promotion of China's national interests abroad, namely, companies and businesspeople working overseas.

China's strategy has been to focus on Africa. Its key goal is to shape an image of a responsible big country and to enhance its soft power. Meanwhile, Chinese enterprises, state-owned ones in particular, have flocked to the continent, investing and setting up plants and undertaking various construction aid projects. However, more and more African countries have accused Chinese SOEs of misbehaving, such as driving down wages and failing to improve production conditions, which are detrimental to the construction of a positive image for China. The Chinese government's strategic partnership with Africa is to participate in Africa's economic and political rejuvenation and to create a sound environment for Chinese enterprises through economic assistance and diplomacy and to encourage enterprises to enter the African continent. However, as China becomes more reliant on these enterprises to carry out this strategy, contradictions between the government and enterprises have exerted a profound influence on the international image of China and the overall strategy of upgrading its global soft power.

To overcome the negative impact caused by the economic activities of enterprises, it is imperative to regulate their economic and diplomatic behaviour. First, while engaging in economic activities, enterprises and commercial associations should have the sense of economic diplomacy. After all, enterprises exist across regions, borders, nations and cultures. Such mixed features result in the fact that enterprises in the era of globalisation are connected with different regions, nations, countries, ethnic groups and languages. Their economic activities are better able to show the national image than traditional diplomatic activities of government, promoting economic development and giving rise to a "multi-win" result.

Second, while conducting economic activities, enterprises should build up their sense of corporate social responsibility (CSR). Former United Nations secretary general Kofi Annan vigorously advocated CSR, stressing human rights protection, freedom of labour and environmental protection, etc. All this means that enterprises should pursue sustainable development, abide by laws and regulations, social norms and business ethics, effectively manage the influence of an enterprise's operation on interested parties and the natural environment as well as the behaviour of maximising comprehensive social and economic value. Only in this way can enterprises better assume their functions of economic diplomacy in transnational economic activities.

Finally, while conducting activities of economic diplomacy, the enterprise can act as a disseminator of thoughts and value and a cultural "ambassador" of its home country. Though economic activities have no national boundary, the behaviour pattern of entrepreneurs, members of commercial associations and business practitioners can reflect the characteristics of a country. Against the backdrop of globalisation, enterprises and commercial associations are an important carrier of and a platform for cultural transmission and collision.

To sum up, if enterprises and commercial associations aim to achieve good economic benefit in economic activities, they must win the recognition and support of the host countries. To this end, the corporate culture should be identical to mainstream social values. The effective transmission of corporate culture through public diplomacy will improve national image and the global transmission of the core social value so as to improve the national image.

From this point of view, enterprises and commercial associations are one of the important components of economic diplomacy.

VI. Think tanks and other research institutions

The "think tank" appeared in China only recently. However, it has deeper roots in the West. In the US, think tanks such as the Brookings Institution and Rand Corporation have played an important role, known as the "revolving door" mechanism. The think tank offers advice and suggestions to the federal government, the State Department, senators and representatives and other politicians. By virtue of the knowledge and prestige they accumulate, think tank scholars also have access to policy-making bodies of the government and hold administrative and advisory posts. In the diplomatic field, the think tank plays a crucial role in America and has cultivated well-known diplomatic figures such as Henry Kissinger and Condoleezza Rice.

The operation of major Chinese think tanks is still in the process of growing up. Some scholars hold that Chinese think tanks may date back to ancient times, such as assistants to a ranking official or generals in old China. Founded in 1677, the Southern Study, for example, was composed of elites whose main duties were to offer the emperors policy suggestions in the Qing dynasty (1616-1911).

In modern China, major think tanks fall into several categories.

The first category is made up of research institutions under government agencies, such as the Development Research Centre under the State Council and the China Institutes of Contemporary International Relations. Think tanks in this category conduct research through materials and channels in the system, and regularly submit research reports to government agencies above them. These research institutions have close academic exchanges with the outside world. Their researchers actively participate in domestic academic discussions. In this sense, they are an important component of the public academic opinion environment.

Category two comprises research institutions under institutions of higher education, such as the Centre for European Studies at Renmin University of China. Most of these think tanks have no systematic, regular researchers. Instead, they use academic resources and reserves of talent in nearby universities and colleges to conduct research and make academic exchanges between scholars more accessible. As academic institutions in colleges and universities have no official capacity, unlike government agencies, they enjoy more freedom in initiating academic activities and easily accept new ideas and concepts that they incorporate into their research. As such, they are an important category of think tank.

The third category is comprised of non-governmental independent think tanks and research institutions founded in recent years that have formed channels for public policy consultation and suggestion. Unirule Institute of Economics in Beijing is one example. Chaired by the renowned economist Mao Yushi and composed of many prominent economists, jurists, sociologists and scholars from other disciplines, the Institute has developed into one of the most influential think tanks in China. It regularly holds academic forums, organises research projects and publishes papers and journals. Though most of its members have other roles - working in research departments of government agencies or as college teachers, for example - the Institute as a non-governmental think tank provides scholars with a platform for concentrated discussions and exchanges, and has made many achievements of great social influence.

As a specialised institution offering public policy and decision-making services, the main functions of think tanks are to provide research products, build a platform for dialogue, cultivate decision-making personnel and give guidance to public opinion. In form, they may be classified as governmental think tanks or non-governmental think tanks. In terms of their contents, they may be classed as comprehensive think tanks or professional think tanks.

Think tanks play an important role in economic diplomacy.

The most popular and most common form of think tank participating in economic diplomacy is to organise cooperation and exchanges between think tanks or symposiums for think tank scholars, which is widely known in diplomatic circles as "track II diplomacy". "Track II diplomacy", first proposed by

Joseph Montville, an American diplomat, refers to non-governmental diplomatic negotiations and exchanges in which non-state actors participate.

Chinese think tanks actively take part in "track II diplomacy", which has become an indispensable part of economic diplomacy.

In 2011, while the China-Africa Co-operation Forum was convened, the first meeting of the China-Africa Think Tank Forum (CATTF) I was held in Hangzhou, Zhejiang province. More than 200 renowned scholars from famous think tanks attended the gathering, along with high-ranking government officials, entrepreneurs and media workers from China, 27 African countries, African regional organisations such as the African Union (AU) and other countries and regions. In the three-day forum themed "Sino-Africa Relations during the Second Decade of the New Century", scholars held heated discussions on bilateral economic and trade exchanges. In contrast to the official atmosphere of governmental cooperation forums, the Think Tank Forum gathered scholars and researchers from all fields involved in Sino-African economic diplomacy, expanded consensus in public opinions of both sides and offered suggestions on Chinese enterprises' investment in Africa and African enterprises entering the Chinese market. Many of these suggestions were adopted in practical exchanges by government agencies and business people. This helped realise the transformation from academic concept to practical action.

Following the encouragement of governments of many countries, the Sino-Africa Think Tank Forum has been stipulated as a regular non-governmental dialogue mechanism. It is held once a year in China and Africa alternately, bringing the roles of think tanks in economic diplomacy into full play.

The second type of form in which think tanks get involved in economic diplomacy provide services such as offering advice and suggestions to the government, and proposing options on diplomatic policies for the reference of the government.

In September 2003, the East Asia Think Tank was founded in Beijing. It is composed of prestigious think tanks from 10 countries of the ASEAN, plus China, Japan and Korea. This think tank aims to establish working groups according to different research issues and submit the unified research reports of the groups to the "10+3" Conference and countries concerned so as to assist them in coordinating their diplomatic policies, which of course include policies on economic diplomacy.

Ever since its establishment, the East Asia Think Tank has offered many suggestions on the policies on economic diplomacy of China and other member countries. It also takes part in decision-making in economic diplomacy and has scored some notable achievements. For example, at its first annual meeting, the East Asia Think Tank conducted detailed and in-depth research on financial and monetary cooperation in Asia. Its research achievements have been adopted by the governments of many countries, which help them to form policies on economic diplomacy of their own. Another example came at the annual meeting held in Shanghai in 2005, when participants exchanged views on internet financial cooperation and submitted the consensus reached at the meeting to governments of the countries. This directly led to the resolutions at the following leaders meeting.

At the 2004 East Asia Think Tank, scores of experts and scholars took part in a national seminar themed "East Asia Community: Prospects and Problems". The meeting reached a consensus that it is an indispensable choice to push forward regional integration and that China should play an active role in this process.

While participating in economic diplomacy, the think tank maintains close ties with major participants and actively offers advice to Chinese enterprises abroad.

They do this in the following ways. First, think tanks hold regular training programmes to provide first-line practitioners of economic diplomacy with knowledge and experience and help enterprises to have a good command of foreign countries so as to improve their economic benefits. In addition, an enterprise's corporate social responsibilities should also improve, thus becoming an important component of China's economic diplomacy. Think tanks regularly publicise research results and reports based on the wisdom of scholars who are most experienced in diplomacy and have a solid foundation of economic theory. This is a valuable reference tool for enterprises' "going global". Finally, Chinese think tanks exchange views not only with each other but also with foreign think tanks, providing an opportunity for these enterprises and even government agencies to have close contact with scholars and researchers who influence policy making of other countries so as to help them have a good understanding of international rules and do a better job in economic diplomacy.

To sum up, think tanks and similar research institutions indirectly influence other actors of economic diplomacy. With the development of Chinese social sciences, especially economics and international politics, think tanks will play an increasingly important role in economic diplomacy. It is likely that China's "revolving door" will appear in diplomatic circles.

VII. Media

If the government is the behaviour agent of traditional diplomacy, then the

NPC, CPPCC, think tanks and research institutions assume the functions of communication and coordination in economic diplomacy. They provide opinions and suggestions to other roles of economic diplomacy. As the local government is the decision maker of local issues including local economic diplomacy oriented to other parts of the country or the world at large, they may be viewed as the "decision maker" of economic diplomacy. Enterprises and commercial associations act as the "output terminal" of economic diplomacy, embodying their image outside and influence of China's economic diplomacy.

The media is another force that plays an important role in economic diplomacy.

Governments of almost all countries have viewed the media as an essential component of diplomatic activities to show and publicise their foreign policy concepts. Yet media coverage itself influences diplomacy. In other words, the force of public opinion represented by media is crucial to the success or failure of diplomacy. This is especially true in contemporary society where there are a great variety of media and abundant platforms. As a result, governments of almost all countries or other diplomatic behaviour bodies have more channels to generate publicity. Yet, these actors have to face with pressure of public opinions from all sides.

From the perspective of economic diplomacy, owing to the fact that economic activities are a priority for the media, coupled with the ongoing economic globalisation, economic diplomacy has become a mainstream diplomatic activity. Every act of the government is viewed by the media and reflected in the media.

The media's influence on economic diplomacy is manifested in the transmission of news information. This is the basic function of media in economic diplomacy and other fields. Whether it is the government or other actors of economic diplomacy, the major channel of obtaining information in contemporary society is to rely on the media. Journalists are under pressure to transmit information as fast as possible. Particularly, online media are so developed today that media information has changed the way people understand and judge the world and naturally changed the decision-making mode of the agents of economic diplomacy.

However, compared with think tanks and research institutions, the media are faced with a huge challenge, that is, lack of background knowledge. In fact, media provide first-hand information, and rarely have the resources to study and analyse it. The problem for media is that information is easily over-exposed, which causes much difficulty in decision making. As a matter of fact, diplomatic actors might make misjudgements without a comprehensive understanding of the information.

The second way the media influence economic diplomacy is diplomatic topic setting. That is, the media arouses public opinion through intensive reporting so as to directly influence diplomatic topics and policy orientation of the government. European countries adopted an anti-dumping policy against China as a result of the media's setting of diplomatic topics. Due to the low growth rate of the European economy and rising unemployment, some media outlets used China as a scapegoat. As a result, acres of newsprint were devoted to the exaggerated impact of cheap products made by Chinese enterprises on the European market, at the expense of traditional industries. Consequently, the government had to respond. The fact is that while China has increased exports, it has also increased the proportion of imports of high-tech products from Europe. From this perspective, China provides Europe with business opportunities. If this was reflected in the European media, it is certain that the topics of economic diplomacy of European countries would have changed. The result would be quite different. Some scholars believe that this phenomenon shows that the media plays both positive and negative roles. The extreme of the negative role is that some Western governments adopt policies according to media coverage but lose sight of what the media fail to notice.

Another way in which the media influences economic diplomacy is to change the pace of diplomatic activities.

Some Chinese enterprises, guided by the "going global" strategy, actively engage in overseas mergers and acquisitions. In some cases in the US, the media often launch a war of propaganda to compel Congress to conduct repeated deliberations over a proposed acquisition. As a result, several cases wither before they get going. The reason is that when diplomatic activities that have something to do with their immediate interests are broadcast across the front page of newspapers, the degree of public concern will escalate. The government is forced to respond even if it does not have to hand any mature policy tools to cope with the situation.

It is highly important for economic diplomacy to use the media as a tool for publicity, and to create momentum and set the agenda.

The government may use the media to draw people's attention to a policy of economic diplomacy, and to raise expectation and thus win their support. In certain circumstances, the government may take advantage of the functions of media to add to the weight of political, economic and diplomatic activities. For example, when the signing of treaty on the Panama Canal between the US and government of Panama came to the final stage, the former used domestic media to champion some special clauses and then used the media coverage to demonstrate the "will of the American people" to put pressure on the latter to make concessions.

In conclusion, the media has become a force that plays a decisive role in economic diplomacy. Therefore, a good command of the interaction between media and government in activities of economic diplomacy is of vital importance to perform a good job in economic diplomacy in contemporary international community.

Chapter 3

Economic diplomacy in different policy fields

Section 1 Financial diplomacy

The outbreaks of the US financial crisis in 2008 and the European debt crisis in 2009 had profound global influences in both political and economic fields. They also elevated the importance of finance as a factor that influences international relations. To brave the huge challenges brought about by these two crises, China, as an emerging country, has spared no effort in global financial diplomacy at a global, regional and bilateral level so as to safeguard its financial interests and security in this era of globalisation. From then on, financial diplomacy, a new concept in China, has gained good momentum. It has become an essential part of China's overall diplomatic activities and has propelled the transformation of China's overall diplomacy in the era of globalisation.

This chapter gives a basic definition of financial diplomacy on the international stage and analyses its historical process of evolution. Then, from multilateral, regional and bilateral perspectives, it expounds China's practice in financial diplomacy after the two crises. Finally, it summarises the basic features of China's financial diplomacy from 2008 to 2012.

I. Financial diplomacy in the international arena

Diplomacy is an external communication behaviour of the central government of a country and its representatives by peaceful means. It has a long history. Financial diplomacy, however, is a new form of traditional diplomacy, which is evolving all the time. Specifically, financial diplomacy refers to official financial interactions conducted by a central government and its subordinate executive agencies oriented to international actors such as governments of other countries, international organisations and transnational corporations. It aims to facilitate international cooperation and effective governance in financial issues, or realise other goals by affecting international financial relations. These official communication activities include: the transmission of financial information, the coordination of financial policies, negotiations on financial issues and the signing of financial agreements. Its specific forms are mainly manifested in transnational visits and international conferences.

Financial diplomacy focuses on the core issues of two aspects: one is intergovernmental transnational capital credit and short-term liquidity supply; the other is the international use of currency and transnational negotiations on the exchange rate. Both are directly the responsibility of the ministry of finance and the central bank. Therefore, with the rapid development of financial diplomacy, both the ministry of finance and the central bank have become important performers in a country's foreign dealings. In this sense, a country's financial diplomacy may be interpreted simply as the diplomatic activities of the ministry of finance and the central bank. Since currency is the core of finance, financial diplomacy in the narrow sense is also called "monetary diplomacy".

Financial diplomacy has three basic features, the first of which is official. Among several actors, at least one side is the official representative of the central government or an international organisation. To say the least, the actor of financial diplomacy must be semi-governmental organisations or private institutions that have clear official purposes. The most typical manifestation of financial diplomacy is the contact between government officials in charge of finance under the central government or between governments and international organisations. Pure contacts between private financial institutions are not financial diplomacy.

The second feature is political. Though many financial issues are somewhat technical, financial diplomacy is highly political. This political element stems from three sources. First, the executive body of financial diplomacy is not a commercial institution but an official body. As a matter of fact, under the hierarchical bureaucratic system, the actions of government agencies will go through a political process. Second, the purposes of financial diplomacy often involve political consideration that is beyond the scope of finance, namely, realising other goals by means of financial relations. Third, diplomatic goals often need to be realised by political means such as issue correlation, diplomatic pressure and the exchange of interests. Therefore, financial diplomacy is not market behaviour but political behaviour.

The third feature is one of intersection. Financial diplomacy, posing challenges to both the norms of traditional diplomatic behaviour and the governance of financial affairs, is the intersection and combination of finance and diplomacy. Executors of financial diplomacy should have a good professional knowledge of financial services (including financial politics), as well as a basic knowledge of diplomatic activities. In short, financial diplomacy should abide by some basic laws of diplomacy and finance simultaneously. If the appearance of professional diplomacy makes diplomacy a highly professional activity, financial diplomacy makes it more specialised.

Financial diplomacy became a fixed international phenomenon since the Bretton Woods conference in 1944. This comprehensive and large-scale conference of financial diplomacy ended the international financial chaos since the Great Depression, and gave birth to a new global financial order that played a crucial role in the economic recovery after the Second World War.

Just as the Westphalian conference symbolised the birth of modern diplomatic activities, so the Bretton Woods conference symbolised the rapid development of financial diplomacy on the international stage. Since then, the development of financial diplomacy can be divided into three stages according to different features.

The first stage was the Bretton Woods Era featuring US financial hegemony. The core feature of international financial diplomacy at this stage was that the US led the international community to establish and safeguard an international financial order whose core contents were "pegging the US dollar with gold and other currencies pegged to the dollar, and adopting a fixed exchange rate (abbreviated as "two peggings and one fix)". The main contents of financial diplomacy in this period were: using various financial means to facilitate the rejuvenation of European countries; diplomatic activities of major countries focusing on international liquidity to create Special Drawing Rights (SDRs); and a diplomatic struggle initiated by France against US dollar hegemony. This stage started in 1944 and ended with the collapse of the Bretton Woods system in 1973, ushering in the beginning of the floating exchange rate system.

The second stage was the era in which big Western powers harmoniously existed with G7 as the platform. The core feature of international financial diplomacy at this stage was that Western developed countries realised joint governance over international financial issues by establishing a new international coordination mechanism. The mechanism of annual dialogue between finance ministers and central bank governors provided an institutional guarantee for the "routinisation" of financial diplomacy. The main aspects of financial diplomacy in this period was the coordination of exchange rates between developed countries, especially between Japan and the US including Plaza Accord, and coping with regional financial crises such as debt crisis in Latin America, the Mexico currency crisis, and the Asian financial crisis. In addition, as the course of European monetary integration promoted the development of financial regionalism, regional financial diplomacy became a new feature. This stage began with the birth of the G6 (in the next year it became the G7) and concluded with the first convening of a G20 summit meeting at the end of 2008.

The third stage started after the global financial crisis in 2008 from which the international financial system has entered the joint governance of developed and emerging countries. The core feature of international financial diplomacy at this stage is that emerging countries have become involved in international financial issues in a comprehensive way through the G20 political framework and have asked for a change to an international financial system that is dominated by Western countries. International financial governance is split into the G7 and BRICS Group, which is characterised by cooperation and conflict. Regional financial diplomacy has developed with the emergence of financial regionalism.

Due to the relative isolation of its financial system, China had for a long time little involvement in international financial relations. In fact, China was very inexperienced in financial diplomacy. It only started to gain experience in 1980, when China resumed its seat at the World Bank and the IMF. For a long time after that, China's limited financial diplomacy was focused on these and other international financial institutions. At the time, China was a follower of the existing international financial system, but it was not very active in financial diplomatic activities

In the 21st century, China has become more involved in international financial diplomacy, especially after the Asian financial crisis in 1997 and the increased appreciation pressures on the renminbi after its entry into the WTO. The global financial crisis in 2008 and the European debt crisis that started in Greece in 2009 highlighted the necessity for China to safeguard its financial interests and security in this era of globalisation. Against this backdrop, China's financial diplomacy has undergone significant development in the past four years and made great achievements on a global, regional and bilateral basis. Today, it is an established and important field in China's overall diplomacy.

II. System reform: China's global financial diplomacy

In 2008, after global financial crisis broke out in the US, Western developed countries needed to deal with the crisis with the aid of emerging countries. The G20 Ministerial Conference, founded in 1999, was upgraded to a summit meeting, becoming an important platform for countries to coordinate their stances and policies in the course of coping with this crisis. It was officially confirmed as a core platform for international economic cooperation at the Pittsburgh Summit in 2010. This led to the transition of the international financial governance mechanism from the "G7 era" to the "G20 era", and symbolised an important institutional change in international finance.

The marginalisation of the G7 at the expense of the G20 made redundant the nearly-10-year discussion on whether China should join the G7. The international financial governance mechanism tackled the problem concerning the participation of emerging countries in international financial diplomacy. As an important member of the G20, the G20 summit meeting and its subordinate meeting of the Group of 20 Finance Ministers and Central Bank Governors, China has an important platform to conduct global financial diplomacy; hence, this marked the beginning of China's large-scale global financial diplomacy.

On this new diplomatic stage, as China's financial security faced severe threat in this financial crisis, it cast away its usual role as a "silent junior partner" and began to question the validity of the US$-dominated international monetary system and took a more active part in proposing the reform of the international monetary system and the establishment of a more diversified international monetary pattern. In March 2009, prior to the convening of the G20 summit meeting, the governor of the PBC Zhou Xiaochuan published an article, calling for the creation of a "supra-sovereign international reserve currency" to replace "a single international reserve currency". His criticism targeted US abuses of its dollar privilege as the international currency.

At that time, the financial crisis reached such a pitch that Zhou's article shocked the world. The article was widely believed to be China's first open challenge to the US dollar's global dominance.[5] It marked not only a turning point in China's role on the international financial stage, but also the country's dissatisfaction with the existing international financial order. The proposal received an enthusiastic response from emerging countries such as Russia, Brazil, India, Argentina and Indonesia. And that was not all. In order to show its concern over China's financial strength, France, the rotating presidency of the G20 in 2011 held a seminar entitled "Reform of The International Monetary System" in Nanjing, China, where finance ministers and central bank governors, representatives of relevant international organisations and prestigious scholars in international economic and monetary circles gathered.

At the following G20 summit meetings and ministerial meetings, China acted hand in hand with other countries through financial diplomacy to propose reform of the international financial system, successfully achieving the goal of elevating the share rights of emerging countries in the two major international financial institutions, the IMF and World Bank. After this reform was put into practice, China, surpassing Germany, France and the UK, became the third largest shareholder in these two international financial institutions. This was China's greatest achievement in international financial diplomacy during the crisis.

In addition, China made great progress in participating in the management of international financial institutions. Lin Yifu, a Chinese economist, took the post of

---

[5] Daniel W. Drezner, "Bad Debts: Assessing China's Financial Influence in Great Power Politics," *International Security*, Vol.34, No.2, Fall 2009, p.39

vice-governor of the World Bank in 2008, and Zhu Min, vice-governor of the PBC, was appointed special adviser to the president of the IMF in May 2010. A little over one year later, Zhu Min was nominated to be vice-president of the organisation by the new president of the IMF. This greatly amplified China's voice in the IMF.

The institutional change from the G7 to G20 resulted from the political demands of major emerging countries in participating in international financial governance. Confronted with the major financial participants that had dominated the international financial arena for decades, emerging countries were disadvantaged by their lack of experience and insufficient strength. They were not well prepared in areas such as setting agendas, reform goals and policy schemes. Against this backdrop, China supported the establishment of the BRICs cooperation mechanism with a view to forming a coordinated stance and enhancing the diplomatic action capacity of BRICS countries in the G20.

On 16 June 2009, the BRIC countries, Brazil, Russia, India and China, held the first summit meeting at Yekaterinburg, Russia, announcing the establishment of the BRICs cooperation mechanism, which symbolises the ascendancy of BRIC countries on the international stage as a country union. Not only that. BRIC countries set up the meeting mechanism of Finance Ministers and Central Bank Governors to coordinate their stances in global financial diplomacy. In addition, they have made a series of calls for issues that oppose the hegemony of the US dollar, increasing the share of rights of emerging countries in establishing international financial institutions and improving the international financial supervision system in a bid to enhance their influence and right of speech on the international stage of financial diplomacy.

In 2011, after Dominique Strauss-Kahn resigned as managing director of the IMF, BRIC countries collectively expressed their consensus on his successor. Though BRICS did not take any substantive joint action on the selection of the new IMF managing director, and nor did they succeed in changing the appointment of a European to that post, their joint declaration had some symbolic significance. Under pressure from emerging countries, the campaign for IMF managing director went through the procedure for a nomination of candidates, which was the first time in its 60-year-plus history. With China's efforts, the BRIC mechanism admitted South Africa as a new member at the BRICS Summit in Sanya, China, in 2011, which added weight to the mechanism.

In the global dimension, some of China's financial diplomacy goals were unsuccessful. For example, the Chinese government has striven to bring the renminbi into the Special Drawing Rights (SDRS), and energetically lobbied European countries for support. However, it was not successful due to opposition from the US.

III. Regional mutual assistance: China's financial diplomacy in East Asia

After the Asian Financial Crisis in 1997, financial diplomacy in the region came alive. At that time, East Asian countries, to cope with the crisis, launched a series of creative diplomatic activities for regional mutual assistance. The chief one was the establishment of the ASEAN, China, Japan and ROK (10+3) summit, which had regional mutual financial assistance at its core.

China has been an active participant in mutual financial assistance in East Asia. During the crisis, the Chinese government resisted pressure to devalue the renminbi. Compared with the considerable depreciation of the yen and the harsh strings attached to American aid, China's international monetary behaviour showed the image of a responsible big country that had won the trust of the region over China's monetary policy. This was the first time China had showcased its financial influence. [6] Moreover, in 1998, the then Chinese premier Zhu Rongji proposed to establish a financial dialogue mechanism under the "10+3" framework that financial ministers and vice governors of the central banks meet regularly. His proposal won approval and was passed.

However,, in that period, China did not have a mature strategy on financial diplomacy towards East Asia. Furthermore, influenced by traditional diplomatic thinking, China did not support Japan's proposal to found the Asian Monetary Fund (AMF). Several years after the Asian Financial Crisis, China's diplomacy in East Asia was insignificant. What was more striking was the commercial diplomacy led by the Ministry of Commerce to push forward the construction of the China-ASEAN Free Trade Area. It gave ASEAN countries considerable economic aid in exchange for their political support, that is, it adopted the "enriching neighbours" policy to create a stable environment in China's neighbourhood". Though Japan's proposal to establish the AMF eventually withered, it became the leading financial diplomacy tool in East Asia through "the Miyazawa Plan", which aimed to aid Southeast Asian countries in 1998, and the Chiang Mai Initiative concerning bilateral currency swaps launched in 2000.

At the "10+3" summit meeting in October 2003, Chinese premier Wen Jiabao was the first to suggest that a bilateral currency swap network be integrated into a multilateral fund assistance mechanism. This suggestion received an enthusiastic response from participating leaders. In May 2006, the "10+3" financial minis-

---

[6] Wang Hongying, "China's Exchange Rate Policy in the Aftermath of the Asian Financial Crisis," in Jonathan Kirshner, ed., *Monetary Orders: Ambiguous Economics, Ubiquitous Politics* (Ithaca: Cornell University Press, 2003), pp.153-197.

ters meeting decided to found the China-and-Thailand-led Chiang Mai Initiative Multi-lateralisation (CMIM)Working Group to conduct detailed research on this scheme. This marked China's active participation in regional financial diplomacy.

Though multilateral currency swaps have marked advantages over bilateral currency swaps, China's proposal of financial diplomacy saw no substantial developments in the following four years. This was mainly because, before and after 2005, China and Japan had an intense regional political disagreement on the institutional form of the East Asia Summit. This disagreement weakened the political foundation for currency cooperation in the region, and also greatly distracted the attention of East Asian countries to push forward currency cooperation in the region. Consequently, the pace of Chiang Mai Initiative Multi-lateralisation was greatly reduced.

The global financial crisis in 2008 and the US government's two rounds of quantitative easing policy stimulated Chinese government thinking on how to reduce its dependence on the US dollar. Soon afterwards, renminbi internationalisation policies were introduced and China's strategy for international currency shifted from following the dollar to containing it. Many Chinese scholars think that, prior to renminbi internationalisation, the renminbi should go through regionalisation, especially under the framework of East Asia financial and currency cooperation. For this reason, China began to make energetic efforts in financial diplomacy in East Asia.

The global financial crisis brought about a rare opportunity for China to realise its proposal on regional financial diplomacy. In this crisis, the American government provided the insurance company American International Group (AIG) with US$180bn of financial aid. After the European debt crisis, Greece and Ireland received bailout funds of US$157bn and US$ 121bn, respectively. [7] In contrast, during the Asian Financial Crisis in 1997, Thailand, Indonesia and South Korea received from the international community aid funds totalling just US$116.8bn with harsh political conditions attached. Faced with crises, the amount of aid received was widely different, which propelled East Asian countries to accept China's proposal. [8]

Against this backdrop, China, taking the meeting of "10+3" summit and Finance Ministers and Central Bank Governors as a platform, engaged in active financial diplomacy to bridge the different opinions of various parties, leading the fast-

---

[7] C. Randall Henning, "The Future of the Chiang Mai Initiative: An Asian Monetary Fund?" *Policy Brief*, PB09-5, Peterson Institute for International Economics (Washington, D.C.), February 2009

[8] Ramkishen S. Rajan, et al., eds., *Exchange rates, Currency Crisis and Monetary Cooperation in Asia* (London: Palgrave Macmillan), p.209

track establishment of The East Asian Foreign Exchange Reserve. In February 2009, the Special "10+3" Finance Ministers' Meeting proposed that the scale of regional foreign exchange reserves under preparation be enlarged from the scheduled US$80bn to US$120bn. Three months later, all member countries reached consensus on the main contents such as contribution share allocation, contribution structure, loan commitment and decision-making mechanism. On 24 March 2010, the East Asian Foreign Exchange Reserve officially came into effect. A regional crisis rescue mechanism was set up. In addition, at the financial ministers' meeting in 2012, all parties decided to double the size of the foreign exchange reserve to US$240bn.

The establishment and expansion of the East Asian Foreign Exchange Reserve is a great success of China's regional financial diplomacy. This success made Japan reassess China's financial strength and it began to share with China leadership in financial and currency cooperation in East Asia. According to the original contribution scheme, the relative contributions of Japan, South Korea and China were 3:2:1, with China ranked third in the funding parties. Later, China advanced a claim to raise its ratio of contributions. Through active diplomatic manoeuvring and bargaining, in the final contribution scheme, China and Japan both contributed US$38.4bn, with each accounting for 32% of the total funds. South Korea contributed US$19.2bn, 16% of the total, while ASEAN countries funded the remaining 20%.

In April 2011, the "10+3" Macroeconomic Research Office (AMRO), which is in charge of supervising economic operation in East Asia, was established in Singapore to assist in the operation of the East Asian Foreign Exchange Reserve. East Asian countries, especially China and Japan, were at odds with each other over the candidate of the director of AMRO. Through diplomatic efforts, China's Wei Benhua was eventually appointed the first director of the AMRO.

Having gone through a series of games of financial diplomacy, in the course of building up the regional financial order of East Asia, China has evolved from an ordinary participant in the Chiang Mai Initiative period into today's core leader.

IV. Currency cooperation: China's bilateral financial diplomacy

Currency diplomacy is the core content of bilateral financial diplomacy. Therefore, the PBC plays a leading role in China's bilateral financial diplomacy.

Before the financial crisis, China's bilateral currency diplomacy was concerned with dealing with US pressure of the appreciation of the renminbi. If the 10-year trade negotiations with the US over China's accession to the WTO in the 1990s directly facilitated the flourishing of China's commercial diplomacy, the dispute over the renminbi exchange rate between China and the US, which continues today, directly led to the elevation of China's currency diplomacy and reinforced the diplomatic functions of the PBC.

That is not the whole story, however. In the first decade of the 21th century, Sino-US currency diplomacy bestowed an important positive legacy to both sides. By promoting dialogue and cooperation in finance and other fields, both sides have established a new institutional framework, namely, the original Strategic Economic Dialogue and today's Strategic and Economic Dialogues (S&ED). This mechanism has become a key platform for communication between China and the US.

The outbreak of the global financial crisis in 2008 uncovered many disadvantages caused by China's long-term dependence on the US dollar. The "dollar trap" became one of the most important topics among political and economic circles of the two countries. Propelled by the PBC, China has conducted a broader and more active bilateral currency diplomacy. The currency diplomacy is mostly targeted to its neighbouring countries and emerging nations that have kept good political relations and frequent economic ties with China. Its main contents are to sign currency swap agreements and to push forward local currency settlement services. Their common goal is to realise the grand strategy of renminbi internationalisation and to reduce the use of the US dollar in foreign economic relations.

Since the PBC and the Central Bank of South Korea signed a currency swap agreement on 12 December 2008, the former has signed currency swap agreements with 18 countries and regions in the following three years, involving a total value of Rmb803.5bn. All these agreements use the domestic currency as the currency of price. On the one hand, it helps the contracting parties to steer clear of the US dollar, thus relatively weakening the dollar currency rate's influence on the economies of those countries concerned and weakening the US dollar's international status in specific regions. On the other hand, it facilitates the renminbi's distribution and circulation through official channels, which is conducive to raising the valuation and settlement proportion of the renminbi in bilateral trade. The renminbi is even used by some countries as an international reserve currency.

Bilateral swap agreements signed by China

Unit: Rmb

Time	Target countries for currency swap	Swap scale	Time	Target countries for currency swap	Swap scale
12-Dec-08	Republic of Korea	Rmb180bn	May 6 2011	People's Republic of Mongolia	Rmb5bn
20-Jan-09	Hong Kong, China	Rmb200bn	June 13 2011	Kazakhstan	Rmb7bn
8-Feb-09	Malaysia	Rmb80bn	22-Nov-11	Hong Kong, China	Rmb200bn

(continued)

11-Mar-09	The Republic of Belarus	Rmb20bn	22-Dec-11	Thailand	Rmb70bn
23-Mar-09	Indonesia	Rmb100bn	23-Dec-11	Pakistan	Rmb10bn
29-Mar-09	Argentina	Rmb70bn	17-Jan-12	United Arab Emirates	Rmb35bn
9-Jun-09	Iceland	Rmb3.5bn	21-Feb-12	Turkey	Rmb10bn
23-Jul-07	Singapore	Rb150bn	22-Mar-12	Australia	Rmb200bn
18-Apr-11	New Zealand	Rmb25bn	26-Jun-12	Ukraine	Rmb15bn
19-Apr-11	Uzbekistan	Rmb700m			

Date source: website of the PBC, Monetary Policy Department II

The signing of these currency swap agreements has abundant diplomatic and strategic logic. For one thing, most of them are China's neighbouring countries such as Mongolia, Kazakhstan, Thailand, Pakistan, Malaysia and South Korea. Some of them have important political and strategic partnerships and some regard China as their major economic partner. For this reason, they have become an important geographical foundation of renminbi internationalisation. For another, some signers of these currency agreements are pivot countries in key regions such as United Arab Emirates (UAE), The Republic of Belarus and Turkey, all of which are of great importance in or the financial centres of their regions, such as Dubai and Istanbul. To conduct currency swap cooperation with these countries is to facilitate the expansion of the renminbi in their regions.

On 22 March 2012, China and Australia signed a currency swap agreement with a total contract value reaching US$31bn. Australia is the largest economy that has signed an agreement of this kind with China. This cooperation marks China's great leap towards the elevation of the image of the renminbi in the market of developed countries.

In addition to signing currency swap agreements, another key aspect of currency diplomacy of the PBC during the financial crisis was to push forward local currency settlement and reduce the use of the US dollar. From 2002 to 2009, the PBC signed bilateral currency settlement agreements for bilateral trade with the central banks of Vietnam, Mongolia, Laos, Nepal, Russia, Kyrgyzstan, North Korea and Kazakhstan, permitting the use of local currencies or the renminbi in border trade settlement with neighbouring countries. Apart from these sporadic and large-scale border trades, China's foreign trade has been settled in foreign currencies. After the financial crisis, China began to adjust domestic monetary policy and enhance currency diplomacy with foreign countries to lift the scale of foreign trade and local currency settlement.

In June 2009, the PBC began its Pilot Programme of Cross-border Renminbi Trade Settlement and from then on it has continuously expanded the scale of the pilot.

This is regarded as a key step of the renminbi's internationalisation. To coordinate this policy, the PBC conducted a series of diplomatic activities to advance local currency settlement. All parties made joint efforts to expand the scale of local currency settlement. In this process, as emerging countries such as Russia and Brazil have weak currencies, they relied on the US dollar for a long time. As the US dollar was faced with a high risk of depreciation, these countries, just like China, had common interest with China in pushing forward local currency settlement and reducing the use of the dollar. For this reason, they became the most important countries towards which the PBC conducted bilateral currency diplomacy.

Likewise, Russia, which traditionally has friendly political and strategic relations with China, is also always on the frontline. The economic development of Russia has been highly dependent on oil trade, which has been in the grip of the "oil dollar". For this reason, Russia has been actively pushing forward the internationalisation of the rouble. During the financial crisis, the central banks of China and Russia had fruitful cooperation.

On 23 November 2010, Chinese Premier Wen Jiabao and Russia's Prime Minister Vladimir Putin held a meeting, announcing that China and Russia would gradually reduce dollar settlement in bilateral trade and use domestic currencies as trade settlement currencies. This was one of the most important achievements in the 15 meetings between prime ministers of both sides. Less than one month later, it was decided that Sino-Russia trade contacts would be realised through local currencies without the US dollar as an "intermediary". The rouble became the second new currency after Malaysia's ringgit, which is freely listed and traded. The listing and trade of the rouble and the renminbi are preparations for larger-scale local currency settlement in bilateral trade, enabling the application scope of the renminbi to expand gradually from being limited to border areas to a broader field in Sino-Russia trade.

On 23 June 2011, the central banks of China and Russian signed a new bilateral agreement on local currency settlement, which expanded the pilot range of bilateral trade settlement by using local currencies. The agreement stipulated that agents of economic activities of both countries may make the decision for themselves to use freely convertible currency, the renminbi and rouble to settle and pay for goods and services. After the signing of the agreement, the local currency settlement of China and Russia will expand from border trade to general trade, accompanied by a greater territorial scope. This marks a crucial step in both countries reducing their reliance on the US dollar in foreign trade.

Besides Russia, Brazil is also an important target country with which China cooperates in local currency settlement and currency. During the London G20 Summit,

Brazilian President Lula met with Chinese President Hu Jintao and proposed for the first time that both sides negotiate on bilateral economic and trade agreement on the renminbi settlement mode. While President Lula paid a visit to China in May 2009, local currency settlement for trade between China and Brazil became the highlight of this bilateral diplomatic activity. In February 2012, Chinese Vice-premier Wang Qishan and Brazilian Vice-President Michel Temer co-hosted the second meeting of the Sino-Brazil High level Committee on Coordination and Cooperation in Brasilia, capital of Brazil. Both sides reiterated their desire to "maintain dialogue on issues including local currency settlement for bilateral trade" and "welcome financial institutions of both countries to establish institutions and conduct business in the other side."

From the perspective of geopolitics and the prospect of economic development, "local currency settlement" between China and Brazil is of profound and far-reaching significance. Brazil is a sponsor of the Rio Group as well as a country whose economy has experienced the steadiest and fastest growth in Latin America. For this reason, it has a huge influence on Latin America and Portuguese-speaking countries. On the other hand, China and Brazil have common interests in international affairs and take a very similar stance. Therefore, "local currency settlement" between the two sides is likely to be a good example of financial cooperation between developing countries and will be further promoted.

Apart from Russia and Brazil, Sino-Japan relations improved. In February 2012, Vice-premier Wang Qishan met Japan's Finance Minister Jun Azumi at Zhongnanhai. Both sides expressed a desire to push forward local currency settlement in trade. To lower the risk of doing business in the US dollar, China and Japan set up a working committee composed of institutions of both countries that are in charge of encouraging investment in the banking system and a great amount of foreign exchange transactions and examining relevant stipulations. Both sides considered establishing an F.O.B. renminbi transaction centre in Tokyo Foreign Exchange Market. Local currency settlement will lower the reliance on the US dollar in Sino-Japan trade.

Currency internationalisation is not only the natural product of market expansion but also reliant on a solid international political foundation. Therefore, China's currency diplomacy, centred on currency swaps and settlement in the local currency, has laid a solid political foundation for renminbi internationalisation.

V. Basic features of China's financial diplomacy

In the early years of the 21st century, especially after the outbreak of financial and debt crises in America and Europe, China's economy and finance became more integrated into the global economic and financial system. The Chinese government deployed a variety of successful financial diplomatic acts at bilateral, regional and global levels. This active financial diplomacy marked an end to China's international image as a "silent junior partner" in global financial governance.

In terms of the diplomatic goals, China's financial diplomacy reflects very clear strategic goals: reforming the existing international financial system centring on the US and dollar and sub-centring on Europe and the euro; changing the excessive reliance on the US dollar; serving the grand strategy of renminbi internationalisation but stressing that the institutional transformation should be done in step-by-step rather than radical manner.

By contrast, China's foreign trade has developed rapidly since its accession to the WTO. As a beneficiary of the existing trade system, China's commercial diplomacy has not been revolutionary in nature. Likewise, politically, as a permanent member of the UN Security Council, China has kept a diplomatic low profile, and its political diplomacy is not aimed at overthrowing the establishing international political order.

The outbreak of the financial crisis in 2008 revealed the risk of China's excessive reliance on the dollar. In 2008, China surpassed Germany in terms of the size of its gross domestic product (GDP); two years later, it overtook Japan to become a real power in the international economic system. These two events made China's decision-makers realise that it was highly dependent on the dollar in foreign economic relations, as a result of which its dual costs in the economy and politics were too high. The US dollar system could no longer be viewed as a "free ride" to hitch. The American financial crisis uncovered the instability of this "free ride". In addition, the sudden increase in China's economic size led to a higher cost while taking the "ride". This "cost" is reflected in the fact that China, the largest holder of the US dollar outside America, pays the US government an extremely high seigniorage and inflation tax. In 2009, a great debate was launched in China over purchasing treasury bonds and China's "dollar trap". As an economically rejuvenating country, China was faced with severe "exploitation" of wealth brought about by dollar hegemony.

This stipulated that the Chinese government should make great efforts to adjust its international monetary policy. Its core content was to change the previous policy of following the US dollar and in favour of checking and balancing the US dollar. Pushing forward renminbi internationalisation has become the core objective of China's foreign financial strategy.

Therefore, whether it is to push forward reform of international financial institutions at global level, or press ahead with the establishment of an East Asian financial order at regional level, or advance currency cooperation that centres on currency swap and local currency settlement at bilateral level, all aim to reduce the reliance on the US dollar and help realise the goal of renminbi internationalisation.

Though China's financial diplomacy lays emphasis on reform of the established international financial system, it stresses that it should be achieved by progressive rather than radical means. This is interconnected with China's overall diplomatic strategy featuring integration and participation, which it has adhered to for more than 20 years. [9] Moreover, under the BRICS framework, compared with the radical position of Brazil and Russia, China has been more mild-mannered in transforming the dollar-centred international monetary system.

Implementing a "supra-sovereign international currency" scheme is not an easy task, either technically or politically. Zhou Xiaochuan's proposal is more an act of strategic diplomacy against Washington than a pragmatic operation, compelling the US to constrain its monetary policy and remould the credit standing of the dollar. Though the voices of developing countries are not loud enough to shake the dollar hegemony, they have pooled into a new force calling for monetary reform and will permanently influence the evolution of the international monetary system.

China's financial diplomacy lays emphasis on institutionalised channels of communication, especially stressing the existing international system framework, and establishing a bilateral institutionalised dialogue mechanism. Conference diplomacy is the main form of China's financial diplomacy.

In international finance governance, there are some institutionalised international organisations or institutions such as the IMF and World Bank. However, the majority are loose international conferences such as the G20. Nevertheless, in most cases, highly institutionalised international organisations make decisions on key issues through regular ministerial meetings or international summits. Therefore, attending international financial conferences has become the main form and channel for China to conduct financial diplomacy. What's more, at the bilateral level, China has taken the initiative to establish some financial dialogue mechanisms. Therefore, compared with other diplomacies, China's financial diplomacy is largely fulfilled through some regular institutionalised platforms.

In the early stages, China conducted financial diplomacy mainly by attending biannual meetings of finance ministers and central bank governors. Later, after the

---

[9] Alastair Iain Johnston, *Social States: China in International Institutions, 1980-2000* (Princeton: Princeton University Press, 2008)

G7 Finance Minister Meeting proposed to establish a ministerial meeting of the G20 in 1999, the annual finance ministers and central bank governors meeting became another major platform for China's financial diplomacy. In 1999, proposed by China, the "10+3" financial dialogue mechanism was established under the ASEAN, China, Japan and South Korea Summit Mechanism. This constitutes a major platform for China to conduct financial diplomacy in East Asia.

Nevertheless, the G7 is still the core platform for global financial governance. China is not a member of the G7. At the initial stage, China's global financial diplomacy was just like its global political diplomacy before the country joined the United Nations and similar to its global commercial diplomacy before acceding to the WTO, in that they lacked a broad stage. In 2004, at the invitation of the G7, Jin Renqing, the then minister of China's Ministry of Finance, and Zhou Xiaochuan, governor of PBC, had the first unofficial dialogue with finance ministers and governors of central banks of the G7 in Washington. China, considering the arrangement unequal, was full of misgivings. Due to the disagreement on the renminbi exchange rate, in 2005 China downgraded its participation level and sent vice-minister of finance Li Yong and vice-governor of the central bank Li Ruogu to attend the dialogue to show its dissatisfaction with the mechanism.

After the outbreak of the financial crisis, the G20 was elevated from a ministerial meeting to a summit meeting that defined itself explicitly as the core platform for the mechanism of global financial governance, thus upgrading the platform for China to conduct global financial diplomacy. Meanwhile, with the official establishment of the BRICS mechanism, finance ministers and governors of central banks meeting under its framework became another new multi-lateral platform of China's financial diplomacy.

International mechanisms on which China's financial diplomacy is based (parts)

Global dialogue mechanism	Spring conference and annual meeting of the World Bank/IMF	Every autumn, the two institutions hold an annual meeting which finance ministers and governors of central banks of all member countries attend; every spring, government officials, private entities, scholars and journalists attend the spring conference at Washington.
	G20 Meeting of Finance Ministers and Governors of Central Banks/ Deputies	It was founded in 1999 and is held once a year.
	Meeting of Finance Ministers and Governors of Central Banks of BRICS	It is held at non-scheduled times through platforms including the annual meeting and spring conference of the World Bank/IMF and the annual meeting of the G20.
	APEC Finance Ministers Meeting	It was founded in 1993 and is held once a year. In August 2012, the 19th Finance Ministers Meeting was held in Moscow. Vice-minister of Ministry of Finance Wang Jun headed a Chinese delegation to attend the meeting.

(continued)

Regional dialogue mechanism	Finance Ministers and Governors of Central Banks of ASEAN and China, Japan and South Korea	It was formerly known as ASEAN, China, Japan and South Korea Financial Dialogue Mechanism (Deputies Meeting), founded in 1999. In May 2012, it developed into a conference of Finance Ministers and Governors of Central Banks of ASEAN and China, Japan and South Korea.
	Europe-Asia Meeting of Finance Ministers	It was founded in 1997 and is held once every two years. Since 2001, it has been held annually. It is a part of the Asia-Europe Meeting.
	The 4th Trilateral Finance Ministers' and Central Bank Governors' Meeting	It was founded in 2008 and is held once every year. In August 2012, the 4th Trilateral Finance Ministers' and Central Bank Governors' Meeting was convened in Dalian, China.
	SCO Meeting of Finance Ministers and Governors of Central banks	In 2009, its first meeting was held in Kazakhstan. Its second meeting was held in Beijing in 2012.
	Governors' Meeting/ Deputies' Meeting of Executives' Meeting of East Asia and Pacific Central Banks (EMEAP)	It was founded in 1991. A governors' meeting is held in the middle of every year to hear the work reports of deputies' meetings and working group mechanism.
	Governors Meeting of South East Asian Central Banks (SEACEN)	It was founded in 1966. PBC officially joined SEACEN in 2011.
Bilateral dialogue mechanism	US-China Strategic and Economic Dialogue (economy)	It was founded in 2009 and was formerly known as the Sino-US Strategic Economic Dialogue, which was founded in 2006. Both sides take turns to hold it annually.
	Sino-US Joint Economic Committee mechanism	It was founded while Deng Xiaoping visited the US in 1979. China and the US take turns to hold it in their capitals. It is co-hosted by finance ministers of both sides.
	China-UK Economic and Financial Dialogue mechanism	Launched in 1998, it was originally the China-UK Financial Dialogue Mechanism and held non-scheduled. In 2008, it was upgraded to vice-premier-level dialogue and from then on is held once a year.
	Sino-Europe Financial Dialogue Mechanism	It was founded in 2005. Ministry of Finance of the PRC and European Commission hold a meeting every year.
	Sino-Russia Financial Ministers Dialogue Mechanism	It was founded in 2006. It used to be held once a year. Now, it is held once every two years.
	Sino-German Financial Stability Forum mechanism	It was founded in 2011. Vice-governors of central banks of the two countries have a dialogue.
	China-Japan Finance Minister Dialogue Mechanism	Founded in 2006, it is held once every two years. In April 2012, the fourth meeting was convened in Tokyo.
	Sub-committee of Finance of China-Brazil High-level Coordination and Cooperation Committee	In September 2009, vice-ministerial Sub-committee of finance of China-Brazil High-level Coordination and Cooperation Committee was established to replace Sino-Brazil Financial Dialogue mechanism which was set up in 2006. It is held once a year.
	Sub-committee of Sino-Kazakhstan Financial Cooperation	Founded in 2004, it is the regular meeting under the vice-premier cooperative mechanism of Chinese and Kazakhstan governments.

After the outbreak of the financial crisis in the US in 2008, China strengthened its efforts in building bilateral financial dialogue mechanisms, which found its expression in upgrading several ministerial-level dialogue mechanisms to vice-premier level and changing non-scheduled meetings into scheduled ones. For example, in 2008, China upgraded the non-scheduled ministerial level Sino-UK Financial Dialogue Mechanism founded in 1998 to vice-premier level and held it every year. In September 2009, China and Brazil established vice-ministerial subcommittee of finance under China-Brazil High-level Coordination and Cooperation Committee to replace the China Financial Dialogue mechanism founded in 2006. The dialogue is held once a year by vice-ministers of both sides in charge of international affairs. Third, in 2011, the deputy-level Sino-German Financial Stability Forum Mechanism was set up through which vice-governors of central banks of both sides have dialogue.

In terms of targets, China's financial diplomacy is more focused on emerging and neighbouring countries. In China's traditional diplomacy, relations with big powers were put in first place. In particular, China has all along used major diplomatic resources to deal with big powers such as developed economies in Europe and North America. Since the financial crisis in 2008, China's financial diplomacy focus has shifted to emerging and neighbouring countries. Globally, while participating in G20 activities, China prioritises political coordination and communication with non-G7 bodies. What's more, China actively participates in establishing the BRICS mechanism, in which it has invested a great amount of diplomatic resources. At regional level, China is committed to establishing a new financial order with its neighbouring countries. At bilateral level, those who conduct currency swap and local currency settlement are mostly its neighbouring and emerging countries.

China has sided with these countries because they have similar interests in the international financial system. After all, today's international financial system is centred on the US and the dollar, with Europe and the euro as the sub-centre. They are the controllers of the current system. By contrast, emerging countries and China's neighbours are at a disadvantage in the international financial system. Even Japan, despite its manufacturing strength, it is under the control of Europe and the US in finance.

In terms of diplomatic executive bodies, the Chinese government has made unremitting efforts in strengthening its domestic institutional foundation of financial diplomacy. A unique decision-making and implementation system of financial diplomacy has taken shape. Since the founding of the PRC in 1949, China's diplomatic system has undergone several changes. It is an integral part of China's modern state-building. However, such an institutional change is focused on a decision-making system of traditional diplomacy. In contrast, the institutional construction of the decision-making system of China's financial diplomacy started over again because the functions of China's financial diplomacy originated from traditional organisations in charge of domestic financial issues. They are weaker than the Ministry of Foreign Affairs and even the Ministry of Commerce in fulfilling diplomatic functions.

In this decision-making and implementation system, the Ministry of Finance and the PBC, which have long dealt with domestic affairs, are the twin engines of the country's financial diplomacy. They are in charge of various daily activities of financial diplomacy. Owing to their functional differences, the Ministry of Finance focuses more on transnational financing while the PBC is dedicated to currency in financial diplomacy. In recent years, in order to carry out financial diplomacy more vigorously, both the Ministry of Finance and the PBC have made internal institutional reform to adapt themselves to the ever-expanding pattern of China's financial diplomacy.

First, the Ministry of Finance changed the name of Department of the World Bank into the Department of International Affairs, which means an expansion of its functions and power in handling international affairs and a reinforcement of its ability to handle international financial issues. In addition, to deal with increasing various bilateral financial dialogue mechanisms, the Ministry of Finance set up the Foreign Financial Communication Office at departmental level, which is in charge of bilateral financial diplomacy. Second, like the Ministry of Finance and in order to handle ever-increasing external affairs, the central bank renamed the Department of International Financial Organisations to the more comprehensive Department of International Affairs. Furthermore, it set up the Monetary Policy Department II which is in charge of issues such as renminbi internationalisation and renminbi exchange rate. Both ministries had one or two vice-ministerial level officials who are in charge of international affairs. This adds weight to international affairs in the two ministries.

Apart from the internal institutional reform of the Ministry of Finance and the Central Bank, on 9 October 2012, the Ministry of Foreign Affairs officially established The Department of International Economic Affairs to get more involved in economic diplomacy, including financial diplomacy. China joins in international organisations and mechanisms such as the G20, APEC and BRICS, all of which are important platforms for international economic governance. The establishment of the Department of International Economic Affairs ushered in the Ministry of Diplomacy's involvement in economic and financial diplomacy.

Above the level of ministry is the State Council. As the Chinese economy has gradually integrated with the world economy over the past 10 years, a convention has taken shape that a vice-premier is in charge of issues concerning economic diplomacy, including financial diplomacy, to facilitate coordination between departments. For example, both Wu Yi and Wang Qishan are the core participants and executants of China's economic diplomacy. The former has a background in foreign trade and economics while the latter has a finance background. Though it seems to be by chance, it is a manifestation of the characteristic of Chinese economic diplomacy: gradually shifting from trade to finance.

As in other issues, the core leadership of China's financial diplomacy is the head of the state and the premier of the State Council. As the premier is mainly in charge of overall economic affairs, while the head of state attaches more importance to political diplomacy, the premier lays more emphasis on economic diplomacy in diplomatic activities, including financial diplomacy.

Overseas offices and diplomatic envoys are the inevitable products of the historic development of diplomatic relations. Apart from the Ministry of Foreign Affairs, institutions concerning foreign affairs also dispatch some staff members and agencies that fulfil their duties under the unified leadership of the overseas offices. For example, the Chinese People's Liberation Army sends a military attaché to the diplomatic mission, the Ministry of Commerce has commercial counsellors and the Ministry of Education has counsellors for education. Though there is no financial counsellor stationed abroad in financial diplomacy, financial diplomacy towards foreign countries is often the additional duty of the commercial counsellor. However, China has sent a great number of financial officials to act as executive directors in more and more China-funded international financial institutions that use their power on behalf of the Chinese government. Usually, China's executive member to the World Bank is sent by the Department of International Affairs of the Ministry of Education. The PBC is responsible for sending officials to institutions such as the IMF and ADB. They become professional financial diplomatic officials stationed abroad. The increasing number of teams of financial officials stationed abroad will further enhance the executive capacity of financial diplomacy.

A series of institutional reforms in China's financial diplomacy mentioned above is a driving force of financial globalisation on China's domestic system.

VI. Conclusion

The upsurge in the development of China's financial diplomacy in recent years is an important part of China's diplomatic transformation in the era of globalisation. Following the surging development of commercial diplomacy, it has greatly enriched the forms of China's diplomacy. With the further opening up of China's financial industry, it will get deeply involved in financial globalisation. In the future, China's financial diplomacy will become more active and its contents richer.

Influenced by the global financial crisis and the rejuvenation of emerging countries, the international financial system is faced with huge transformation pressures. The traditional financial order will be difficult to maintain while a new financial order is now emerging. Moreover, as China has begun a new phase to realise its rejuvenation by shifting from trade to finance, it has greater interest in the international financial system. Therefore, China's financial diplomacy will be subordinate to the grand goal of financial rejuvenation. Specifically, China's financial diplomacy in future will be devoted to realising three goals: reform of the global financial system, establishment of regional financial order and renminbi internationalisation. In this course, success in China's financial diplomacy will depend on both global political mobilisation and domestic financial development.

Section 2 Energy diplomacy

In recent years, the phrase "energy diplomacy" has often been on the lips of Chinese and foreign scholars. Energy diplomacy" means economic diplomacy centring on energy cooperation and transactions, and competition and sanctions. It is the policy, behaviour and process by which sovereign states or international organisations obtain energy safety and economic benefit by diplomatic means or gain political and security interests by means of energy.

"Energy" is placed together with "diplomacy" in that it has its particularity, importance and sensibility, which makes energy-related issues an indispensable part of international politics. The rise and decline of a nation and energy structure are intertwined. According to Susan Strange, a British scholar of international political economy, energy is an "indispensable condition" considering power operation in the world political economy (IPE). Moreover, security and wealth are linked together with national economic safety by reliable energy supply. As a matter of fact, the upsurge of energy diplomacy is closely associated with the struggle in vying for power, interest and security between the new and old big powers.

Energy diplomacy and the development of the oil industry are closely interrelated. It was not until after the Second World War that energy diplomacy began to flourish. By contrast, China's energy diplomacy started late. China's has abundant coal supplies but a lack of oil and natural gas, coupled with low utilisation rates of hydroenergy, wind energy and solar energy, makes it largely dependent on foreign energy. In the early years of the founding of the PRC, and in order to break through the blockade of Western countries and get oil, the Chinese government combined energy with diplomacy. Actually, the development of China's energy diplomacy started with the implementation of the reform and opening-up policy. In the 1980s, oil and natural gas accounted for a small proportion of energy consumption. In that period, though Chinese economy underwent rapid growth, it could meet its needs in oil and gas. In 1993, China became a net importer of oil. From then on, China gradually adjusted its energy policy and energy development strategy. It began adopting the "extravert-type energy development strategy", which meant vigorously developing oil and gas resources in its surrounding sea areas and in foreign countries and regions and importing oil and gas through many channels. Moreover, China supported oil and gas enterprises to go global. In the 21st century, the international energy situation has seen drastic change and there is an acute shortage of energy supplies on the global market. Consequently, energy geopolitical conflicts and competition are intensifying; new energy sectors have witnessed explosive growth; in short, energy has become more politically significant and energy issues have been elevated to the height of overall national strategy.

I. Organs of China's energy diplomacy

China's energy management system has undergone chronic reform and many twists and turns. Before the establishment of a national energy steering group in 2005, there was no unified energy management department during the 10th five-year plan period, and the NDRC was in charge of energy management. In 2005, an energy steering group was set up, which had a subordinate administrative body known as the Office of the National Energy Leading Group. However, the effectiveness of the office was found to be insignificant in subsequent years. In 2008, the State Council launched an institutional reform and decided to set up the National Energy Administration (NEA) and a high-level coordinating body, the National Energy Commission. In the same year, the functions and duties of the Office of the National Energy Leading Group were incorporated into the newly-established NEA. Hence, the NEA became the competent department in charge of energy issues. However, as a vice-ministerial-level institution, the NEA, faced with key energy issues, proved to be inadequate in making overall plans for and coordination with departments. In view of this, the National Energy Commission was established in 2010 which has the authority and governance lacking in previous energy institutions.

On 27 January 2010, the State Council decided to establish the National Energy Commission. It is highest coordination and deliberation institution established for China to enhance its decision-making and coordination in energy issues. Its main responsibilities include: studying and drawing up a national energy development strategy, deliberating key issues in energy safety and development, and making overall plans for and coordinating big issues concerning energy development and international energy cooperation. Premier Wen Jiabao took the concurrent post of director of the National Energy Commission. The reestablishment of the National Energy Commission is a manifestation of the highly important status vested to energy safety by the Chinese government in recent years. From 2002 to 2012, the Chinese government became more and more adept in energy diplomacy which has become more and more important in China's foreign policy.

II. China's strategy for energy diplomacy

Between 2002 and 2012, China's energy diplomacy was led by the state, under the auspices of the NDRC and with the participation of nation-owned energy enterprises and other groups, such as environmental NGOs and trade associations.

During the decade, China's economy grew rapidly. As demand for energy increased, more of it had to be sourced from abroad. As a result, energy supply and safety became a decisive factor in the quest for the sustainable development of China's economy. The forms of energy most used in China are oil, gas and other fossil fuels, which are mostly imported. For this reason, China's energy security is vulnerable. In the early years of the 21st century, the US and other Western countries kept control over the Gulf area, a major production base of oil and gas. Moreover, some oil production countries in the Middle East such as Iraq experienced political unrest, which seriously affected oil supply. As China became the world's second largest oil consumer in 2004, the West began to refer to "China's energy threat". Big powers wrestled in the energy field and anti-China forces among oil-production countries hindered China's cooperation in energy with foreign countries. About 85% of oil exports are transported by sea, which has tremendous risk. Therefore, the Chinese government has sought to build up onshore oil transportation channels.

Such a tough energy situation both at home and abroad makes China's energy safety a prominent problem that cries out for a solution. Energy safety depends more on the protection by political and military means. On the other hand, with the rapid growth of China's political and economic strength, it is necessary for China to deepen its economic and diplomatic friendly relations with other countries and unfold its image as a "responsible big developing country" so as to push forward a new order of international energy that features "harmony, stability and win-win".

The new international situation forced China to formulate a clearer energy strategy and implement more effective energy diplomacy. In 2001, the Outline of the 10th Five-Year Plan for National Economic and Social Development (2001-05) was adopted which put forward a new energy strategic guideline: "to actively use overseas energy resources; oil and natural gas supply bases will be established abroad, and oil will be imported through various channels. The national oil strategic reserve system will be established to safeguard national energy security." After 2002, the Chinese government has looked closely at sources and channels of energy imports, and investigated ways of international energy cooperation. It has also supported Chinese oil and gas enterprises to "go global" in fields such as diplomacy, finance and trade with a view to carrying out a multi-agent and all-dimensional diplomatic strategy. In July 2006, at a dialogue meeting between leaders of the G8 and developing nations held in St. Petersburg, Hu Jintao, the then Chinese president, put forward a "new concept of energy security": to safeguard global energy stability, safety and sustainable development: "We should build up and carry out "mutually beneficial cooperation, pluralistic development and collective guarantee. China will make proper use of international energy market and enhance cooperation with all countries of energy production and consumption by following the principle of equality and mutual benefit with a view to safeguarding global energy safety."

The strategic goal of China's energy diplomacy is to ensure national energy safety, promote sustainable social and economic development and safeguard and expand national political interest and security. The overall plan for China's energy diplomacy may be summarised as: first, implement "new concept of energy security" and national energy strategy and diplomatic strategy. Second, safeguard national and even international energy security, sustainable social and economic development and national interests pertinent to energy. Third, make full use of domestic and overseas resources, and domestic and overseas markets; give consideration to both traditional and non-traditional energy for common development, to energy exploitation and progress in energy utilisation, and to energy development and ecological safety.

While pursuing its interests and safety objectives, China, as a peace-loving and responsible country, will conduct energy diplomacy by respecting ownership and following the principle of equality, mutual benefit and common development.

III. Practice of China's energy diplomacy

The practical forms of energy diplomacy include: direct import; enterprises' overseas investment and mergers and acquisitions; combined construction of energy engineering projects; personnel and technical assistance; offering low-interest loans; rule-making through multilateral negotiations; energy threats for political, economic and military purposes; and political, economic and military threats for energy. China has not resorted to the last two forms in its energy diplomacy. In most cases, it chooses direct import and bilateral cooperation.

China's traditional modes of bilateral cooperation in energy diplomacy include entering into contracts and share acquisitions. In recent years, China has created a new mode, known as the "loan-for-energy deal", which involves China providing a loan to a country that has abundant energy resources. In exchange, the loan-receiving country exports a certain amount of energy resources to China. Countries using energy in exchange for loans from China include Russia, Brazil, Venezuela and Kazakhstan. "Loan-for-energy deals" help both sides take what they need, and they also avoid the problems of fluctuating resource prices and exchange rate depreciation. In this way, both sides can achieve mutual benefits and win-win results through cooperation.

In terms of types of energy, China's energy diplomacy focuses on the field of fossil energy such as oil and natural gas. So far, China has made some achievements in the field of unconventional energy as represented by hydroenergy, electric power, nuclear energy and shale gas and oil sand.

In terms of energy production, China has achieved good results in energy diplomacy in the last decade. First, it has made great achievements in exploiting upstream energy resources. For example, CNPC acquired all listed shares of Petro Kazakhstan. Second, progress has been made in midstream energy resource transportation; by 2012, a strategic pattern of four major oil and gas intake vents had taken initial shape: a China-Russia crude oil pipeline in northeast China and a China-Kazakhstan crude oil pipeline in northwest China, a China-Burma oil and gas pipeline in southwest China and Dongnan Shipping. Third, achievements in downstream oil and gas refining and chemicals include a joint venture project involving Sinopec, Exxon Mobil and Saudi Aramco, Fujian Refining and Ethylene Project (FREP) and petroleum products marketing.

The following section outlines China's achievements in energy diplomacy (2002-12) in terms of regional (bilateral) and multilateral diplomacy. Russia, central Asia, the Middle East, north Africa and Latin America are key areas for China's energy diplomacy.

1. China and Russia

From 2002 to 2012, the most remarkable achievement in energy diplomacy between China and Russia was the completion of the China-Russia crude oil pipeline that forms part of the East Siberia-Pacific Transportation Pipeline that aims to export Russian crude oil to the Asia-Pacific market. Currently, negotiations on natural gas pipeline transportation are still going on between the two sides.

Negotiations on a crude oil pipeline between China and Russia began in 1997, but for a number of reasons, the negotiations did not run smoothly. Both sides signed an agreement in 2009 that China will provide a loan of US$25bn to Russia. In return for this, China will import 15m tons of crude oil from Russia every year for the 20 years starting from 2011. As part of the agreement, China and Russia decided to lay a pipeline starting in the Russian town of Skovorodino and running to Daqing, Heilongjiang province. On 27 September 2010, construction of the pipeline was completed. Since 1 January 2011, the pipeline began to transport 300,000 barrels of oil a day. This is an example of a "loan-for-oil deal" project.

Figure 1 Sino-Russian oil and gas cooperation (2002-12)

2002	Transneft (Russia)and CNPC (China) decided to make joint efforts to build Angarsk-Daqing pipeline.
October 2004	Russia gives up the Angarsk-Daqing pipeline project
July 2005	Russian President Vladimir Putin decides to give China preference in transporting oil
October 2006	CNPC and Rosneft Oil jointly establish Vostok Energy
March 2007	Vice-minister of the Russian Federation Industrial and Energy Administration Andrey Dementiev: fulfilling the contractual liability that Russian companies supply oil to China is the preference of East Siberia-Pacific pipeline.
October 2008	China and Russia sign an agreement on the China branch line of the Siberia Oil Transportation pipeline
2009	"loan-for-oil deal"
September 2010	Completion of Skovorodino-Daqing oil pipeline
November 2010	China and Russia sign Memorandum of Cooperation in Expanding Oil and Gas Exploration and Development (Upstream) between CNPC and Vostok Energy. China and Russia to make joint efforts in exploring and developing three land oil and gas blocks and one land hydro-pneumatic suspension maritime block
Apri 2011	Hand over the engineering operation right of management of Daqing-Mohe Line of China-Russia crude oil pipeline

Prior to the completion of the crude oil pipeline, the oil that China imported from Russia took up only a tiny proportion of China's oil import volume. The main inhibiting factor for Russia to increase oil exports to China was transport. Russia exported oil to China mainly via land transport. However, the road and rail infrastructure in Russia's far eastern regions was very weak. Besides, railways in China's north east were overloaded. Crude oil pipelines have proved to be very effective in removing the traffic barrier. Since the implementation of the agreement on the crude oil pipeline, China's oil import volume from Russia has increased dramatically. In 2012, Russia exported 24m tons of crude oil to China, becoming the third largest crude oil supplier of the country.

China and Russia can achieve mutual benefits through cooperation in energy. China is able to meet its energy needs and expand its energy channels, which reduces its excessive dependence on Middle East oil and the Strait of Malacca trade route to a certain extent, and it also diversifies the transportation channels of its energy resources. On the part of Russia, cooperation with China relieves a big headache of Vostok Energy and Transnet due to a shortage of funds caused by the financial crisis. Russia's strategy for tapping the Asia-Pacific market (with China as a representative) and strategy for developing its far east and east Siberian regions are gradually being implemented. Moreover, cooperation facilitates Russia's export diversification and reduces the risks brought about by Russia's traditional reliance on the European market.

Apart from cooperation in energy transportation, the Chinese and Russian governments established energy cooperation and dialogue mechanisms at different levels in this period. In these 10 years, the Subcommittee of Energy Cooperation of Sino-Russia Premier Regular Meeting Commission was held once a year to settle problems in bilateral energy cooperation and push forward the implementation of cooperation projects. In July 2008, the Sino-Russia Vice-Premier Energy Negotiation Mechanism was initiated, through which cooperation issues in areas such as oil and gas, nuclear energy and electric power were handled efficiently.

Substantial progress in energy diplomacy has propelled Sino-Russia relations, the only deficiency being that energy cooperation between the two sides is only limited to the oil and gas trade. Little achievement has been made in downstream oil and gas refining and chemicals. On the other hand, as both countries are major energy players, they will promote their bilateral political ties to develop their energy relations into more mature energy diplomatic partnership in the future.

2. China and the central Asia

Central Asia here refers to the five countries: Kazakhstan, Kyrgyzstan, Uzbekistan, Tajikistan and Turkmenistan, all of which are endowed with abundant oil and natural gas resources. What's more, they are adjacent to China and are of vital geopolitical importance.

From 2002 to 2012, the most remarkable achievement in energy diplomacy between China and the countries in central Asia was the construction of the China-central Asia natural gas pipeline. The original intention of laying the pipeline was to extend the China-Kazakhstan petroleum pipeline. The completed natural gas pipeline provides China with an ample and steady supply of natural gas. The China-central Asia natural gas pipeline promotes the economic development of central Asian countries. Its significance to China and the central Asian countries is similar to that of the Sino-Russia crude oil pipeline project.

Figure 2 China-Central Asia natural gas pipelines

Nov-05	Completion of China- Kazakhstan petroleum pipeline
Dec-09	Completion of the China-Central Asia natural gas pipeline (Line A)
Dec-09	Completion of the China-Central Asia natural gas pipeline (Line B)
Dec-12	Invitation for bids for the China-Central Asia natural gas pipeline (Line C)

A pattern of oil and gas cooperation between China and the central Asian countries has already taken initial shape. China has cooperated with Kazakhstan in oil, natural gas, electric power and nuclear power, with Turkmenistan and Uzbekistan in natural gas, and with Tajikistan and Kyrgyzstan in electric power.

Figure 3 Some energy cooperation projects between China and central Asian countries

Country	Time	Project	Building contractor
Kazakhstan		Aqtobe project	CNPC
		PK project	
		Sino-Kazakhstan petroleum pipeline project	
		Sino-Kazakhstan natural gas pipeline project	
		North Buzachi project	
		ADM project	
		KAM project	
		Nathans project	CITIC Group
		East Moire Tucker oil field project	
		Right of Mining of Sazankurak oil field	Sinopec
		Five exploration areas around the Caspian Sea	
	April 2008	Contract: contract for the building of the Maina hydropower station	
	November 2008	Contract: exploit uranium mine of Kazakhstan and build nuclear reactors in China	
Turkmenistan	July 2007	Contract on product sharing of natural gas on the right bank of the Amu Darya of Turkmenistan; Sino-Turkmenistan agreement on purchase and sales of natural gas	
		Well repairing cooperation project	Sinopec
		Oil and gas exploitation	CNPC
		Natural gas pipeline project	

Thanks to the good relations between China and the five countries in the central Asia, as well as the "balancing strategy" they adopt to the big powers, China's energy diplomacy has run smoothly. However, China is also faced with some challenges: The "three evils" (terrorism, separatism and religious extremism) have played havoc with collaborative projects; the US and Russia compete in central Asia which create imponderables for China; and the potential political uncertainty that exist in central Asia.

3. China and Middle East and north Africa

The Middle East and north Africa are the most important sources of energy supply in the world, and also the "heartland" of China's oil imports. For example, the Gulf Area is endowed with three largest oil fields in the world. Saudi Arabia, Iran, Iraq, Kuwait and the United Arab Emirates (UAE) are among the top 10 countries in terms of oil reserves in the world. Currently, China cooperates with the Gulf

Area in energy mainly in the following areas: oil trade, oilfield development and management, project contracting and joint efforts in building refineries. In all, the Gulf Area is China's most important source of crude oil import.

Figure 4 China's top 10 suppliers of imported crude oil

Unit: million tons

2005			2011		
Country	Import volume	Proportion (%)	Country	Import volume	Proportion (%)
Saudi Arabia	22.18	17.49	Saudi Arabia	50.28	19.81
Angola	17.46	13.77	Angola	31.15	12.27
Iran	14.27	11.25	Iran	27.76	10.94
Russia	12.78	10.08	Russia	19.72	7.77
Oman	10.84	8.55	Oman	18.15	7.15
Yemen	6.84	5.39	Iraq	13.77	5.43
Sudan	6.62	5.22	Sudan	12.99	5.12
Congo	5.53	4.36	Venezuela	11.52	4.54
Indonesia	4.09	3.23	Kazakhstan	11.21	4.42
Equatorial Guinea	3.70	2.92	Kuwait	9.54	3.76

Data source: Yin Dongqing & Wu Binghui: *Turbulence in Middle East and North Africa and China's Petroleum Import Safety*, International Petroleum Economics, Vol 10, p13, 2012

From 2002 to 2012, China's energy diplomacy in the Middle East and north Africa involved the direct trade of oil and gas, winning several oil-gas exploration projects, building up joint oil refinery projects and enhancing cooperation in engineering equipment

Figure 5 China's major investments in oil and gas in Middle East and North Africa

Country	Project	Date	Company
Saudi Arabia	Rub Al Khal B Block natural gas field	February 2004	Sinopec
	Red Sea Oil Refining Company	March 2011	Sinopec
Iran	Yadavaran oil field	December 2007	Sinopec
	North Azadegan oil field	January 2009	CNPC
	North Paz oil field	May 2009	CNPC
	South Paz oil field	June 2009	CNPC
	Refinery construction	2010	CNPC
Iraq	Abdab oil field	November 2008	AL-WAHA PETROLEUM CO.LTD
	Rumaila oil field	June 2009	CNPC
	Halfaya oil field	December 2009	CNPC
	Missan oil field	March 2010	Sinopec, CNOOC

(continued)

Economic Diplomacy in Different Policy Fields

Qatar	Qatar Offshore BC Block gas field	August 2009	CNOOC
	Memorandum of understanding on natural gas	November 2009	CNOOC, CNPC
Sudan (before the independence of South Sudan)	Block 15	2005	CNPC
Oman	Block 36, 38	October 2004	Sinopec
Kuwait	Block 69, 71	2004	Sinopec
Algeria	Adrar upstream and downstream integration project	July 2003	CNPC
	Block 112/102A & Block 350	December 2003	CNPC
	Risk exploration		
	Block 438 B	July 2004	CNPC
	Design service for Octouat oil field productivity construction	September 2004	CNPC
	Construction of Skikda gas condensate refinery	May 2005	CNPC
Oman	Exploration of Libya Block 17—4	December 2005	CNPC
Yemen	Well abaa-1, Block 71	2010	Sinopec

Data source: Wang Yongbo, Cai Yongguo: *Recent Situation in the Middle East and North Africa's Influence on China's Energy Safety, Journal of Honghe University,* Vol 4, p74, 2011

While China has made great achievements in this region, it also faces great energy safety challenges. Several years before 2010, as regimes in north Africa gradually loosened foreign investment conditions, Chinese enterprises invested heavily in this region. At the end of 2010, as several regimes in the Middle East and north Africa collapsed and the political situation became highly unstable, Chinese oil and gas enterprises suffered drastically, increasing risk in investment and racking up enormous losses. For example, the turmoil in Libya broke off the investment projects of Chinese enterprises, causing direct losses that amounted to tens of billions of US dollars. Furthermore, as China and Western countries competed with each other keenly in north African energy, some Western countries blocked Chinese interests. For instance, the US intervened in China's normal trade with Iran. Chinese investment, opposed by some local people, was viewed as "neo-colonialism". For example, the Rumaila oil field was opposed by a trade union in Iraq.

In view of this, it has become urgent for China to establish how it can effectively protect the safety and interests of its energy, enterprises and workers on the principle of maintaining neutrality and not interfering in the internal affairs of other countries.

4. China and Latin America

Latin America abounds in oil and natural gas. Some regions are also endowed with shale oil and gas. Energy resources are mainly found in Venezuela, Mexico and

Brazil. Therefore, Latin America is one of the important targets of China's energy diplomacy, and in particular Venezuela, Columbia, Peru and Ecuador, Venezuela is a representative case.

Venezuela has the richest reserves of oil and gas in Latin America. Hugo Chavez, the former head of state, attempted to break away from the influence of the US Moreover, because of his urgent need for funds to fulfil his political commitment to his countrymen, Venezuela and China became ever closer. In 2004, China and Venezuela began energy cooperation on the basis of a "loan-for-oil" agreement. Venezuela allowed Chinese petroleum enterprises to invest and exploit oil in 15 of its domestic oil-producing areas. In November, 2007, China founded the Overseas Chinese Investment Fund to assist Venezuela. The latter promised to expand oil exports to the former. Just as in other "loan-for-energy" deals, China and Venezuela have achieved mutual benefits through cooperation in oil.

Figure 6 Some of China's energy cooperation projects in Latin America

Date	Country	Project
Decembe 2004	Venezuela	Signed an agreement on energy cooperation, "loan-for-oil" deal
May 2009	Brazil	China Development Bank (CDB) and Petroleo Brasileiro S.A.-Petrobras signed a 10-year bilateral loan agreement valued at US$10bn
March 2012	Venezuela	Petroleos de venezuela sa (PDVSA) and CITIC Group signed a cooperation agreement to invite China to be a shareholder of Petropiar

China's energy diplomacy in Latin America is faced with risks that stem from two sources. On the one hand, the legitimacy of some regimes in Latin America has continuously decreased, which resulted in political turbulence and even affected energy issues. On the other hand, as the US views Latin America as its own "backyard", it has all along played a role in Latin American issues. As a result, the US is prone to intervene in energy partnerships between China and Latin American countries by political, economic and military means. For this reason, China should redouble its caution in energy diplomacy towards Latin America.

5. China and East Asia

Cooperation between China and the Southeast Asian nations is mainly in the fields of natural gas, electric power and water conservancy. The most outstanding achievement from 2002 to 2012 was the oil and gas pipeline connecting China and Burma. In 2009, the Chinese and Burmese governments signed an agreement on laying pipelines. The construction project started in 2010. The natural gas pipeline was completed in 2013 and it began to transmit gas. The Sino-Burma pipeline allows crude oil to enter China overland from the southwest without passing through the Strait of Malacca, one of the world's most pirated waters. This enables China to diversify its petroleum transport modes and lower the risk of transportation.

Southeast Asia boasts a vast marine area and abundant oil and natural gas. However, China's diplomacy in this region is confronted with many difficulties, the greatest of which is the ownership of reefs in the South China Sea. Before the dispute of the South China Sea is settled through political means, there is little space for China to conduct energy diplomacy in this area.

6. China and North America

Figure 7 Some energy acquisition projects of Chinese enterprises' in North America

2005	CNOOC failed in acquiring Unocal, America
December 2009	CNPC acquired 60% of the mining rights of two oil sand projects of Canada's Athabasca Oil Corporation
2010	CNOOC acquired 33% of the stock rights of the shale gas project of Eagle Ford of America's Chesapeake
2010	Sinopec acquired 9.03% of stock rights of Syncrude
April 2011	Sinopec acquired oil sand and shale gas project of Canada's Daylight
July 2011	CNOOC acquired 35% of the stock rights of Long Lake oil fields of OPTI
January 2012	A subsidiary corporation of Sinopec acquired one-third of the five asset rights and interests of shale gas of America's Devon

China's energy diplomacy towards the US and Canada is mainly manifested in cooperation in unconventional energy projects such as shale gas and oil sand, as well as in mergers and acquisitions. Currently, the US and China compete with each other in the energy field. Besides, the two are sensitive to the interests in political, economic and military fields. Therefore, cooperation of both sides is limited to technical areas such as production and processing. Though Canada is endowed with rich oil, natural gas and uranium reserves, its industrial policy and the alternate governance of different political parties hinder Sino-Canada energy cooperation to a considerable extent.

7. China and South Asia

China and Nepal began cooperating in hydropower in 2008. China and India have cooperated to establish an energy coordination mechanism. As "all-weather friends", China and Pakistan cooperate closely in energy. Energy cooperation projects between the two sides include: China assisting Pakistan in constructing Gwadar port (2002-07), constructing the second-phase project of Chashma nuclear power station and a tar coal power project.

8. China's multilateral energy diplomacy

From 2002 to 2012, China established relations with some international energy organisations. In 2002, it began to cooperate with the Energy Charter. In 2005, China and the Organisation of Petroleum Exporting Countries (OPEC) officially established a High-level Energy Round-table Conference Dialogue Mechanism. In 2008, China and the Gulf Cooperation Council (GCC) held the China-Arab Energy Cooperation Conference. During the 10 years, China deepened its relations with international organisations such as the World Energy Council (WEC) and World Petroleum Congress (WPC).

Nevertheless, China's multilateral energy diplomacy is still at its initial stage. So far, China has only joined coordination-based or dialogue-based organisations. It has not entered into alliance-based or collaboration-based international energy organisations.

IV. Looking to the future

In view of the current situation, the Chinese economy will continue to develop rapidly in the years to come. Development and utilisation of new energy is still ongoing. Fossil energy will remain its major consumption energy. Therefore, China will encounter a tougher challenge in energy and energy shortfalls will continue to widen. Furthermore, the political situation in the Middle East and North Africa is still uncertain. There is a possibility that social instability may appear in the Middle East, Eastern Europe and Latin America. In view of all this, China's oil and gas supply is still in jeopardy. In terms of the international energy environment, fossil energy will remain the major energy in the short run. The contradiction between supply and demand of oil and natural gas will become more acute. Competition between countries, big powers in particular, will become more intense. Energy is more closely related to political and military affairs. Energy diplomacy will play a more important part in economic diplomacy. On the other hand, international cooperation will increase, centring on formulating rules on energy exploitation and transaction, research and development of new energy, energy production technology and energy collective security pre-warning.

Section 3 Oil diplomacy

I. Emergence of oil diplomacy

Since 1993, China has developed from an oil exporter into a net oil importer. With the sustained and rapid development of its economy, China's oil consumption has risen and the extent of its foreign oil dependence has increased year by year. Statistics show that, by 2012, China's degree of dependence on overseas oil had already amounted to 57%. The oil giant BP published a report in 2013 that pointed out that, by 2030, China's degree of dependence on overseas oil is likely to reach 80%.

Since the 1990s, China's rapid increase in oil imports has attracted the attention of the central leadership. President Jiang Zemin and Premier Li Peng elevated China's oil shortage to a new strategic height. Though China did not have a special document expounding its policy on oil diplomacy, statements concerning the country's strategy for oil safety have become increasingly common in government documents since 2000. As early as 1993, the Central Committee of the Communist Party of China (CPC) and the State Council explicitly stated: "We should make full use of both domestic and overseas resources and markets to develop our oil industry." In March 2000, the third session of the 9th National People's Congress put the "going global" strategy on a national strategic level. In the following year, the "going global" strategy was written into the Outline of the 10th Five-Year Plan for National Economic and Social Development (2001-05). In 2003, *Nine Countermeasures for National Oil Security* was drawn up by the SDRC as China's oil security strategy. Apart from supporting the domestic development of oil and gas, carrying out the "going global" strategy, setting up oil reserves and popularising petroleum substitutes, five new strategies were put forward in the Nine Counter-measures for National Oil Security. Among them, "oil diplomacy" was the first, demanding efforts to be made to maintain the low price of international oil through oil diplomacy. The strategy is to help China establish good relations with three categories of groups: major oil-producing countries, major oil consumption countries and those countries that control the waters through which China's oil imports are transported.

Oil diplomacy had long been in existence long before China's oil safety strategy officially appeared in government documents in 2000.. In the early 1990s, three major Chinese oil companies - PetroChina, Sinopec and China National Offshore Corporation (CNOOC) - carried out the "going global strategy". In the mid-1990s, China began its "diversification" strategy in oil importing and reduced oil imports from the Asia-Pacific region. Instead, it began to increase oil imports from Europe, America and Africa. In terms of corporate structure, the government has reformed the oil industry since 1998. PetroChina and Sinopec were reorganised into two oil companies featuring vertical integration. The rapid development of PetroChina, Sinopec and CNOOC is a remarkable achievement for China as it strives to create first-class oil companies. Moreover, as far back as in 2003 when the NDRC issued its report, China's policy has been to maintain the stability of the economy and ensure sufficient supply of overseas oil. For example, in 1999, President Jiang Zemin paid a visit to Saudi Arabia, the world's largest petroleum-exporting country. During the visit, China and Saudi Arabia established a "strategic petroleum partnership". All this indicates that China's petroleum safety strategy achievements are the result of the efforts of Chinese oil companies and the Chinese government since the early 1990s. What's more, the promulgation of these documents provides a necessary strategic basis and policy support for China's oil diplomacy in the future.

II. Three efforts in oil diplomacy

Traditionally, diplomacy is defined as "the international activities that a country conducts, such as taking part in international organisations and conferences, exchanging ambassadors, negotiating, signing treaties and agreements, etc". However, in oil diplomacy, the word "diplomacy" has additional connotations. The participants of diplomacy are not limited to the government of a country. Instead, non-state actors such as multinational companies and international organisations play a role and have functions and influences of their own. Therefore, "oil diplomacy" often refers to diplomatic activities in which the state takes the leading role, and oil enterprises and other actors participate, taking oil either as a purpose or a means. Taking oil as a purpose, oil diplomacy is to safeguard the economic interests in oil development, transport and consumption. When taking oil as means, oil diplomacy uses oil to fulfil other foreign policy goals. Generally, the two are determined by whether the state is an oil-importing country or an oil-exporting one. The former takes oil diplomacy as a purpose while the latter uses it as a means. But, of course, this correspondence is not absolute; instead, it can change according to specific situations.

One of these specific situations in China occurred in 1993. Once China had become an oil-importing nation, the pursuit of oil safety and overseas oil supplies was a clear purpose of its oil diplomacy. The Chinese government became engaged in multi-dimensional oil diplomacy. Xia Yishan, chief energy expert at the Institute of China Studies, expounded in an interview by *China Report* several essential factors of this multi-dimensional diplomatic policy. According to Mr Xia, the purpose of China's energy diplomacy is to maintain the stability, safety and sustainability of energy supply and to safeguard China's energy safety to the largest extent.

To achieve these three goals of oil diplomacy, the Chinese government has made efforts in three areas: oil diplomacy for ensuring safety of supplies, oil diplomacy for ensuring transportation safety and oil diplomacy for ensuring cooperation safety.

1. Oil diplomacy for ensuring safety of supplies

The first focus is on countries that are rich in oil resources. Here, the focus of China's diplomacy is to hope that these countries can continuously provide reliable and stable oil resources and create more opportunities for Chinese state-owned companies to invest there to ensure the safety of oil supply. As China is more reliant on imported oil, the Chinese government takes oil-supplying countries as the focus of its oil diplomacy. In terms of geographical distribution, these countries can be divided into five regions: the Middle East, Africa, Russia and Central Asia, Latin America and the Asia-Pacific region. The supply volume of these regions takes up 45.2%, 31.5%, 12.8%, 6.4% and 3.6% of China's total oil import volume, respectively. These regions are the core areas of overseas investment of China's state-owned oil companies. To help these companies expand investment and ensure China can get reliable and safe oil supplies, the Chinese government has formulated a proactive oil diplomatic strategy through bilateral and multi-lateral channels. In terms of bilateral channels, the Chinese government often conducts oil diplomacy through high-level official visits. Other modes, such as development aid, reducing and cancelling debts, interest-free loans and basic development financing, are use to support and expand this policy. In addition to actively conducting bilateral co-operation in oil, China has been exploring new ways on how to use the multilateral mechanism to safeguard its overseas oil supply and has created a set of strategic approaches of its own. In central Asia, the SCO provides China with a multilateral mechanism that pushes forward cooperation between China and the important oil-producing countries in the former Soviet Union. Apart from the SCO, China has established other regional organisations that facilitate multilateral oil diplomacy between China and other regions. For example, in 2004, while visiting Egypt, President Hu Jintao proposed to establish the China-Arab Cooperation Forum which soon became a state-to-state cooperation organisation, and later also a platform for China to mobilise Arabian countries that have abundant oil reserves to join in the multilateral cooperation mechanism. In addition, the Sino-Africa Cooperation Forum established in 2000 and the Sino-OPEC Energy Dialogue Mechanism established in 2005 and many others provide a good platform for China to conduct oil diplomacy and oil trade with countries that have abundant oil reserves.

2. Oil diplomacy for ensuring transportation safety

The second focus concerns dealing with frontier countries along transport corridors. One goal of China's oil diplomacy is to ensure the transport safety of oil imports. Second only to securing access to oil resources, China's main concern is the security problem of offshore oil supply chains. Currently, maritime transport is the weakest link of China's oil safety. In 2002, 93% of China's gross petroleum import volume was transported by sea while only 10% was transported via China's own oil tankers. Four-fifths of China's imported crude oil is transported via the Strait of Malacca. This has become a potential safety hazard, for that area is rife with piracy and chronic border disputes. Besides, the straits are highly congested with vessels. The huge number of cargo vessels, passenger vessels and fishing boats has a strong impact on the navigation safety of ships. What's more, its location is far beyond the patrol range of the Chinese navy. Excessive reliance on foreign oil tankers and the potential safety problems in surrounding waters have made the Chinese government deeply worried about its fragile oil transportation system.

Therefore, the transportation safety of overseas oil imports has become a priority of China's oil diplomacy. To reduce its reliance on the Strait of Malacca, China has adopted two approaches: building land oil petroleum pipelines and enhancing cooperation with countries along the oil channels. The Chinese government has explored five different oil transport routes: the Sino-Russia pipeline, the Sino-Kazakhstan pipeline, the Kela Canal, the Sino-Burma pipeline and the Pakistan energy corridor. The Sino-Russia pipeline project has experienced several ups and downs. In September 2012, China and Russia concluded an agreement after 15 years of negotiation and the pipeline is currently under construction. The Eastern Siberia-Pacific petroleum pipeline, China Branch (Skovorodino-Daqing) will become a "main artery" of energy resource transportation of China and Russia.

To gain the initiative in these negotiations on pipelines, China has explored other transport routes. Since June 2003, President Hu Jintao paid a visit to Kazakhstan, and the timetable for construction of a Sino-Kazakhstan oil pipeline was accelerated. In addition to these two oil pipelines, the Chinese government has been studying the feasibility of the Sino-Thailand Kela Canal, the Sino-Burma pipeline and Pakistan energy corridor, for which great diplomatic efforts have been made.

While actively exploring oil pipelines that reduce the impact of the "The Malacca dilemma", China has focused its short-term attention on enhancing friendly relations with countries along the oil corridors. On the basis of respecting the sovereignty of coastal states of the straits, and under various frameworks (such as ASEAN 10+3, China-Asean Free Trade Zone and the East Asia Summit), China, as a stakeholder, raises its concern over security across the Strait of Malacca and strives to participate in maritime security arrangements in the area. If the security issue of the Straits of Malacca is put under the framework of East Asian energy security cooperation, China will play a more active role in this aspect.

3. Oil diplomacy for ensuring good international relations

The third focus is on other major oil-consuming countries, or third-party countries as stakeholders. For example, Chinese oil companies explore and develop oil in Iran, which caused the resentment of the US. Therefore, in dealing with these countries, China's oil diplomacy aims to coordinate relations with countries whose oil interests clash with those of China, that is, realising safety of oil co-operation. China is active in its oil diplomacy in that it strives to guarantee its oil safety. However, while securing oil interests, China inevitably gets involved in strategic conflict and competition with other major oil-consuming countries. Chinese state-owned oil companies have undergone rapid expansion overseas, which may cause some unexpected consequences to the oil diplomacy strategies of countries with rich oil reserves or those situated along oil transport corridors. To reduce such consequences, diplomatic efforts are designed to promote cooperation and coordination between all countries concerned, prevent cut-throat competition between major oil consumers and reduce international doubts over China's efforts in pursuing oil interests overseas.

Other large oil consumers include the US, Japan, India and the EU. China actively cooperates with these countries and stresses the concept of common energy security. In July 2006, at the G8 summit in St. Petersburg, Chinese President Hu Jintao stated that every country had the right to make full use of its energy resources to develop itself. Only through international cooperation can the overwhelming majority of nations ensure their energy safety. At the meeting, Hu proposed China's "new energy safety concept" and stressed that international cooperation should be conducted in three aspects. First, strengthen mutually beneficial cooperation in the development and utilisation of energy resources. Second, establish a system for the research, development and popularisation of advanced energy technology. Third, maintain the existing political environment for energy safety and stability. This clearly indicated China's explicit call for sound cooperation between energy-producing countries and energy-consuming countries. Meanwhile, China, noticing that its state-owned oil companies encounter political turmoil overseas and that oil transport is faced with challenges, proposed that the international community make joint efforts to maintain the stability of energy-producing countries, especially those in the Middle East and some other regions, to ensure the safety of international oil corridors. Furthermore, China holds that efforts should be made to avoid geopolitical conflict in global energy supply and that conflicts should be resolved not by politicising energy issues but through negotiation and dialogue. In addition, China's oil diplomacy also includes making joint efforts with major energy-consuming countries to stabilise oil prices. For example, against the backdrop of rising oil prices in 2006, the Chinese government organised for the first time a high-level meeting of government officials of major oil-consuming countries. At the meeting, ministers of energy from the US, Japan, South Korea, India and China agreed to enhance cooperation in five fields: diversifying energy resources, promoting energy conservation and energy efficiency, improving the strategy of oil reserves, sharing energy information and raising market transparency as well as development and utilisation of renewable energy.

III. Participants in oil diplomacy: Chinese state-owned oil companies

Stanislav Zhiznin, a famous Russian energy expert, thinks that energy diplomacy refers to the practical activities conducted by departments of foreign policy, economy and energy to fulfil the goals and tasks concerning foreign energy policy and that in most cases, these activities involve energy companies. One of the characteristics of modern energy diplomacy is the close cooperation between diplomatic departments and energy companies. These companies may also play an active role as independent "players" on the international stage. Governments use diplomatic resources to support energy enterprises in expanding their interests overseas, which is a major means of international energy diplomacy. China is no exception.

1. Interaction between the government and companies

Since China became a net importer of oil products in 1993, China's three large state-owned oil companies, CNPC, Sinopec and CNOOC, have assumed the important responsibility of providing a surging domestic economy with sufficient oil and gas supplies. In the past 20 years, Chinese state-owned oil companies, which used to be little known, have developed into eminent multinational companies. In 2007, CNOOC appeared for the first time in the Fortune 500, in 469th place. In 1999, Sinopec and CNOOC ranked 73rd and 84th, respectively. By 2007, they had risen to 17th and 24th place, respectively. By 2012, they featured among the top 10, ranking fifth and sixth respectively. Chinese state-owned oil companies have become a force to be reckoned with in the global oil market.

The Chinese government encourages Chinese state-owned oil companies to develop themselves abroad. When these companies are pursuing resources and opportunities internationally, the Chinese government will use diplomatic means to cultivate close relationships with countries that are endowed with rich oil resources, concluding bilateral agreements and establishing alternative transport corridors as well as ensuring opportunities for overseas investment. As we have seen, before Chinese state-owned oil companies make an overseas investment, Chinese leaders pay visits to foreign countries, establishing bilateral "strategic partnerships", providing economic aid or low-interest loans, mitigating or cancelling debts to China that are behind in payment, and promising to assist in building infrastructure projects or agreeing to enhance bilateral trade. Meanwhile, Chinese state-owned oil companies take advantage of their professional skills in oil to contribute ideas and make other contributions to the oil diplomacy of the country. For example, enterprises often play a leading role in the selection of regions for overseas investment in oil and business negotiations on oil cooperation.

2. "Companies" as independent participants in diplomacy

China's major oil companies may be state-owned, but they are run as independent business entities. The government collects taxes, shares profits and appoints members of the boards of directors without intervening in corporate management. Therefore, Chinese oil enterprises conduct activities overseas mainly based on economic principles. The overseas activities of these enterprises are conducted in the form of pursuing the maximum profit. In this regard, Chinese state-owned oil enterprises are more and more like international oil companies in behavioural pattern and diplomatic influence.

State-owned oil enterprises are playing an increasingly important and independent role in China's oil diplomacy. On the one hand, they have made a considerable contribution in economic development and created strategic assets for China's economic and modernisation drive. On the other hand, with the expansion of economic strength and international influence, they participate in overseas operations of China's diplomacy as practitioners of the country's foreign policy, but also influence the formulation of China's foreign policy in a more independent manner.

First of all, Chinese state-owned enterprises are developing rapidly throughout the world, imposing greater requirements on the diplomatic ability of the Chinese government in areas such as safeguarding personal safety and the overseas assets of Chinese citizens, managing external assets and balancing overseas economic interests and international responsibilities.

Second, Chinese state-owned enterprises participate in the formulation of diplomatic policy in both formal and informal ways. Corporate executives have the right of speech in formulating foreign policy and directly taking part in policy formulation through official mechanisms. For example, outstanding experts from three major Chinese oil companies play a part in the formulation of policies concerning oil safety of the country. They convey their opinions to the central leadership through their professional research and knowledge.

Finally, they have become a medium of the diplomatic game in the international arena. They are often driven by external forces and thus influence China's decision-making on foreign affairs. Multinational companies often act as an intermediary between the government of the host country and their home country. The host country may express their interests to China through negotiations with Chinese state-owned enterprises. This game of oil diplomacy is not only played by China and the host country, but also by the third party as a stakeholder. For example, the US, as the largest oil consumer in the world, has already taken Chinese state-owned oil companies as an important parameter in the diplomatic game, no matter whether it participates directly in some practice of China's oil diplomacy or whether the overseas development project of Chinese state-owned enterprises involves American elements. In such cases, the US takes counter-measures to influence China's diplomacy by studying the acts, motivations and logic of these

Chinese companies. For example, Erica S. Downs, a researcher from the Brookings Institution, suggests that the US deals with Chinese oil companies by implementing a "stick and carrot" approach so as to influence China's attitude towards Iran on the nuclear issue. [10] On the one hand, the US warns of or even unilaterally imposes sanctions on Chinese oil companies, admonishing them to withdraw from Iran. On the other hand, it gives China larger investment and cooperation opportunities in the North American market with a view to gradually replacing China's investment in Iran.

IV. China's oil diplomacy: looking to the future

In the mid-1990s, China began implementing the "going global" energy strategy. Through nearly 20 years of efforts, the Chinese government and state-owned enterprises have made a tremendous contribution to safeguarding the stability, safety and sustained supply of overseas oil. It is due to their joint efforts that China has succeeded in avoiding the dilemma of energy shortage since China became a net oil importing country in 1993. Moreover, supported by the "going global" strategy and Chinese foreign policy, these state-owned oil companies have enjoyed rising international influence. Besides, China's overseas investment has been on the increase and their overall competitiveness has been enhanced. By 2011, Chinese oil enterprises had undertaken about 84 relatively large "going global" projects. Among them, 17 were in the Middle East and Africa, four in central Asia and the Commonwealth of the Independent States (CIS), eight in America and five in the Asia-Pacific region. In addition to bilateral oil cooperation with other countries, China's multilateral oil diplomacy has also developed rapidly. So far, China has established energy partnership with major international energy institutions, covering an extensive cooperation fields. Among them, the International Energy Agency and OPEC are key targets of China's multilateral energy diplomacy.

However, China's oil diplomacy is characterised great uncertainty. Though the government has formulated some active policies on oil diplomacy, and China's state-owned oil companies have taken the initiative to expand overseas in the past 15 years, long-term oil supply contracts comprise fewer than 10% of total imports. This means that 84% of China's crude oil imports still rely on the international spot market. From this we can see that the Chinese economy has not escaped the impact of the price fluctuations of the international oil market. In terms of oil transport safety, China's earnings are subjected to great limitation. Though China has actively conducted diplomacy along the oil corridors, more than 90% of crude oil is transported to China by sea, and 90% of that is shipped by foreign oil tankers.

---

[10] Downs, Erica and Maloney, Suzanne. Getting China to Sanction Iran [J]. Foreign Affairs, March/April 2011, Volume 90 (No 2)

By 2011, despite the Sino-Russia, Sino-Kazakhstan and Sino-Burma oil pipeline being in operation simultaneously, more than 75% of crude oil still needed to be shipped by sea. This situation is likely to persist for a long time, which means that China's oil diplomacy still has a long way to way.

Apart from all this, there is still plenty of scope for the Chinese government to improve its supervision over the overseas investment of its state-owned oil companies. The behaviour of these companies overseas is mainly based on economic principles. However, in some special circumstances, the internal economic interests of the companies fail to take into consideration China's foreign policy and its expectations for a unified energy strategic arrangement.

China's oil diplomacy has undergone 20 years' development. Great achievements have been made, especially in the last decade. However, China is still faced with a long-term and arduous task in its oil diplomacy. As China's energy cooperation strategy started late, it is imperative that it evaluate the experience and draw lessons from failures so as to improve China's practice of oil diplomacy in future.

In terms of the development direction of oil diplomacy, China, while obtaining resources through existing efforts in diplomatic cooperation, should make efforts in the construction of international rules. It will continue to safeguard the stability of the world's energy market, participate in international energy safety mechanisms, ensure the smoothness of international energy corridors and complement each other's advantages in industrial technical cooperation. China should also seek more meeting points of interests with energy-exporting countries, energy-importing countries and energy transit countries with a view to seizing the advantage of energy cooperation and pushing forward bilateral and multilateral cooperation. It is to be noted here that Chinese state-owned oil companies, which play an important role in China's oil diplomacy, have attracted worldwide attention. Whether China is able to effectively integrate its national interests overseas and fulfil its responsibility as an international player will be a test of its diplomatic ability and administrative capacity as a big power. While establishing strategic oil reserves, China is willing to play an active and constructive role in promoting common security. Meanwhile, China shows its willingness to make concerted efforts with the international community in settling political issues such as crisis in Darfur and the Middle East peace process. As a matter of fact, China's efforts do not aim to blindly seek oil interests. Nor do China's interests clash with those of Western countries. In the future, the Chinese government will surely attach great importance to establishing a unified and efficient regulatory system of the oil industry, assuming the government's leading role and enhancing the supervision over and standardisation of overseas investment of the enterprises with a view to ensuring that their commercial operations are not detrimental to the image and interests of the country. For their part, Chinese state-owned oil companies should enhance their ability in transnational management, coordinating with host countries with China's overall development planning. By doing this, the Chinese government will surely work together with its state-owned oil companies to play a stabilising role in the international energy market.

Section 4 Environmental diplomacy

I. Development background of China's environmental diplomacy

Environmental issues are of great global concern, and they have much to do with the basic condition of existence and quality of life. In the 21st century, environmental issues have become increasingly global. Environmental problems centring on air pollution, water pollution and water resources utilisation, disease transmission and climate change are faced by nearly every country. Some environmental problems have evolved into an important cause of international disputes and have hindered the harmonious development of the international community.

In the past decade, China's environmental diplomacy has undergone tremendous change. In the 20th century, with the signing of the Kyoto Protocol, all countries concerned could achieve a general consensus on environmental cooperation and environmental diplomacy mainly focused on a single key issue - global climate change. What China currently faces is an international environment featuring more extensive contents, diversified layers, multi-faceted interactive modes and more intense argument.

International environmental diplomacy in the past decade has been richer in content. Topics on environmental diplomacy have expanded from the original one-sided concern over climate change into all aspects of the environment. On each environmental issue, disputes over details between countries concerned have tended to increase. Moreover, the width and complexity of environmental diplomacy have increased drastically, while the participation level of international environmental diplomacy continues to diversify. Apart from sovereign states, social forces such as international organisations, regional groups and non-governmental organisation (NGOs) have become involved in environmental diplomacy. In view of this, China's environmental diplomacy needs to give consideration to more interests and participate in more intense competition.

Against this backdrop, China, as a responsible big nation, has the obligation and need to conduct cooperation in environmental prevention and control on the international stage. Behind the technical level, it is more important for a country to coordinate its internal interests, rationalise relations between the government and enterprises so as to make public policies that serve the will of the state and then seek a consensus in environmental management on the international stage. In view of this, it is imperative for China to integrate its national resources and participate from a strategic perspective in the management of international environmental issues on the basis of state sovereignty and in the form of environmental diplomacy.

China is on the front of development in international environmental diplomacy. For example, China was present at the first multilateral environmental diplomacy, the Stockholm Declaration at the United Nations Conference on Human Environment in 1972. It became one of the pioneer countries of international environmental diplomacy. Later, China played an active role in the United Nations Framework Convention on Climate Change (UNFCCC) and the Kyoto Protocol. Indeed, China's environmental diplomacy has kept up with international development and has won the recognition of the whole world.

However, the development of international environmental diplomacy has by no means been plain sailing. As a matter of fact, the practice of environmental diplomacy in the post-Kyoto Protocol era has bristled with difficulty, including conflicts over sovereignty, a the lack of funds and the blocks on of technical transfers. Confrontations in environmental diplomacy have escalated due to the rising importance and degree of involvement in the issues being discussed. Faced with such an intricate international environment China needs to work out how best to clarify its interests and stand its ground.

II. Theoretical development of environmental diplomacy

There are numerous and complicated definitions of environmental diplomacy in academic circles. One recognised definition is: the general name of various activities in which the actors in international relations adjust international environmental relations through negotiation, cooperation and other means. Environmental diplomacy includes two layers of meaning. One is that government agencies and staff members, with the sovereign state as the main body, settle and adjust all environment-related behaviour in international relations (such as exploring the ways of enhancing international environmental cooperation, formulating international environment laws, implementing international environmental conventions and settling conflicts and disputes in international environment through diplomatic means including negotiation and concluding treaties). The other refers to "using environmental issues to realise specific political goals or other strategic intentions". In other words, environmental diplomacy is the interaction between diplomacy and environmental issues. It is, in essence, the extension and realisation of national interests in the environmental field.

To sum up, environmental diplomacy has the following characteristics. First, it covers a wide range of areas, involving all aspects of international environmental issues. Second, the goals of environmental diplomacy are multilayered, covering the environmental interests of one country and also striving to realise those of the whole world. In diplomatic activities, consideration is given to other interests in the country. Third, the means of environmental diplomacy are peaceful and diversified. In terms of the practice of China's environmental diplomacy, it mainly covers three areas: participating in conferences on international environmental cooperation and establishing bilateral, regional and multilateral cooperation dialogue mechanisms; taking part in legislation such as international environmental conventions, resolutions by international organisations, declarations between governments and bilateral agreements; and establishing regional organisations of environmental protection so as to share information and technology concerning environmental protection.

Most theoretical studies on China's environmental diplomacy are articles on international political economics and policy suggestions. So far, no scholars have conducted systematic integration for the theory and practice of environmental diplomacy. Nor has any "grand theory" in this field been created. Furthermore, Chinese theory on environmental diplomacy holds that, apart from realising the environmental interests of a country and the world, environmental diplomacy has a spillover function that facilitates diplomacy in other fields. For instance, in the interaction of environmental diplomacy, all countries may consolidate their environmental interests in the name of national security. Active and effective environmental diplomacy may not only enhance the soft power of a nation, but also improve its image before the international community. Environmental diplomacy can also bring about positive economic benefits by vigorously giving impetus to the research and development of domestic technology of environmental protection and production of relevant equipment.

III. Practice of China's environmental diplomacy

China's stand on environmental diplomacy has changed with the times and in response to the international environment. In 1999, China declared that it could not assume the obligation of reducing greenhouse gas emissions until it had become a moderately developed country. However, with the deterioration of the international environment and the expansion of its economic strength, China has gradually changed this position. In 2001, China declared that effective financial aid and technical transfer are an essential condition to improve the ability of developing countries in dealing with climate change, officially expressing its active standpoint on global warming. In 2009, China proposed a long-lasting principal which emphasised the different historical responsibilities among developed and developing countries. Developed countries should play a leading role based on the principle of fairness, while developing countries should be supported by funds and technology. The clarification of "common and differential liability" has been used in China's environmental diplomacy in past decade. Funds and technology are the prerequisites for the fulfilment of environmental liability. China emphasises international strategic cooperation on environmental diplomacy.

Based on this position, China has conducted many practices in international environmental diplomacy. President Hu Jintao and Premier Wen Jiabao attended many regional summits, attaching great importance to the environment and development. In global multilateral environmental diplomacy, China has actively attended and hosted important conferences, taken part in international negotiations and fulfilled international environmental treaties conscientiously. So far, a multilayer pattern of environmental diplomacy - bilateral, regional and global - has taken shape. For example, at the dialogue meeting of G8+5 in 2005, President Hu expounded China's three principles on international cooperation in climate change: persist in the guidance of the United Nations Framework Convention on Climate Change and the Kyoto Protocol; uphold the concept of coping with climate change within the framework of sustainable development; reaffirming the importance of science and technology. In June 2007, China issued its National Climate Change Programme, explaining the country's attitude towards climate change, including reducing greenhouse gas emissions to the greatest extent, coping with climate change, enhancing exchange in international environmental protection and technical transfer, conscientiously assuming the obligations stipulated in the United Nations Framework Convention on Climate Change and the Kyoto Protocol, and actively cooperating with relevant regions. It can be seen here that China's environmental diplomacy, based on the spirit of existing international resolutions and documents, is conducted in an active and innovative manner with international conferences as the platform.

In the post-Kyoto Protocol era, China's environmental diplomacy is faced with a grimmer situation in that the principle of "common and differential liability" is rejected by developed countries. They insist that China assume more international obligations, while China says that it should be treated with a different level of liability by sticking to the spirit of the Kyoto Protocol. From the Bali climate change conference in 2007, to those in Copenhagen, Cancun, Durban, Doha and finally to the Warsaw climate conference in 2013, this conflict has accompanied the development of China's environmental diplomacy, leading China to a situation of chronic competition and negotiation with developed countries after 2007. A series of diplomatic manoeuvres resulted in China's pledge at the Copenhagen climate change conference in 2009 that, by 2020, it would reduce its release of carbon dioxide per unit of GDP by 40% to 45% compared with that of 2005. This demonstrated China's sincerity and constructive attitude towards environmental diplomacy, and it also represented a big concession in its diplomatic manoeuvring with Western countries.

IV. The mechanism of China's environmental diplomacy

During the past decade, China has achieved substantial results in its international practice, and also established a steering group and initial decision-making mechanism to fit in with its practical needs. For example, in response to global concern over international environmental protection, China established the National Leading Group for Climate Change, Energy Conservation and Emissions Reduction headed by Premier Wen Jiabao in June 2007. Three months later, the Ministry of Foreign Affairs established the Leading Group for External Work for Climate Change to unify China's environmental diplomacy and facilitate coordination between departments. In 2008, State Environmental Protection General Administration was upgraded to the Ministry of Environmental Protection, under which the International Cooperation Department of Environmental Protection was set up to coordinate external work concerning environmental protection. In 2013, the General Office of the State Council adjusted the staff composition of the National Leading Group for Climate Change, Energy Conservation and Emissions Reduction. Leaders of more than 30 departments, including the Ministry of Foreign Affairs, NDRC, Ministry of Science and Technology (MOST) and the Ministry of Finance took part in policy formulation for China's environmental diplomacy, leading to the creation of an initial working mechanism of environmental diplomacy.

Apart from the official agencies, China's environmental diplomacy has absorbed social forces. These include quasi-official clubs and organisations such as the China Institute of Environmental Sciences and the China Environmental Protection Foundation, and also industrial associations such as the China Promotion Association of International Transnational Corporations. Social forces strive to propel Chinese transnational companies to fulfil their environmental responsibilities through international cooperation such as the International Forum on Food and Drug Safety and the Clean Coal Demonstration and Promotion Project. Through 10 years of effort, the pattern of China's environmental diplomacy has taken its initial shape in which official organisations take the lead and non-governmental associations play a supplementary role. China's environmental diplomacy is pressing ahead in a systematic and professional way.

V. Assessment of China's environmental diplomacy

Despite suffering many setbacks in the past decade, China's environmental diplomacy has made great achievements. First, it has taken on greater significance, from the margin to centre stage. China's environmental diplomacy has been heightened to a core national interest. The 17th National People's Congress of the CPC report proposed "ecological civilisation construction" which has become one of the five core principles of the Scientific Outlook on Development, which guides the country's development. Second, China is increasingly active in international environmental diplomacy. From Kyoto to Warsaw, from bilateral meetings to multilateral forums, China has become an indispensable participant of global environmental diplomacy. Third, the main body of China's environmental diplomacy has taken its initial shape and achievements have been made in the participation of social forces and information accumulation of talented personnel. Finally, China's environmental diplomacy has made some substantial achievements such as the signing of the Kyoto protocol and deepening cooperation in energy conservation and emission reduction involved in the US-China Strategic and Economic Dialogue (SED).

However, as China's environmental diplomacy is still in its infancy, it faces many problems and flaws. First, China's environmental diplomacy still develops in a passive way. Besides, it lacks strategic initiative and theoretical innovation. China's environmental diplomacy develops simply by following the international trend but lacks active strategic innovation and relevant practice; in most cases, it is focused on domestic environmental management. Such an introspective approach largely restricted the practice of China's environmental diplomacy. Second, as the mechanism of China's environmental diplomacy is still immature, the functions of professional talents cannot be reflected in policy making. Though China has established a decision-making body for environmental diplomacy, it is still occupied by official or semi-official organisations. The environmental opinions of scholars, enterprises and the general public are still marginalised. Third, China's environmental diplomacy is too inflexible and it is wasteful in terms of its resources. Moreover, the practical effect of China's environmental diplomacy tends to focus on domestic environmental benefits. The social, economic and political benefits of environmental diplomacy, however, have been left undervalued. There is no denying that, as China's environmental diplomacy is still in its initial stage, there are inevitable shortcomings in diplomatic practice. Nevertheless, on the whole, China's environmental diplomacy has achieved great progress in the past 10 years.

VI. Major challenges facing China's environmental diplomacy

China's environmental diplomacy is faced with many challenges. According to practical experience and the research findings of scholars, three major factors - institutional, structural and identity - have shaped China's environmental diplomacy.

Institutional factor refers to the restrictions of domestic institutional environment to the practice of environmental diplomacy. Vertically, the central government, local governments and domestic enterprises and their overseas agencies have different interests. The environmental diplomacy decision-making structure is still highly decentralised. From the perspective of institutional efficiency, insufficient stock of knowledge, theories and information concerning environmental diplomacy along with legislative defects and a lack of environmental awareness impede the formation of a unified opinion in China. These institutional factors harm the state's ability to form a clear consensus on the goal of environmental diplomacy and even weaken the effect of its executive.

Structural factor mainly refers to that fact that countries attempt to shuffle their responsibilities to each other and get a free ride. In the absence of major environmental problems, countries enjoy this state of affairs without having to pay a price. In this case, they obtain positive externality and the environment becomes a public product. However, once the environment is polluted and it affects other countries, those countries have to pay a price. In this case, they bear negative externality. Environmental management can eliminate negative externality. Therefore, as long as one country invests in environmental management, other countries can benefit from it. Following the logic of rational calculation, as every country hopes to obtain positive externality without any input, they often shuffle their environmental management responsibilities to each other, in the hope that one country will shoulder the responsibility and offer public products. However, there is no single government that can supervise all countries. Besides, all countries hope to gain an advantage by hitching a free ride. Consequently, the international community has fallen into the prisoner's dilemma in shouldering environmental liability. Under such circumstances, all countries implement a diplomatic policy that involves making little effort while urging other countries to assume responsibilities.

Identity factor mainly refers to the influence of identity on interests and identity positioning. China positions itself in its environmental diplomacy as both a developing country and a responsible big country. However, such a dual identity has brought about a contradictory benefit positioning to China. On the one hand, as a developing country, China should not assume too much responsibility on the principle of "common and differential liability". In this sense, it is a beneficiary of the existing international environmental system. On the other hand, China, as a responsible big country, should shoulder its international obligations and take its responsibility in environmental protection. However, such a positioning of dual identity leads to the defining of vague benefits in China's environmental diplomacy. This is particularly reflected in the fact that China, more often than not, fails to justify itself in answering the question, "Should China assume limited liability or primary liability?" Consequently, other countries often take this as an excuse to challenge China's policy on environmental diplomacy. If the issue of identity positioning is not settled, China's image and right of speech concerning China's environmental diplomacy will inevitably be affected.

VII. Development prospect of China's environmental diplomacy

In the coming decade, the environmental pattern of the world will continue to follow the trend of multilayer, multi-field and increased competition. As the environment will surely deteriorate in the foreseeable future, environmental issues will become a major topic in international exchanges. Moreover, the urgency of environmental diplomacy will be more pressing and its status will be improved. Scientific and technological strength will become the core competitive force of a nation's environmental diplomacy, which will gradually become the main channel through which countries showcase their soft power and shape their national image. With the upgrading of China's overall national strength and international status, it is faced with greater identity pressure. China will inevitably assume more international responsibilities to justify its identity and status as a big power. To promote the sound development of China's environmental diplomacy, protect the state's environmental safety and interests, and lead the developmental trend of environmental diplomacy, China should reform its environmental diplomacy in the following fields.

1. Pinpoint dual identity and define national interests

As China's dual identity as a developing country and a responsible big power will continue in the following 10 years, it should stick to the principle of shouldering responsibility featuring "common but differential liability" in its environmental diplomacy. In dealing with developed countries, China should continue to position itself as a developing country and strive to fulfil its environmental responsibility that matches its technological capabilities. In exchanging with under-developed countries, China should demonstrate its demeanour as a responsible big power, construct regional power by providing more public goods and assume obligations within its capability. As China improves its science and technology and deepens international cooperation, it should gradually take the initiative to fulfil more obligations. China will take the lead in building up international regulations for environmental governance in order to promote its voice and gain the right to formulate rules. In the long run, it should assume more international liabilities and providing more public goods, such as the regional fund for reducing carbon emission..

2. Establish and improve the system of environmental diplomacy

Although China has built up a systematic framework for its environmental diplomacy in the past decade, "the National Leading Group for Climate Change, Energy

Conservation and Emissions Reduction" as the core decision maker is not powerful enough. Besides, its rights and liabilities are ambiguous and policy implementation is incoherent. Over the next decade, China should make great efforts to establish and improve its system of environmental diplomacy and strive for basic coordination of internal interests in forming its diplomatic policy. It should also coordinate external opinions and ensure sufficiency and effectiveness in political authorisation. Furthermore, China should: make full use of bodies such as institutions operating abroad, overseas enterprises and transnational companies to form its information network; encourage main bodies at all levels to take part in decision making and implementation of environmental diplomacy; increase both the rationality of decision-making of environmental diplomacy and the efficiency of its implementation process.

3. Coordinate public policy and diplomatic policy

China's environmental diplomacy strives to be rational in decision-making and secure real effect in its implementation. However, the central government cannot accomplish this all on its own. In the coming decade, China's environmental diplomacy will surely be to serve national interests. A great number of enterprises have a stake in government environmental policies. Relations between the government and enterprises will directly influence the execution and impact of environmental diplomacy. On this basis, China should adopt diplomatic policies concerning the environment that will benefit both enterprises and the state.

4. Push forward domestic environmental protection

Over the past 10 years, the institutions of environmental diplomacy of China's central government have been standardised and environmental awareness has been cultivated. However, local governments pay little attention to cooperation in environmental protection. Besides, the external cooperation mechanism for environmental protection is far from mature. Therefore, China should make unremitting efforts in raising the environmental awareness of enterprises and the general public and enhancing the publicity of non-governmental environmental protection so as to make people want to play a part in environmental protection. China should support the activities of non-governmental organisations in institutional management and bring into full play the unique role of social forces in environmental protection and diplomacy.

5. Play an active role in all-directional environmental diplomacy

All-directional diplomacy is the basic requirement for China's overall diplomacy. In future, China should more actively participate in international interactions concerning environmental diplomacy with multilateral diplomacy at the forefront and bilateral and regional diplomacy as supplementary methods. This is where China is able to demonstrate its status as a big power. In terms of bilateral environmental diplomacy, China should adopt flexible policies in dealing with different countries. In the coming decade, it should conduct interactions with countries in Latin America and Africa. In addition, South-to-South cooperation should be used as a platform to extend its environmental diplomacy.

6. Abandon zero-sum thinking and promote overall diplomatic development on the basis of environmental diplomacy

The primary goal of environmental diplomacy should be to promote the prevention and control of environmental pollution. As China is vulnerable to acute environmental problems, the benefits of environmental diplomacy should conform to its own interests. China should not strive to obtain comparative advantage over other countries. Instead, it should play an exemplary role in environmental control. China is expected to forge an image as a responsible big power by fulfilling its responsibilities and endeavouring to expand environmental diplomacy in coordination with other aspects of diplomacy.

China's environmental diplomacy has achieved good momentum since the beginning of the 21st century. In 10 years, China's mechanism for environmental diplomacy has taken initial shape and exerted a lasting effect on the international stage. However, due to insufficient coordination and a lack of experience in international activities, China's environmental diplomacy still has much room for improvement. In the coming 10 years, diplomatic disputes are bound to continue in global environmental diplomacy. Therefore, China should explicate its national interests through its dual identity strategy, improve the mechanism for environmental diplomacy, and rationalise its domestic relations so that it can realise its national interests on the multifaceted diplomatic stage.

Section 5 Aid diplomacy

China is a developing country with a long history of providing aid to foreign countries. For years, it has adhered to the guiding principle of equality and mutual benefit, stressing practical results, keeping up with the times and giving aid without any political conditions attached. While committed to developing itself, China has always provided assistance to other developing countries and assumed international obligations. This section provides an overview of China's aid to foreign countries from 2002 to 2012, including the history of China's external aid, guiding ideology and major modes of external aid, policies on and effects of foreign aid as well as problems encountered.

I. History of China's external aid

China's external aid started with helping neighbouring countries. In 1950, China began to render material assistance to North Korea and Vietnam. After the reform and opening-up, economic cooperation between China and other developing countries turned from providing aid to mutually beneficial cooperation. In the 1990s, during its transformation from a planned economy to a socialist market economy, China began a series of reforms to its foreign aid policy, the focus of which was to push forward the diversification of the capital sources and modes of aid funds.

Since 2004, in step with the rapid and sustained economic growth and expansion of overall national strength, China's foreign aid contributions have kept increasing. The average annual growth rate of foreign aid funds from 2004 to 2009 amounted to 29.4%. The Report of The Seventeenth Party Congress stated: "We will continue to enhance solidarity and cooperation with developing countries, deepen our traditional friendship, expand pragmatic cooperation and provide assistance to the best of our ability and safeguard just demands and common interests of developing countries." In addition to deciding through consultation on aid programmes through traditional bilateral channels, China has strengthened collective negotiation with recipient countries at the international and regional level. The Chinese government announced a package of niche targeting policy measures of external aid at conferences of regional cooperative mechanism such as the UN High-level Meeting on Development Financing, the High-level Plenary Meeting on the Millennium Development Goals, the Forum on China-Africa Co-operation (FOCAC), Shanghai Cooperation Organisation (SCO), a meeting between Chinese and Asean leaders, the China Caribbean Economic and Trade Cooperation Forum, the China-Pacific Island Countries Economic Development and Cooperation Forum and the Forum for Economic and Trade Cooperation between China and Portuguese-speaking Countries. These meetings led to enhanced Chinese aid in areas such as agriculture, infrastructure, education, medical treatment and public health, cooperation in human resources development and clean energy.

On 15 October 2005, the Seventh G20 Finance Ministers and Central Bank Governors Meeting was convened in Beijing. President Hu Jintao attended the meeting and delivered an important speech entitled *Strengthening Global Cooperation to Promote Common Development*, putting forward four proposals on balanced and orderly development of the world economy. The fourth proposal was to help developing countries accelerate development. He said: "It is, therefore, imperative for us to enhance the North-South dialogue, proceed with the gradual establishment of a new type of long-term and all-inclusive North-South partnership. We also need to improve the development assistance mechanism and encourage more development resources to be diverted into developing countries. Hu also pointed out that China would pledge new assistance measures in five areas including taxation, debt relief, concessional loans, public health and human resources development. After the outbreak of the international financial crisis in 2008, the world economy slumped to a low ebb. However, "China, as a responsible big developing country, has all along taken common development as the important content of its diplomacy policy and tried its best to provide support and aid to other developing countries, thus honouring its commitment to the United Nations Millennium Declaration. So far, China has rendered assistance to more than 120 countries, exempting the cumulative debts of 49 heavily indebted poor countries and least developed countries. In addition, China has given zero-tariff treatment to more than 40 least developed countries." President Hu Jintao made the commitment that China would "conscientiously honour all promises and measures of foreign aid in a responsible manner and provide developing countries, the least developed African countries in particular, with more assistance to the best of its ability.

On 27 June 2010, the fourth Leaders' Summit of the Group of Twenty (G20) was held in Toronto, Canada. At the summit, President Hu said: "To realise long-term and sustained growth of the world economy, we must help developing countries to fully develop themselves and narrow the gap between the North and the South. In the international financial crisis, developing countries suffered a severe impact and are faced with untold difficulties in tiding over the crisis. Most of the member countries of G20 are developed countries, countries with an emerging market economy and highly industrialised developing countries, whose GDP accounts for 85% of the world's total. However, we cannot afford to ignore the developmental appeal of other developing countries that account for 85% of the number of countries on this planet. Therefore, the G20 has the obligation to provide more political impetus, more economic resources and a better institutional guarantee." In August 2010, the Chinese government held a National Conference on Foreign Aid to summarise its experience in foreign aid and clarify the key tasks in furthering and improving efforts in foreign aid. Since then, China's foreign aid has entered a new developmental stage. By the end of 2009, China had provided assistance to 161 countries and more than 30 international and regional organisations. A total of 123 developing countries were in regular receipt of Chinese aid, of which 30 were Asian countries, 51 African countries, 18 countries from Latina America and the Caribbean, 12 countries from Oceania and 12 from East Europe.

On 21 April 2011, the Information Office of the State Council issued a white paper entitled *China's Foreign Aid*, introducing policy, fund, mode, distribution and management aspects of foreign aid as well as international cooperation in this area. This was the first time the Information Office had issued a white paper on

China's aid to other countries. In March 2011, the Chinese government aided Japan after it had suffered from a powerful earthquake and tsunami with goods and materials valued at Rmb30m and 20,000 tons of fuel oil. On 21 August 2011, the United Nations World Food Programme (WFP) announced in Beijing that the Chinese government had given it US$16m, which was the single largest sum of its kind to support its famine rescue operation. In 2011 alone, China's donation to the WFP amounted to US$20m.

In recent years, China has enhanced its support to the WFP in its fighting famine all over the world. On 15 September 2011, responding to a request from Zimbabwe, the Chinese government decided to provide Rmb90m of emergency food assistance to the country to help relieve the famine caused by drought. Before then, the Chinese government had announced that it would provide US$70m of emergency food aid to the drought-stricken countries in the Horn of Africa. In October 2011, the Chinese government decided to provide Rmb50m of humanitarian emergency assistance to Cambodia after it was severely affected by floods, including drugs, medical supplies, medical apparatus, bedding and mosquito nets. On 11 April 2012, the Chinese government provided US$2m of humanitarian emergency assistance to Syria through the International Committee of the Red Cross (ICRC) headquartered in Geneva. On 23 May 2012, the China's vice-minister of the Ministry of Foreign Affairs, Zhai Juan announced at the "Friends of Yemen" meeting held in Riyadh, Saudi Arabia, that China would render assistance gratis of Rmb100m to Yemen.

During the 10 years from 2002 to 2012, China provided large amounts of economic aid to many countries and regions which not only greatly relieved the shortage of badly-needed goods and materials in the aid recipient areas but also achieved notable results.

II. Guidelines and major types of China's foreign aid

China's foreign aid is based on its realistic national interests. By providing aid to foreign countries, China helps unite a large number of people, and also increases its influence in the world. A country provides aid to other countries and regions for the sake of its own national interest. Economic interest, an essential part of national interest, is the material foundation of the country's survival and development. Reviewing the economic motive of foreign aid since World War II, we are able to find the following rules. First, from the logic of the market economy, foreign aid can help aid recipient developing countries eliminate poverty, while at the same time helping aid-providing countries to pursue their economic interests so as to promote good trade and investment relations with aid recipient countries. This is rational and normal behaviour in foreign aid. Since the adoption of the reform and opening-up policy, China has adjusted its policies on foreign aid from ideology concern to international cooperation, in order to highlight mutual benefit.

Factors influencing the foreign aid of a country vary according to changes in its domestic political and economic environment. Therefore, its foreign aid policy keeps adjusting over time. Against the backdrop of growing economic globalisation, poverty has become a "systematic risk", being a breeding ground for issues such as terrorism and armed conflict. Consequently, poor countries have become a root cause of global challenges in the new century. Moreover, the problems these countries face have spillover effects, such as civil war and genocide that can shift across national borders and threaten the safety of other countries. Foreign aid is an important means to tackle these global challenges. Accordingly, it is imperative that China formulate its goals for foreign aid in a broader international climate. In addition, its current mode of foreign aid conforms to its national conditions and stage of economic development. As the largest developing country in the world, China is faced with problems such as a huge population and weak economic foundations, low average per capita income and uneven economic development. Therefore, development remains a long-term and arduous task for China. For this reason, equality and mutual benefit and common development will be the principle that China should abide by in the years to come.

Fundamentally, China provides aid to foreign countries to promote development and to facilitate cooperation through development. China's thinking in foreign aid has been constantly evolving. The course of China's foreign aid is penetrated with ethics such as keeping a low profile, striking a balance between obligations and interests, maintaining independence and keeping the initiative in our own hands, pursuing common development, creating a responsible big country and a harmonious world.

Currently, China provides aid to foreign countries and regions in eight principal ways: complete sets of projects, ordinary materials, technical cooperation, cooperation in human resources development, foreign aid medical teams, humanitarian emergency assistance, foreign aid volunteers and debt relief. China's aid funds fall into three main categories: non-reimbursable assistance, interest-free loans and concessional loans. By the end of 2009, the cumulative amount of China's foreign aid had totalled Rmb256.29bn, of which non-reimbursable assistance accounted for Rmb106.2bn, interest-free loans Rmb76.54bn and concessional loans Rmb73.55bn. The priority targets of China's foreign aid have been low-income developing countries. Asia and Africa, with the largest number of poor people, received about 80% of China's total aid. This aid is distributed in various areas such as agriculture, industry, economic infrastructure, education, healthcare and, in recent years, climate change. China's foreign aid is focused on providing bilateral aid and support and participates to the best of its ability in development assistance of multilateral institutions such as the UN. China takes initiative to conduct exchanges in development assistance with multilateral organisations and other countries and explores new avenues for pragmatic cooperation. The decision-making power of China's foreign aid rests with the central government, and the Ministry of Commerce is the competent department authorised by the State Council to be in charge of foreign aid. In 2008, the Ministry of Commerce made joint efforts with relevant departments and institutions under the Ministry of Foreign Affairs and the Ministry of Finance to officially establish an inter-ministerial liaison mechanism for foreign aid. In February 2011, this mechanism was upgraded to an inter-ministerial coordination mechanism.

III. Policy and effects of China's foreign aid policy

China's foreign aid policy complies with its national conditions and the development needs of aid recipient countries. Back in the 1960s, China proposed its Eight Principles for Aid to Foreign Countries, which became the basic principle in this field and has been enriched and improved in practice. China, the largest developing country in the world, has a huge population and a poor economic foundation, coupled with uneven economic development. Therefore, development has been a long-term and arduous task, which determines that China's foreign aid is a part of South-to-South Cooperation which, in essence, refers to cooperation between developing countries. The main contents of China's foreign aid policy are:

1. Insist on helping recipient countries to improve their capacity for self-development. Experience has shown that a country can develop itself best by its own efforts. While providing foreign aid, China endeavours to cultivate local talented personnel and technical strength for the recipient countries, help them in infrastructural construction, develop and utilise their national resources so as to lay a solid foundation for development by their own efforts.

2. Provide aid without any political strings attached. China has all long adhered to the Five Principles of Peaceful Coexistence and respected the right of recipient countries in choosing independently the social system and road to development, believing that they can explore a development mode suited to their national conditions. Under no circumstances will China take aid as a means to interfere in the internal affairs of other countries and to seek political privileges.

3. Pursue common development on the basis of equality and mutual benefit. China perseveres in taking foreign aid as mutual aid between developing countries, attracting great importance to the actual effects of the aid and respecting the

interests of others. China strives to promote friendly relations and mutual benefits and win-win results through economic and technical cooperation with other developing countries.

4. Do what China's strength allows. In terms of the scale and modes of foreign aid, China provides aid to the best of its ability. In addition, China, relying on their comparative advantages, strives to meet the actual demands of the recipient countries to the maximum.

5. Keep pace with the times in reform and innovation. China provides foreign aid in line with the dynamic domestic and international situations, attaches great importance to summing up experience, creating new modes of foreign aid, adjusts and reforms the management mechanism promptly so as to improve continuously the work of foreign aid.

While aiding other countries and regions, China helps them overcome their social and economic difficulties, improve their access to overseas markets, thereby helping the export of Chinese products. Moreover, China's foreign aid products are mostly high quality and made in China. This gives Chinese products a window for promotion overseas and makes them more popular in local markets. For example, China's medical assistance to Africa is viewed as a tool to publicise Chinese pharmaceutical products.

China has stressed that its foreign aid is a part of South-to-South cooperation and that it should be viewed as mutual help between developing countries. Some aid projects in areas such as infrastructure, technical cooperation, personnel training and specialist support help aid recipient countries better understand Chinese enterprises, products and technology, which promotes the development of bilateral relations. Therefore, China's foreign aid plays an important role in enhancing its friendly relations with developing countries and trade and economic cooperation, facilitating the development of China's foreign economic relations and creating a harmonious and stable environment for international development.

To sum up, China's foreign aid expands its influence in the international arena. On the one hand, China provides aid to other countries to maintain the stability and prosperity of its neighbours. On the other hand, Chinese aid brings domestic enterprises to the international market and enlarges China's global trade share, thus creating a favourable external environment for its economic development. China's foreign aid promotes bilateral trade and investment, becoming an important component of China's foreign aid strategy and even the "grand economic and trade" strategy as well as the "going global" strategy.

IV. Problems of China's foreign aid and prospect analysis

Over the past 50 years, China's foreign aid policy has scored some tremendous achievements, yet also encountered quite a few difficulties and reverses. China's foreign aid policy has been reformed and adjusted over time. China's foreign aid has received a considerable amount of foreign criticism. Some say that China's foreign aid lacks openness and transparency, while others argue that China's aid may increase the debt burden of African countries, or that it support "rogue states" and gives rise to unfair business competition to Western countries. Governments of some Western countries and non-governmental organisations even impose pressure on China, requiring China make some changes in its foreign aid policy to serve their interests. All this has posed challenges to China's diplomacy. In future, as China will surely have more international dialogue and communication in the field of foreign aid, it must strike a balance between its insistence on defending its own interests and gaining the understanding and cooperation of the outside world.

In the course of providing foreign aid, there have been some undoubted failures. For example, excessive emphasis has been given to the economic interests of foreign aid. As a result, national interests are confused with corporate interests, which is detrimental to the national image. Furthermore, while carrying out foreign aid projects, some Chinese enterprises attach excessive importance to corporate interests without paying attention to the protection of the legitimate rights and interests of local workers. Nor do they bother to fulfil their corporate social responsibilities. All this is detrimental to China's national image. It is for this reason that some Western countries compare the momentum of China's aid, trade and investment in Africa to a revitalised East India Company. Meanwhile, some Western media defame China's aid and investment in Southeast Asia as a tool to regain control over its backyard, thinking that China attempts to found an "empire". Influenced by all this, China's aid in some Southeast Asian countries fails to win the hearts of the local people.

In view of this, we should take a comprehensive attitude towards the opinions of the international community. On the one hand, some organisations are heavily influenced by some developed countries and some local groups intentionally provoke trouble for the sake of their partial interests. On the other hand, as some enterprises implementing China's foreign aid projects know little about the local political environment and make little effort to publicise the aid projects, the local people and social groups misread China's assistance. With the expansion of China's economic strength and the upgrading of its international political and economic status, China should adjust its major goals of foreign aid and gradually weaken the influence of economic factors. By doing so, China will, with a broader international view, enhance the position of foreign aid in its overall foreign relations.

President Hu Jintao stated: "With the deepening of economic globalisation, human communities have never been so closely interconnected in interests and destiny. Therefore, to realise common prosperity conforms to the fundamental interests of the people of all countries concerned. The most urgent task we face now is: strengthening international cooperation in development, narrowing the North-South gap to ensure the realisation of the United Nations' millennium development goals...Chinese people are willing, together with the people of the other countries in the world, to build up the 21st century into an era in which all people enjoy prosperity and development opportunity." Guided by this view, we should further improve the new mechanism and modes of China's foreign aid, coordinate the development of foreign aid and foreign trade and investment so as to make it the strategic thinking of China's foreign aid.

China joined the International Development Association (IDA) in 2007. From then on, the country turned from an aid recipient into an aid donor. Therefore, China should actively participate in global governance, foster an image as a responsible big power, enhance collective negotiation and formulate fair, rational, effective and multi-win measures and rules in international cooperation and assistance. In 2008, the Ministry of Commerce, working together with the Ministry of Foreign Affairs and the Ministry of Finance, established an inter-ministerial liaison mechanism for foreign aid. Three years later it was upgraded to an inter-ministerial coordination mechanism. Owing to the establishment of the foreign aid mechanism, there are still some problems in coordination between the ministries and the commissions of the central government, between the central government and the local governments and between the government and the market. Research is to be undertaken on how to realise the unity of political tasks and market efficiency at the same time. Efforts should also be made to integrate foreign aid with foreign direct investment. The state should provide concessional loans to help strong enterprises carry out "going global" projects, especially service-based enterprises such as financial and insurance enterprises. In addition, relevant laws and regulations should be formulated without delay to enable enterprises to perform their duties in accordance with laws while implementing the projects. Moreover, efforts should be made to enhance supervision and assessment and to fight against violation of laws. Second, we should combine foreign trade with foreign aid, especially expanding imports from recipient countries so as to gradually improve their commodity structure. In addition, we should further increase the recipient countries' proportion of service trade, such as technical services and educational services. This is conducive for them to improve their education and technology and to promote service trade of both sides. Third, while rendering aid to foreign countries and regions, China should attach great importance to its own sustainable development and that of recipient countries through rational use of natural resources. In providing foreign aid, China should combine non-reimbursable assistance with reimbursable assistance so that it can help develop the economy of recipient countries as well as facilitate the development of China's foreign trade and foreign direct investment.

China bears a heavy responsibility in the provision of its foreign aid. The Chinese government should make unremitting efforts to optimise the structure of foreign aid, improve its quality and effectiveness, further enhance capacity for self-development of aid-receiving countries and attach specific aims to the aid. Furthermore, China should promote South-South cooperation, increase foreign aid to help realise United Nations' millennium development goals and make its due contribution to the peace, common prosperity and construction of a harmonious world.

Chapter 4

China's economic diplomacy in international organisations

Section 1 The WTO

The year 1978 marked the beginning of China's pursuit of reform and opening up. More than 30 years has passed. While it represents only a short span in human history, this period when China charted its journey of endeavour towards a socialist market economy with Chinese characteristics was a mixture of joy and hardship.

I. A remarkable transformation and catching up from behind

Since the implementation of the reform and open policy in 1978, economic exchanges between China and the rest of the world have been expanding. Meanwhile, as the Cold War ended in 1990s and a new round of globalisation has accelerated, China realised that it could not afford to simply observe these important world economic developments. Therefore, conditions were ripe for China to request resumption of its status as a contracting party to the GATT and later to accede to the WTO. As one of the three pillars of global governance envisaged in the Bretton Woods system, the multilateral trading system provides an invaluable platform for China to actively participate in the global economy, exploring opportunities to realise greater development potential and keep pace with the rest of the world.

Two major events took place in 2001 in world trade. One was China's accession to the WTO at its fourth ministerial conference in Doha, Qatar, becoming the 143st member of the organisation. The second was the launch of a new round of multilateral trade talks, commonly known as DDA (Doha Development Agenda), putting a development dimension in trade talks. This was triggered by a widespread desire to help developing countries to effectively participate in the multilateral trading system and benefit from globalisation.

These two events - the accession to the WTO of one of the world's largest developing countries and the decision to place development at the centre of a new round of multilateral trade talks —were of great historical significance.

The road towards China's resumption of its GATT membership has been hard and winding. Those who negotiated entry were frustrated by negotiations that were complicated by economic as well as political considerations. Nonetheless, China remained firm and resolute in its quest for membership. This reflected the Chinese leadership's wise decision to take strategic moves in light of global changes and the attention it paid to the issue with long term vision and statesmanship. It also reflected the skill and hard work of negotiators. The experienced gained in the 15 years leading up to accession and the years that have followed have created a strong team capable of multilateral trade negotiations, and paved the way for China's evolving role in the multilateral family.

China's knowledge of the multilateral trading system dates back to the years when the GATT came into being. Nonetheless, it was regarded a "rich man's club" until China decided to resume its seat. Since its accession to the WTO, China has become an experienced member through a process of learning about the rules, applying the rules and making the rules. Today, China has become fairly competent in all three pillar areas of the WTO's work, exercising increased influence in the multilateral trading system.

(1) Advancing the Doha Round

Since its accession to the WTO, China has been playing a constructive role in negotiations. It has submitted more than 100 proposals and made substantial contributions to further world market opening should the Doha round be concluded. In line with its status as a developing country, China pledged to cut its average tariffs by around 30%, further reduce non-tariff barriers and continue to open its services sector, which is already more open than most other developing countries.

As its economy continued to strengthen and its trade volume expand, China was invited to join the G7 core group of negotiations in 2008, together with Brazil, India, the US, EU, Australia and Japan. This contrasted with the Quartet of the US, EU, Canada and Japan that took the leading position in the multilateral trade negotiations conducted within the framework of the GATT, known as the Uruguay Round negotiations. Foreign media commented that China had finally come to the fore, shifting the power balance and configuration of negotiations. Some refer to China as a big elephant in the Green Room, which is the informal name of the WTO director-general's conference room where meetings of the heads of around 30 delegations take place. Of course, its core group status also places increasing responsibilities on China, as it seeks to maintain a proper balance between rights and obligations.

(2) Honouring China's commitment shown in trade policy reviews

Free trade, non-discrimination and transparency are core principles of the WTO. While any member is entitled to enforce domestic regulation given the national context, it should ensure that all such measures do not distort trade or push other members into unfair competition. Members have to notify the WTO about any measures that will affect trade, particularly subsidies under WTO jurisdiction, and will need to go through regular trade policy reviews. According to WTO rules, the leading four members in terms of world trade will have to go through a trade policy review every two years.

Even though trade policy reviews are not legally binding, members that go through reviews put their policies and measures under the spotlight. They are likely to receive comments or even criticism from other members as they undertake this through performance evaluation.

So far, China has gone through four reviews. Members took great interest in learning about China's trade regime and policies. On average, there are about 1,200 questions in advance and for the fourth review in 2012, China attracted some 1,700 questions, twice as many as those for other members. Even so, China took the review openly and seriously, using this important platform to advocate its policy and appease the doubts of members. Members spoke highly of China's effort to fully meet its WTO commitment and obligation; the director general, Pascal Lamy, even gave China an A+ for its excellent performance during the period under review.

(3) Maintaining fair trade through a dispute settlement body

In comparison with other international organisations, the WTO is an international treaty. Since taking over from the GATT, it has institutionalised a dispute settlement board (DSB) allowing all members, big or small, to bring their cases for arbitration and settlement. Members that breach their commitments will follow a ruling by the DSB to rectify their improper policies and measures. If the recommendations or rulings are rejected by the respondent, the WTO allows the complainer to retaliate.

Between its WTO accession and April 2011, China was involved in 29 disputes cases, initiating eight complaints against others and was taken to the DSB by other members on 12 occasions. China won on some occasions and lost in others. By participating in consultations, panel procedures and appellate rulings, China has trained its own team to the extent that it has become a reservoir of legal expertise on multilateral trade rules and enabled China to apply legal instruments to safeguard its own interests. China's experience in winning a case against dairy products of a major member is just one example.

Since the financial crisis in 2008, China has become a primary target of trade disputes, experiencing an increase in the number of cases. Trade protectionism has been the main reason, perhaps understandably since the country has risen to become the world's largest trading nation. Even so, the number of trade dispute cases has not increased at the same rate as the growth in its trade volume.

China is no doubt experiencing the growing pains of rising, big country. The honeymoon period following its accession to the WTO is over and members are increasingly watchful of China in terms of its compliance with WTO rules. In this sense, the increased number of trade dispute cases should be regarded as normal and expected. We should guard against any protectionist measures under the guise of fair trade while also not over react to the increase in dispute cases.

II. Building harmony in the WTO family

As in other international organisations, there is a divide in the philosophies of developed and developing countries in the WTO. The differing positions of the South and the North often result in a standoff. Due to the nature and traditional beliefs in trade that date back to the founding of the GATT, WTO members' positions are formed and they join different groups to pursue their interests.

For example, the G10 on agricultural products and the NAM-A11 on non-agricultural products are made up of both developed and developing members. The G20 and G33 are developing member groups for agricultural negotiations where countries ally themselves on export or import issues. And so, once an economy joins the WTO, it will find itself in a complex environment of highly interdependent and conflicting interests.

Following its accession to the WTO, China has enjoyed a growing influence in the multilateral trading system. This is mainly due to the fact that China has honoured its words with concrete actions and seriously followed WTO rules, making China a universally respected member of the WTO family.

Those elements in Chinese traditional culture that "respect harmony in diversity and build consensus over differences" have allowed China to adopt flexible approaches in dealing with multilateral issues and through cultural fertilisation to advance a win-win outcome and harvest mutual benefit. China has been regarded as a reliable friend and its support has been valued by many within the WTO family. Here are some examples.

The Doha round has been going on for more than a decade, characterised by frequent clashes of interest in the multilateral trading system. On a number of occasions when the negotiations were on the verge of collapse, China was approached by members seeking advice on a way out. China's culture and philosophy to find the middle ground were appreciated by others and helped to bring the negotiations back on track.

(1) To converge differences on the Swiss Formula

The issue at the core of the Doha round and the fundamental interest of members to engage in the talks is to address the long-standing imbalances in the multilateral trading system: to substantially reduce high tariffs and tariff escalations and to clarify and strengthen the rules. Members, including China, have worked on a formula for tariff reduction, which has been a controversial topic in the NAMA negotiations. From a technical point of view, the "high tariff, higher cut" formula put forward by the Swiss has emerged as a possible workable solution to the problem. However, most developing members believed that even with the Swiss Formula, the resultant cuts would be too large for them to accept. And so, both developed and developing members were seriously divided over the issue and the trade talks fell into an impasse.

In order to break the logjam of negotiations, China did not insist on its own proposal, but instead, reached out to those middle grounders to help build consensus between different interest groups. It also worked closely with developing members to better understand the consequences and impact of the Swiss Formula while maintaining the same stand as other developing countries to safeguard their legitimate rights to special and differential treatment. The developing members finally agreed to accept the formula on condition that developed members committed to granting the special and differential treatment.

(2) To ensure the success of the Hong Kong Ministerial

Due to the failure of the Seattle and Cancun ministerial conferences, there was a felling of despair about prospects for the Doha round. In the first half of 2005, news about the talks was not encouraging and very few had hopes for the forthcoming Hong Kong ministerial conference at the end of the year. As a failed Doha Round would seriously undermine confidence and damage the credibility of the multilateral trading system, China made special efforts to ensure the success of forthcoming talks in Hong Kong.

In the summer of 2005, China's Ministry of Commerce hosted an informal mini-ministerial in advance of the talks in the northeastern coastal city of Dalian. A few deliverables were agreed and public expectations were downplayed. Thanks to the joint effort of all participating ministers, the Ministerial in Hong Kong agreed that developed members and those developing members that claimed to be able to do so, would phase out agricultural export subsidies by

2013 and approved a "work programme" to advance the Doha round. Thus, China's efforts helped achieve concrete, albeit limited, results and reinvigorated the confidence of members to progress with the Doha round towards a successful conclusion.

(3) To advocate China's three principles on trade talks

In July 2008, the WTO ministerial conference on the Doha round again ended with a setback. When Pascal Lamy announced the failure of the ministerial talks, the agriculture commissioner of the EU almost burst into tears during her closing remarks. Nevertheless, the history of multilateral trade talks has shown that all previous rounds were eventually concluded despite all the twists and turns in getting there, and so China has never given up hope for the Doha round and remained committed to pushing ahead with the negotiations.

Looking forward, China holds the view that the work that has gone into the Doha negotiations should not be wasted. At the seventh ministerial conference, China called upon members to remain confident and try their best to advance the negotiations. Media reports highlighted that, when most people were at a loss about what to do, China had sent out a clear and powerful signal demonstrating its firm commitment to advance the Doha round.

China has put forward three principles to continue negotiations: to respect the development mandate, lock in the progress made so far and keep working on the remaining issues based on the negotiation chairs' texts. China's proposal has served as the basic text of declaration and statement of the G20 summit and the APEC leaders since then.

Chinese beliefs and philosophy have enriched the culture of the WTO. Pascal Lamy and many foreign ambassadors love to speak a bit of Chinese or quote a few Chinese proverbs. For example, Lamy called on members to unite as a fort ("zhong zhi cheng cheng") in times of difficulties facing the Doha negotiations. During the third Trade Policy Review of China, a South Korean ambassador quoted an ancient Chinese doctrine that says one is well established when one reaches 30 and understands better when one reaches forty. He quoted the saying to suggest that China's pursuance of reform and opening up had taken 30 years and the international community would love to see China continue its effort well into the next 10 years as it was in the best interests of China. The first Chinese Ambassador to the WTO, Sun Zhenyu, is a highly respected figure whose knowledge, experience, fluency in English and French, and good sense of humour all helped to cross fertilise the culture of the WTO and presented a positive image of the Chinese diplomat in the Geneva-based organisation.

III. Arduous tasks ahead to continue reform and opening up

China's WTO membership of the past 11 years has provided the country with a stable, transparent and predictable external environment. Now, China has entered a new phase of economic development with opportunities coupled with challenges. And so, China will learn from the history and continue its resolve to reform and opening up.

(1) History tells the truth

From a historical perspective, and based on international and national experience, countries with an open economy enjoy faster growth than those with a closed economy. Academic studies have shown that places where poverty has been eradicated are mostly open to trade. In the China context, the Sui and Tang dynasties were among the most prosperous in world history. It has been a long-standing pursuit of the current Chinese leadership to build a country that is among the strongest in the world. In his early days as leader of the Chinese Communist Party, Mao Zedong believed that the world should share both happiness and sorrow. His "liberal" idea encouraged the nation to learn from foreign countries. After the founding of the People's Republic, China's modernisation drive has gone through three periods. The first generation of the Chinese Communist Party called for learning useful things from abroad, such as the implementation of 156 cooperation projects with the Soviet Union, which helped China lay a solid foundation for its drive to industrialisation. The second phase started in the early 1970s, when China managed to develop bilateral trade relations, despite some very difficult circumstances. For example, China set up 26 heavy and chemical industry projects through the "4.3 programme" with industrial countries, such as Germany and Japan. This was also the time when China resumed its seat at the United Nations.

The third phase started in the late 1970s when China adopted its reform and open-door policy. During this time, and especially since it acceded to the WTO in 2001, China has achieved leap-frog development. The success story convinced the Chinese government of the role of trade to stimulate economic growth, job creation, welfare improvement and national development. Its GDP has grown at an annual rate of about 10% for more than 30 years. If calculated in terms of 15,000 jobs generated per US$100m of exports, China's exports generating 255m jobs in 2012. FDI has been a big contributor to jobs. Back in 1978, when the country was embarking on its road to reform and opening up, China's per capita GDP was only US$300. In 2012, China's GDP per capita GDP had jumped to more than US$5,000. China has continued to strengthen its position among the major economies of the world. This augurs well for the WTO's core principles of non-discrimination, fair trade and transparency to serve as a necessary external insurance policy for China's development and enabled the country to better use both national and international markets as well as resources. At the same time, an open economy has played a pivotal role in enhancing people's welfare and this is why China has been the prime beneficiary of the multilateral trading system and also a success story of the developing country's integration into the world economy.

(2) History should be given due credit

The GATT was born out of the ashes of World War II. Due to the prevailing historical conditions and the level of development, its rules were based more on the legal system of industrialised countries. Nonetheless, after six decades of transformation when global economic patterns have undergone constant change and developing countries have contributed more and more to the betterment of existing multilateral rules, such rules have been universally accepted and followed by members. A rule-based multilateral trading system has played a pivotal role in maintaining world trade prosperity and has enabled countries to reduce trade transaction costs, promote fair trade and provide systemic external support for national development and contributed immensely to the prosperity of international trade. The multilateral trade rules even withstood the 2008 financial crisis and have effectively put protectionism at bay.

After 18 years of painstaking negotiations, Russia joined the WTO. The Pacific island of Vanuatu, with a population of just 250,000, joined at the same time as Russia. The fact that these two countries, with such striking differences, both eagerly joined the WTO is a clear demonstration of the attractiveness of the organisation.

(3) History will be enriched with a new chapter

The multilateral trading system is far from outdated and will assume an even greater role in a multi-polar world. However, gaps in the existing rules and a lack of effective responsiveness to the ever-complicated world trade reality have become apparent. Some rigidity in the current rules has failed to effectively address the issues that arise during crises. Currently, trade-restrictive measures have resulted in losses amounting to 30% of total world trade, creating a major impediment to the economic growth prospects and job opportunities in developing countries. Therefore, the long-tested mandate of the WTO needs to be preserved, yet refined with the times to ensure its continued relevance in the 21st century. In particular, the WTO should strengthen and improve the existing rules and at the same time make new rules to consolidate its three pillar areas of work and to fight against protectionism. At the same time, it should take strategic steps to deal with the current challenges such as food security, climate change and energy shortages that have exerted a negative impact on world trade.

Pascal Lamy once outlined a "triangle of coherence", a module of future global economic governance structure. He explained:"On one side of the triangle is the G20, replacing the former G8 and providing political leadership, policy direction and coherence. The second side of the triangle is the United Nations, which provides a framework for global legitimacy through accountability. On the third side lie member-driven international organisations where the multilateral trading system provides expertise and specialised inputs, be they rules, policies or programmes" to promote an agenda that incorporates economic growth, social inclusiveness and environmental friendliness. Recently, a review of the UN millennium development goals has concluded that the achievement of these goals needs a stable, fair and inclusive growth that is indispensible from the multilateral trading system to build an environment that is rule-based, transparent and predictable.

The Doha Round of negotiations has been going on for more than 10 years. Due to a significant divide among major members over the issue of responsibilities, the Doha Round has missed several deadlines and this has led to serious anxieties. There is no sign in sight of reaching the goal that will give more market access to developing countries, particularly market access for their agricultural products, and the chances for the least developed countries (LDCs) to benefit from duty-free and quota-free treatment are even slimmer. This has serious repercussions for the multilateral trading system. Nevertheless, we should not lose heart but work to strengthen the multilateral trading system and further advance the Doha Round negotiation to its successful conclusion.

(4) China's next 10 years

No country will be able to confront the challenges of the 21st century single-handedly. Globalisation has made countries even more interconnected. The difficulties have to be resolved together through collaboration. The development of global value chains, adjustment to world economic patterns, and sustainable national development all require that we continue support the multilateral trading system and intensify reform and opening up.

1. **Full compliance and a more proactive approach** Despite some weaknesses and inadequacies in the global governance architecture as well as some imbalances in the multilateral trading system, people still follow these rules. Therefore we should not attempt to challenge the existing system and fall outside of the international rules, but instead make full use of them while being more proactive in

the rule-making process. It is necessary for China to intensify learning about the WTO and further implement the commitment so as to minimise trade friction and bring the market economy more in line with WTO rules. After decades of reform and opening up, China's voices in these organisations have amplified and it should be better equipped to engage more in multilateral rule-making.

2. **Common but differentiated responsibilities** As China is both a large beneficiary of, and a contributor to, the international system, it should play an active role in global economic governance. At the same time, however, China is still a developing country with regional disparities and income gaps. And so, whatever we do, our point of departure should be set firmly on national conditions and our status as a developing country should be maintained. For a country of 1.3bn people, China's duty-bound commitment to the world community and to maintaining world prosperity means it must work well on the home front and take on its international responsibilities in line with its own level of development.

3. **Further opening up** In response to the challenging areas of reform that are needed to develop a socialist market economy, we need to be firm in intensifying our efforts, target key areas of concerns through deepening reform and further improve our trade regime while providing impetus to the multilateral trading system. We should be pragmatic, open-minded so as to build an open economy that is stronger and broader in scope. A proactive, open strategy will be a driver to changes in economic growth patterns and to promoting and improving a socialist economic system, cultural exchange, social undertaking and environmental and ecological soundness.

As China's national strength has continued to grow and its prestige enhanced, and as the landscape of international trade has undergone change, peaceful development is the logical choice in building a socialist society with Chinese characteristics. We need to better engage in developing an open economy that is mutually beneficial, balanced with diversity and efficiency with safety. This is China's principle stand in dealing with foreign economic and trade relations. This line of thinking will guide our work in response to the very complicated web of interests and to ensure a bright future.

The 21st century inherited the previous century's achievements and challenges. People have high expectations for the future of global governance. An advertisement in the Economist that stated "Underwriting the future" best captures what we should do in the next 10 years: we should be even more supportive of the role of the multilateral trading system and take responsibilities commensurate with our country's status as a developing country and to the level of our development in market access negotiations, in implementing commitment and compliance to

WTO rules and regulations in order to achieve market diversification of our exports, ensure safety and efficiency of our outbound investment. China is committed to further opening up and following WTO rules so that our march towards a healthy, open economy will be solid and steady, nurturing an enabling external environment for our future sustainable development.

Section 2 The IMF

In the early years of the 21st century, China maintained a lukewarm relationship with the IMF but more recently it has played a more active role in the organisation. The turning point came in 2005, when the Chinese government started to attach more importance to multilateral economic diplomacy in which the IMF has played an indispensable role.

During this time, the IMF has undergone unprecedented challenges. During the Asian financial crisis, the IMF was found to be unresponsive and inadequate, leading to growing calls for the body to be reformed. This process started in 2006, and it has been the most far-reaching reform since the IMF was founded in 1944. Unfortunately, while the reform was underway, a financial crisis that swept the whole world imposed an even greater challenge on the development of the IMF, compelling it to re-examine its relations with all countries concerned, the emerging countries in particular. Among them, China has naturally attracted worldwide attention.

I. Development situation of China and IMF in the past 10 years

1. China's "golden decade"

The 10 years from 2003 to 2012 was the "golden decade" of the development of China's economy. It was in this period that China's GDP grew at a remarkable rate, averaging 10% a year. In contrast, the growth rate of the world economy in the corresponding period was only 3.9%. The size of China's economy rose from sixth place in 2012 to second in 2012. Average per-capita GNP increased to US$5,432 from US$1,135 over this period, as China moved to join the list of medium-income countries. The outbreak of the financial crisis in 2008 actually presented China with a rare opportunity. The central government took resolute measures and launched a Rmb4,000bn bailout plan, enabling China to maintain its 8% economic growth rate despite the world economic downturn.

A rapidly expanding economy has required China to take on more responsibilities, which in turn necessitate a transformation in diplomatic style. Economic diplomacy, as an essential part of China's diplomacy, is no exception. In recent years,

China has gradually changed its diplomatic policy, no longer always "keeping a low profile" but striving to make greater efforts in order to "do something". Deciding how to act as a responsible big power became a major factor while China formulated its diplomatic policies, including economic diplomacy.

2. The IMF's "10-year reform"

Compared with China's recent rapid development during the 10 years, the IMF has suffered many hardships. Responsible for the stability of the international monetary system, its actions following the Asian financial crisis were widely criticised, with some even saying that the IMF had actually made the situation worse. Following the outbreak of the crisis, the IMF tried to coerce crisis-stricken countries to implement a tight economic policy with a view to maintaining the stability of the international financial system. However, this measure only served to aggravate economic recession in these countries. Later, it attempted to expand economic opening-up in these crisis-stricken countries to stimulate economic growth. Unfortunately, it made those developing countries suffer greater shocks from the outside world. The IMF was also criticised for misjudgement over the crisis. Though there were clear indications of problems in the economic development of Thailand, the IMF was still optimistic about its growth prospects. Consequently, it frittered away a good chance to bail out its economy and, as a consequence, the country was destroyed by international venture capital.

In response to this criticism, the IMF gradually started deep-seated reform, although it did not happen until2006. As part of this reform, the function of emerging countries was highlighted, in areas such as voting rights, special drawing rights (SDRs), the supervision system and the loan mechanism. There was a perceptible shift in influence from Western developed countries to emerging countries, reflected in a declining number of senior positions being occupied by Europeans and Americans.

However, more work remains to be done. The economic crisis in 2008 was a significant test of the effectiveness of IMF reform. Only after the onset of this crisis did the IMF pay more attention to the role of China and ask it to assume more responsibilities as a big power.

II. China's achievements in economic diplomacy towards the IMF: from constructive participation to actively promoting reform

With China's entry into the WTO and further opening to the outside world, one important topic in Chinese economic diplomacy circles was how the country could better take part in the international system in a comprehensive way so as to provide sustained support to its foreign trade and foreign exchange.

1. Increasing participation (2003-06)

On 1 January 2002, Dai Xianglong, the then governor of the People's Bank of China (PBC), wrote a letter to Horst Kohler, the IMF's managing director, formally filing an application for China's entry into the organisation's General Data Dissemination System (GDDS). This not only represented significant progress in the area of statistics, but also marked an acceleration of Chinese cooperation with the IMF. From then on, China's participation increased further. Zhu Rongji, the then Premier of the State Council, expressed his hope that there would be greater progress in cooperation between China and IMF.

At that time, China was emerging as a major world economy. Given its huge population, which implied huge consumption potential, this was a country that the IMF wanted to see play a more active role. The IMF was able to contribute a lot to the development of the Chinese economy, especially its external economy and international trade. In 2003, some countries campaigned vigorously for an appreciation of the renminbi. Kenneth Rogoff, chief economist at the IMF, stated openly that the organisation would not support such a call. Instead, he proposed that China make the foreign exchange rate of its currency more flexible over a reasonably long period of time. This comment greatly relieved pressure on China to appreciate the renminbi.

At that time, China had already realised that it could not develop itself in isolation of the international mechanism. An international mechanism is a mode through which the international community is regulated and becomes well-organised. The existence of the international mechanism enables countries to coordinate and cooperate with each other at low cost and to help different countries safeguard their interests. This was particularly true of China, which after its entry to the WTO had become such a major trading nation.

In the early years of the 21st century, China had gradually increased its degree of participation in the IMF. Initially, although it was determined to open wider to the outside world, it knew little about the international rules. Nor did it have competent personnel. Only by joining the IMF could China have a good understanding of international finance with a view to helping China lay a solid foundation to cooperate with other countries in the financial field. International trade does not just apply to trade in goods, but also to finance and monetary cooperation. In fact, it is finance that determines the developmental orientation of the world economy. Both the Asian financial crisis in 1998 and the American subprime mortgage crisis in 2008 were triggered by financial problems. Therefore, if China wants to secure a smooth and sustainable development on the international stage of finance, it is essential to have a good command of international monetary rules. Only in this way can China safeguard its interests and make its actions more persuasive and convincing. Of course, it is an indispensable part of international trade to deal with other countries. Since most major countries are capitalist, China must have a good knowledge of this system.

As China has deepened its cooperation with the IMF through means such as entering the GDDS, it has learned more about finance, which has helped it in policy decision-making. In addition, the IMF often gives China suggestions on its development and reform. Though China does not always follow these suggestions, they provide good reference value to its policy choices. In this period, though China was positively inclined towards integration into the international mechanism, it had little knowledge about the workings of the IMF. Therefore, suggestions of the IMF helped China formulate policies that were more mature and adaptable to the international community.

The active participation of the IMF also pushed forward the internationalisation of China's finance. At the end of the 20th century, China's financial structure was still immature. The financial assets held by financial institutions accounted for more than 94% of the total assets. The corresponding proportions in the US and Japan were only 7.6% and 6.9%, respectively. One may say that China's financial assets have already entered the stage of rapid accumulation and next will enter the stage of structural adjustment. Cooperation between the IMF and China facilitated China's efforts in internationalising its finance. To improve its cooperation with the IMF, China reformed many domestic financial industries, including banking, insurance and securities. All this pushed forward China's reform in its economic system.

During the four years from 2003 to 2006, China laid a solid foundation for its integration into the international economy in a comprehensive way through active economic diplomacy, and it also created a favourable social environment for rapid economic development.

2. Pushing forward IMF reform (2006-10)

At the annual meeting of the IMF in September 2006, 184 member states officially passed a reform proposal that involved changing the formula of voting rights. Under this reform, voting rights of emerging countries such as China would increase at the expense those of some strong stakeholders, mainly European countries. Subsequent reforms would tackle SDRs, the IMF supervision system and loan mechanism. This was the largest scale reform since the establishment of the IMF and China played a major role in these events.

(1) Reform in voting rights

As an international financial institution, the IMF has an operational mechanism that is very similar to that of a commercial bank. Member states' rights to vote and to make decisions are determined by the proportion of funds they pay. The proportions are calculated by the IMF according to set formulae. Before the reform, the calculation formula variables included foreign exchange reserves, the value of imports and exports, economic size and an economic fluctuation index. Voting rights included basic voting rights and weighted voting rights. A member state may get one more right to vote for loaning out 400,000 special drawing rights (SDRs). Therefore, developing countries have more voting rights. When a vote is taken, the IMF adopts a majority voting system, with 21 kinds of issues calling for 70% for affirmative votes and 18 other important issues requiring 85% for affirmative votes. Such a voting mechanism is based on "ratio equal", which encourages big powers to assume corresponding responsibilities. Moreover, decisions made under this mechanism win much support from the developed countries, which improves the efficiency of international public products.

However, with the changing international situation, the IMF's voting process has been muddied by political factors. When voting, some developed countries tend to first take into consideration their own interests instead of the stability of the overall international monetary system. For example, the US has more than 15 voting rights, which enables it to exercise a veto with only one vote on some matters of vital importance. This situation is detrimental to China's position in the international system. The US has become increasingly nervous of China's growing strength. As a result, it tries to safeguard its own interests in making decisions on some issues that are also important to China. From this we can see that it has become the main goal of China's economic diplomacy in this period to increase its voting rights and right to be heard.

In the 21st century, China's share of voting rights in the IMF has increased several times, rising from 11th place in 2001 to sixth place in 2006. In 2010, the two-day G20 Finance Ministers and Central Bank Governors Meeting was convened in South Korea. At the meeting, all participating countries reached a consensus on IMF reform, transferring 6% of voting rights to emerging economies. As a result, China's voting rights rose to third place. Though America's voting rights were still as high as 17.67% after the reform and retained the power of veto, the resolution gave recognition to the growing importance of China and other emerging economies in the international economic system.

China played a proactive role in these reforms, as well as in global economic governance. Before its rapid economic growth, China's diplomatic strategy focused on bilateral relations, with multilateral diplomacy playing a supporting role. However, this approach no longer meets its requirements. To develop its economy smoothly and rapidly and to create a more stable international environment, China should attach greater importance to multilateral diplomacy in its diplomatic strategy.

First of all, to realise the grand strategic goal of transforming China's diplomacy, China consistently carries forward its multilateral financial diplomacy. This conforms to the trend of global financial multi-polarisation under the international economic condition, especially after the financial crisis in 2008. Since then, the US, which had adhered to unilateralism, has gradually shifted to multilateralism. Under the new mode of global governance where the G8 has gradually been replaced by the G20, the US has actively taken the G20 as a platform to share rights with developing countries, push forward reform in governance of the international financial system and allow a greater voice for emerging countries. Of course, the US was fully aware that it could not alone extricate itself from what was a world economic crisis. For its part, the IMF has actively pressed ahead with reform of the multilateral governance mechanism. Only by increasing the voting rights and voice of developing countries can the initiative and enthusiasm of these nations be stimulated in taking part in international governance and making joint efforts to recover the world economy. China grasped this opportunity from the very beginning. Multilateral financial diplomacy makes China more experienced in, and enthusiastic about, multilateral cooperation. What's more, multilateral financial cooperation makes has made it possible for China to increase its influence in the IMF.

In addition, China has on many occasions called for honouring the commitment to share reform made at the Pittsburgh conference. It proposed that the IMF abide by the principles of comprehensiveness, proportionality, gradualness and timeliness in the reform. At the G20 summit in April 2009, the then Chinese President Hu Jintao proposed three more specific reforms. First, the IMF should enhance and improve its supervision over the macro-economy of leading economies that issue major reserve currencies. Second, it should improve its governance structure and increase the representation and voice of developing countries. Third, the IMF should improve the regulatory mechanism for the issuance of reserve currencies so as to facilitate the diversification and rationality of the international monetary system. While China paid close attention to the increase of its own vote shares, it also called for the overall reform of IMF, which demonstrates the attitude of a responsible big power.

Finally, China actively coordinated strength and interests of all parties in the course of the reform, which eventually helped to realise the shift of voting rights to developing countries. While the outbreak of the subprime crisis in 2008 played a key role in provoking reform, no one can ignore the role played by China in making sure it happened.

(2) SDR reform

Special drawing rights are the reserve assets and unit of account that were created by the IMF in 1969. Also known as "paper gold", SDR is akin to a super-state currency. After the 2008 financial crisis, people began to assess the risk of holding the US dollar as an international reserve currency. Some people proposed holding SDR as an alternative reserve currency. China was an active advocate. One of its motives was to break the hegemony of the US dollar. It also wanted to ensure the safety of China's foreign exchange reserve of US$2,000bn. China's active role in this area also marked a rejuvenation of the role of developing countries.

Though China was looking after its own interests, it did not entirely support the idea of European countries to end the hegemony of the US dollar. Its actions were motivated partly by a desire to maintain the safety of its foreign exchange rate. From another perspective, China has demonstrated its image as a responsible big power, in facilitating the progressive reform of the International Monetary Fund system, and preventing further impact on the world economic system. This helped China's image in the international community, and also increased its influence in the IMF.

(3) Reform of the supervision system

The IMF was established to maintain the stability of international currency and the global financial system. It supervisory actions help to coordinate the economic development of different countries and prevent actions by some countries for their own national interests at the expense other economies. However, before the reforms, the supervision framework of the IMF was effective only over a certain number of countries. Besides, the coordination of reserve currencies was only realised within the G7, which, although this accounted for a large portion of the global economy, did not represent the interests of all countries. Since the rise of emerging economies, such a supervision mechanism could no longer meet the prevailing needs. Specific aspects of IMF reform proposed by China at the G20 summit addressed this problem. However, for the time being, no substantial scheme has yet been unveiled, and this deficiency is likely to become a focus of China's economic diplomacy towards the IMF in future.

(4) Reform of the loan mechanism

The loan mechanism is a policy targeted mainly at developing countries. Whether it is convenient or not is an important indicator of the position of developing countries in the IMF system. The IMF has been trying to increase the flexibility of a number of loan projects and to reduce unnecessary additional conditions. Although China has not borrowed money from the IMF, should it have international balance of payments difficulties in future, this would be a helpful reform.

In its economic diplomacy to encourage IMF reform, China has begun to explore the transformation of its diplomatic strategy and has made great achievements that will play an active part in China's economic and trade development in future.

3. A responsible big power in the IMF (2010-12)

Since the reform and opening up, China's share of voting rights has increased, but so have its obligations, in areas such as international aid and providing international loans. This brings both challenges and opportunities. Although China is now the second largest economy in the world, its per capita GDP remains outside the top 100. China may be regarded as both a rich country and a poor one, which requires it to strike a balance between foreign aid and its own economic development. China knows it should live up to its international responsibilities, but it also needs to ensure the smooth and sustainable development of its economy.

In terms of opportunity, China's existing international economic status and right to speak have laid a foundation for the internationalisation of the renminbi. This is attractive to China because it would help the country to reduce its dependence on the US dollar in foreign trade. Only in this way can China develop its economy in a safer international environment. Yet, once the renminbi is internationalised, China's international influence will be enhanced, enabling it to play a much deeper and broader role in the world economic system.

III. A prospect for cooperation between China and the IMF

China aims to be a "responsible big power" in its diplomatic policy. Owing to the fact that China has advocated a fair international monetary fund system, it will take a more active stance in participating in IMF reform in the future. To achieve that goal, China should make the best use of the current external system to adjust its relations with the international system and establish the role it has played in international affairs. As a new participant in the system, China will inevitably affect the vested interests of other countries, meaning it must conduct its diplomacy wisely so as to minimise conflicts with other countries.

More specifically, China should continue its efforts to enhance the influence of developing countries in the IMF, in areas such as voting rights and reforms to the SDR, supervision system and loan system. In particular, it should make greater efforts in these last two areas. However, reform is a long journey, in which China should actively promote renminbi internationalisation and reduce its reliance on the US dollar so that it can enhance its safety in international trade. Moreover, China should make great efforts to cultivate inter-disciplinary expertise with a good knowledge of both the international economic mechanism and China's economic situation, and to raise the proportion of Chinese people taking office in the IMF.

However, China will be moderately cautious about the IMF. Even after the reforms, the US still has veto power over important proposals that developing countries don't have. Western developed countries have more than 50% of the voting rights, and they retain the greatest influence. Moreover, while the Chinese economy has developed considerably, its per capita GDP remains relatively low, which poses a challenge for the country to assume expanded international responsibilities and obligations. Therefore, China is still cautious about its fulfilment of relevant responsibilities.

Though China's economic strength has grown, and it has begun to enhance its international prestige and taken an active part in the formulation of the international order, it should not altogether ditch its policy of "keeping a low profile". China should not define itself as a challenger, which in any case is unlikely to bring about much benefit. Instead, it will make China vulnerable to attack. Only by increasing its strength will China secure its long-term development. After all, China cannot entirely depend on a reformed IMF. It must also keep a low profile, be pragmatic and take advantage of the favourable conditions brought about by the reform and assume rational international responsibilities.

In conclusion, China will deepen its cooperation with the IMF in future. It will safeguard its interests by means of its economic diplomacy, and will continue to keep a low profile and take a prudent attitude to become a defender and constructor of the world order. It will not be a challenger but instead it will focus on the sustained and steady development of its economy.

Section 3 The World Bank

2014 was the 34th year of cooperation between China and the World Bank. Both sides have formed a new sustainable mode of international cooperation, featuring close consultation, equality and cooperation, mutual benefit and win-win results. This has greatly pushed forward the healthy and sound development of bilateral relations. The World Bank helps China develop its economy rapidly by providing loans, conducting cooperation in the knowledge economy and by other means. For its part, China has taken the initiative to participate in World Bank decision-making and has advocated reform of the institution so as to inject new vigour and vitality to it.

I. General cooperation between China and the World Bank

China is one of the founding members of the World Bank. However, after the establishment of the People's Republic of China in 1949, China's legitimate status in the World Bank was occupied by the Taiwan authorities. It was not until 1980 that China resumed its legitimate status in the World Bank. On 14 April 1980, the vice-governor of Bank of China, Wang Weicai, signed a memorandum on resuming China's legitimate status in the World Bank. In 1981, China accepted its first loan from the World Bank, marking China's first step towards its integration with the world economy and pressing ahead the process of reform and opening to the outside world. Between 1980 and 1999, the World Bank provided China with a series of aid projects on infrastructure and people's livelihoods. Meanwhile, China worked hard to advance its understanding of the knowledge economy and to work more closely with the World Bank. In 1998, when the Yangtze River basin suffered catastrophic floods, the World Bank provided urgent recovery aid. The whole process, ranging from project approval to its eventual operation, was completed in just 11 months. The IMF, together with other international institutions, provided vigorous support to the post-disaster reconstruction with high efficiency and a pragmatic attitude.

Entering the 21st century, cooperation between China and the World Bank has extended to new areas such as regional balanced development, environmental enhancement and of the promotion of people's livelihood. China became an important donor of the World Bank. With the rapid economic development and the gradual expansion of China's influence in the international arena, knowledge cooperation between the two sides has shifted from one-way input to two-way communication. In this regard, China has shared its successful experience in its development with other developing countries.

Today, China is one of the largest shareholders in the World Bank. World Bank investment in China has exceeded US$10bn. There are 107 World Bank-funded projects in China, more than 90% of which are in the better developed central and eastern parts of the country, with only a few are in underdeveloped regions such as Xinjiang, Qinghai and Gansu. The largest proportion of all investment has gone into transportation projects, accounting for US$4.144bn, or 40% of the total investment. This money has been used to fund large-scale road construction and the Nanning-Guangzhou railway, reconstruction following the Wenchuan earthquake and sustainable development projects in poverty-stricken areas. The second largest investment area covers water resources, health and flood control. Projects in these areas have consumed US$2.9bn of World Bank funds, taking up nearly 30% of total investment. It includes local ecological management and reconstruction projects of important rivers such as the Haihe, the Qiantang, the Hongshui and Pearl River. The third largest category is energy and minerals projects, with investment of US$1.16bn. The Urumqi thermoelectric project and Shandong energy consumption project have both attracted World Bank funds. The three main categories make up 70% of the gross investment amount, covering a great number of infrastructure and social development projects in regions of strategic importance to China.

II. The World Bank assists in China's development

1. Advanced thought and cooperation mechanisms built up by the World Bank

(1) Advanced development concept and modes

Entry into the World Bank was an important step for China to exchange with the outside world. From China's perspective, the World Bank is like a window through which it may appreciate many advanced development concepts. Concepts such as eliminating poverty, frameworks of integrated development, people-oriented development and sustainable development strategy initiated by the World Bank have exerted an important and positive impact on the development of Chinese society, helping to construct a more harmonious society and upgrade the overall national image. China has obtained considerable knowledge, experience and technology through cooperation and exchange with the World Bank, in addition to institutional and theoretical innovations and social transformation. The Chinese government has all along adhered to a number of development concepts such as "development first and treatment later" and "equally priority for ecological construction, environmental construction and economic development" which are complementary to concepts advocated by the World Bank. The World Bank is also an important platform for China and other developing countries to conduct South-South cooperation. In 2007, the World Bank and The Import and Export Bank of China made joint efforts to conduct African aid projects, which not only improved the living conditions of some African people, but also deepened the understanding of the outside world towards China.

(2) Taking South-South cooperation as a platform to promote communication between developing countries

The World Bank is the largest aid agency in the world. Recipients of World Bank aid have historic backgrounds, national conditions and development difficulties that are similar to those of China. Having worked with the World Bank for a number of years, China can effectively share developmental experience and cooperate with developing countries in many fields for mutual benefit. From 2008 to 2009, China and the World Bank successfully held the Sino-Africa High-level Symposium on Sharing Development Experience, which looked at the opportunities and challenges China faced in the course of its development, along with the measures it took and the achievements it made. This symposium, which promoted exchanges in the development experience of China and Africa, is regarded as a successful model of South-South cooperation. In March 2010, the UN High-level Conference on South-South Cooperation and Capacity Development was held in Bogota, capital of Columbia. Madam Ngozi, vice-governor of the World Bank, said that, with the support of China and other developing countries, the World Bank had established an innovation mechanism to provide developing countries with small loans that were used to support knowledge and experience exchange projects.

2. Key project loan assistance provided by the World Bank

(1) The World Bank pushes forward the development of China's key industries and professional fields

In recent years, the World Bank has provided China with a series of loans to support construction in sectors such as transportation, energy and environment. Among them, transportation accounts for 41%, water resources protection 30%, energy 11% and industry 11%. In the transportation industry, projects including the Nanning-Guangzhou railway, Guiyang transportation project, Shenzhen subway and Hunan urban development were carried forward. Major accomplishments in water resources protection were achieved in remote areas in western China, while environmental improvement projects took place in small towns in the Qiantang River valley, for example. In the industrial area, remarkable achievements included an agricultural safety and quality assurance project in Jilin, and a series of projects relating to petroleum, thermal power, natural gas, hydropower and new energy, which are under construction. Furthermore, investments in areas such as education, information and agriculture have improved people's livelihoods and promoted the construction of a society featuring comprehensive, balanced and sustainable development.

(2) World Bank promotes regional coordinated development in China

Entering the new century, as central China begins to address regional inequality through initiatives such as the large-scale development of its western region, the World Bank has increased its investment in central and western parts of the country. Priority is given to enhancing the input for infrastructure construction and people's livelihoods in these regions. Typical examples are a thermoelectric project in Urumqi, a natural heritage and cultural conservation project in Gansu, water resources protection in Turpan, Xinjiang and agricultural technology projects.

(3) World Bank assistance after the Wenchuan earthquake

The Wenchuan earthquake and subsequent reconstruction project have brought about profound transformation and reflection in Chinese society. The World Bank has provided aid totalling US$710m for the restoration and reconstruction of infrastructure and water resources protection. The aid helped the Chinese government in its disaster relief programme and served to highlight the consistent efforts of the World Bank to reduce hardship in poverty-stricken areas and following natural disasters.

III. Virtuous support provided to the World Bank by China

1. China actively pushes forward reform of the World Bank and contributes to the improvement of its governance system

In 2010, China became the third largest shareholder of the World Bank, marking a new stage of cooperation between the two sides. It was a sign of China's growing international status and degree of participation in international affairs. China has implemented many cooperation projects with the World Bank, expanded the areas of cooperation, deepened mutual benefits and promoted decision-making and action by the World Bank in a more scientific and fair manner.

(1) Seeking benefits for emerging economies and increasing developing countries' influence

Due to growing economic strength, China and other emerging market countries have played a more and more important role on the international stage. The World Bank and even the United Nations, founded after the Second World War, tend to be partial to large Western powers and sometimes ignore the rights and interests of developing countries. China has endeavoured to push forward reform of these institutions to promote the establishment of a new international economic order. After the financial crisis in 2008, China has actively participated in discussions and negotiations on the reform of voting rights in the World Bank, vigorously supporting the greater representation of emerging markets and developing countries. Eventually, on 25 April 2010, the World Bank took the lead in carrying out the consensus of the G20 Pittsburgh Summit, by making developed countries transfer 3.13% of voting rights to the emerging markets and developing countries. For example, China's voting rights increased from 2.77% to 4.42%, becoming the third largest shareholder of the World Bank, behind only the US and Japan. The prompt implementation of the reform achievements reflects China's conscientiousness in international affairs as a regional big power, and also the growing power of emerging market countries to play an active role on the international stage.

(2) Playing the role of an important member state and encouraging a more pragmatic World Bank

With its international prestige being enhanced, China has kept expanding its influence on the orientation and contents of decision-making at the World Bank, encouraging the organisation to actively share and learn from the successful diversification experience of all countries in international development cooperation so as to improve its development level and policy-making and fulfil its duties in a more pragmatic way and enhance the impact of its aid to developing countries. In addition, China has taken the World Bank as a platform to actively support and participate in South-South cooperation, helping other developing countries to better integrate themselves into the international economic order. What's more, the Chinese government donated US$300,000 to the World Bank South-South Knowledge Cooperation Fund to help the World Bank make better use of the South-South cooperation platform and narrow the gap between the North and the South.

2. China actively shares its experience in eliminating poverty and initiating new modes of development

(1) Enhancing institutionalised communication with developing countries to share its development achievements

Since 2008, China and the World Bank have co-sponsored the Sino-Africa High-level Symposium on Sharing Development Experience, which has been held every year. This has become a regular exchange mechanism for China and African countries. It helps both sides to learn development experience and modes from each other and deepen mutual trust and understanding. China publicises its "road of peaceful development with Chinese characteristics" through the World Bank, stressing that it respects the autonomy of economic and social development and the diversified developmental modes of developing countries. All this enriches and improves the theory and practice of development of the World Bank, and makes a contribution to its implementation of the goals of global poverty elimination and development.

(2) Pushing forward green development and innovative development

Most developing countries are inhibited by disadvantages such as a large population base, fast population growth, high energy consumption and a deteriorating environment. Due to a lack of scientific development concepts and advanced technology, they have to develop their economy at the cost of environmental quality and resource utilisation efficiency. In fact, China used to take this unsustainable development road for a number of years, which brought about serious consequences. Summing up its historical experience and drawing the lessons, the Chinese government put forward a new mode of development in its 12th five-year plan. The plan stressed that, while maintaining rapid and sustainable economic development, a grand goal is formulated to increase energy efficiency and manage natural resources and sustainable environmental development. Currently, China is endeavouring to push forward a long-term market incentive mechanism with a view to developing domestic large and medium-sized enterprises as a driving force of world innovation and making China's environmental industry the main source of economic growth. Moreover, laws and regulations are used to control the amount and standard of emission reduction, adjust industrial structure, eliminate the development of sunset industries, reduce the consumption of fossil fuels and close down small plants with high energy consumption. However, this mode has some shortcomings. China's economic structure has become complicated and multi-faceted. Traditional tools are still used in several industrial and mining enterprises that employ many people. Therefore, closing down these enterprises does not lead to an obvious improvement in development quality. In view of this, the Chinese government has proposed to learn experience in comprehensive environmental management of the world. The best way is, first of all, to ensure that the market price of products and services reflects the real cost of production and consumption.

For developing countries, there is a huge cost involved in transforming their economic growth modes. Many developing countries, including China, continuously improve their managerial experience by participating in World Bank projects. They learn from the experience of other countries to offset their weaknesses. Economic transformation cannot be accomplished in one move. China's experience in this regard is useful for many countries. For instance, the southwest China poverty relief programme, co-funded by China and the World Bank, yielded many satisfying results. Meanwhile, the World Bank hopes to learn from China's promotion and implementation of the programme so as to help other developing countries eliminate poverty.

3. China participates in World Bank poverty-relief programmes and provides financial support to the World Bank

According to statistics from the World Bank, since China's entry into the WTO, the average rate of contribution of China to the world economy has been 13%. China has become one of the driving forces of the world economy. Since the early 1980s, the World Bank provided China with a great amount of low-interest or even interest-free aid loans, which greatly promoted the development of China's reform and opening to the outside world. By July 1999, the International Development Association (IDA) under the World Bank provided China with soft loans totalling US$10.2bn and 69 projects were undertaken. From July 1999, thanks to its remarkable economic achievements, China emerged from the ranks of underdeveloped countries. Therefore, the World Bank stopped providing loans to China. On 14 December 2007, China denoted US$30m to the IDA, its first donation to the organisation. This indicated that China had already turned from an aid recipient country to a donor country and correspondingly assumed its international responsibilities. This set up a sound and positive international example. After the international financial crisis in 2009, China, as the largest developing country in the world, made joint efforts with the World Bank to confront the new challenges. The international Finance Corporation (IFC) proposed to make a plan for global trade financing. China actively participated in the plan at the G20 Summit in November 2008 to support the trade financing of developing countries. This showed the determination of China and the World Bank to make joint efforts to cope with the financial crisis and promote the recovery of the global economy.

IV. Prospect for cooperation between China and the World Bank

1. China could not develop without the help of the World Bank

Although China has become the second largest economy in the world, its per capita GDP is less impressive. As a matter of fact, there is still a big gap between China and developed countries in this aspect. Besides, China still faces many deep-seated contradictions and barriers in its economic development that are hard to overcome in the short-term. The World Bank, the largest multilateral economic development aid agency in the world, has continued to provide developing countries with aid and guidance in technology, labour services and loans in recent decades. It has already become a driving force for developing countries to achieve healthy development. China needs the vigorous support and coordination of the World Bank to secure its healthy economic development. Currently, China is in a period when its domestic reform is underway, and it must further deepen its mutual beneficial cooperation with the World Bank, draw on the advanced managerial and reform experience so as to improve its ability of governance and realise the goal-oriented "top-level design". In addition, China should take South-South cooperation and North-South Dialogue as a platform provided by the World Bank to enhance exchanges and interaction with various countries at different development levels, extensively conduct exchanges with different development modes and enrich its strategic reserve. China also needs to take this journey in order to realise the "Chinese Dream".

2. Development of the World Bank is closely related to China

In addition to being the second largest economy in the world, China is also the third largest shareholder of the World Bank, second only to the US and Japan. China is pleased to be regarded as a "responsible stakeholder" by many countries. Compared with the US, China's actions are more pragmatic and it takes multilateral interests more into account. Therefore, China, a powerful partner of the World Bank, will bring about more opportunities and achievements to the World Bank. Specifically, China has the ability and experience to play a part in the decision-making and actions of the World Bank in fields such as investment in poverty relief, development in Africa, coping with climate change and promoting growth of the world economy.

3. Advancement in cooperation fields between China and the World Bank

In the past three decades, China has made remarkable achievements in its cooperation with the World Bank. However, some problems remain. The World Bank's investment in China is mostly focused on central and eastern China where the economy is relatively developed. Few aid projects have been given to regions such as Xinjiang and Tibet where the economy is relatively backward. Most aid projects have been undertaken to solve issues concerning people's livelihoods. Government policies are helping to transform the economy of western China, which has become more diversified and therefore better able to receive investment from the World Bank in more fields. While maintaining the existing investment in infrastructure and improving investment in water resources, China devote more resources to education, cultural protection, information communication and finance with a view to further developing the western region.

The knowledge economy is becoming increasingly important. For China, the World Bank is an important carrier representing the knowledge economy. Therefore, in future cooperation, both sides should be more innovative in the platform of the knowledge economy, devoted to pushing forward the construction of a new international economic order, popularising law-carbon economic growth and the establishment of cooperation in other fields.

V. Conclusion

According to Justin Yifu Lin, the Chinese economist and former senior vice president of the World Bank, cooperation between China and the World Bank has been the most successful in the bank's history. Both sides have benefited a great deal in long-term cooperation. In fact, China's' development cannot have been achieved without the support of the World Bank. Meanwhile, China's reform, opening to the outside world and its soaring economic development has greatly pushed forward the development of the World Bank. Robert Zoellick, president of the World Bank between 2007 and 2012, holds that China and the World Bank should enhance and deepen their cooperation. Also, both sides should work hand in hand to confront new problems in areas such as poverty elimination, environmental control and rebalancing economies. As China's development has moved into the post-industrialisation stage, it not only faces problems such as environmental pollution, ecological damage and industrial structure adjustment, but also the "middle-income trap" which is arguably more serious than those mentioned above. China should not only learn more experience in how low-income countries become high-income countries with the help of the World Bank, but also draw on lessons of other middle-income countries. In these respects, economic diplomacy between China and the World Bank should continuously be advanced. On the basis of more than 30 years of cooperation, we have every reason to believe that, in future, China and the World Bank will promote common, sustainable and coordinated development in a comprehensive way.

Chapter 5

China's economic diplomacy towards major countries and regions

Section 1 China's economic diplomacy towards the US

1. Introduction

China-US economic relations enjoyed rapid growth between 2002 and 2012, during which time their bilateral political and diplomatic relations have been promoted greatly. More important, the accomplishments in their mutual economic and trading relations are more and more employed strategically to serve their bilateral political and diplomatic purposes. At the same time, disagreements between the two great powers on issues such as textiles, the renminbi exchange rate, and export control have persisted. Why has this happened? This section tries to answer this question by reviewing and explaining the strategies both countries have adopted during this period.

What is economic diplomacy? There is no universally accepted definition. A literal interpretation equates economic diplomacy to securing diplomatic goals by applying economic pressure. Zhang Xiaotong claims that economic diplomacy is "the mutual transformation between wealth and power", i.e., the transformative actions and processes wielded by a government in its foreign affairs to obtain wealth and power by flexibly utilising strategies, tactics and institutional methods.[11] We analyse Sino-US economic diplomacy according to this concept. In the first part, an overview of China-US economic and trade relations will be presented through several tables and figures. The second and third parts will separately analyse US strategies of economic diplomacy towards China and vice versa. In the fourth part, a state-market-society interactive model will be introduced to compare the two parties' economic diplomacy strategies with one another. Some policy suggestions are also briefly discussed in this section.

---

[11] Zhang Xiaotong. Constructing a Chinese Theory of Economic Diplomacy: A Tentative Attempt. *Foreign Affairs Review*, 2013(6):49-60

2. China's WTO accession: China-US economic & trade relations (2002-12)

There are dozens of indices suggesting that China-US economic and trade relations have been have been more equal since China's WTO accession. First, China has become the fastest growing overseas export market for the US. The bilateral trading volume has consistently risen since 2002 (see tables1, 2 and 3)[12]. The US was China's second largest trade partner in 2012, with China being the third trade partner for the US (See Table 4).

Table 1 China-US visible trade (Chinese statistics)

(Unit: US$ million)

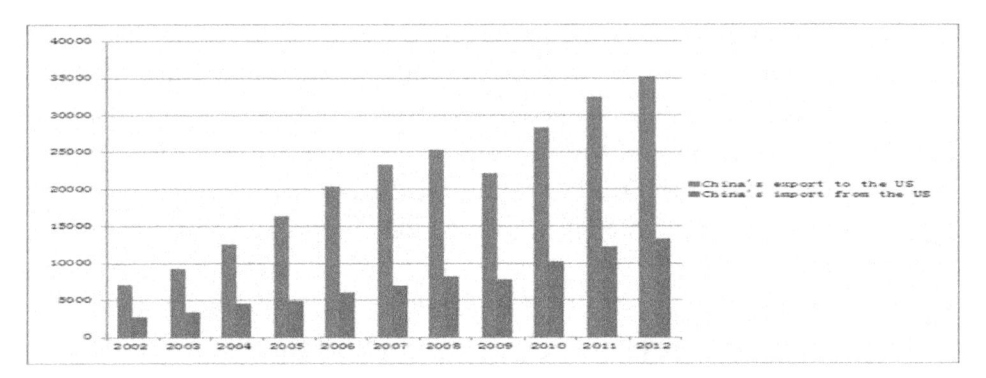

——Source: National Bureau of Statistics of the People's Republic of China, annual data.

Table 2 US-China visible trade (US statistics)

(Unit: US$ million)

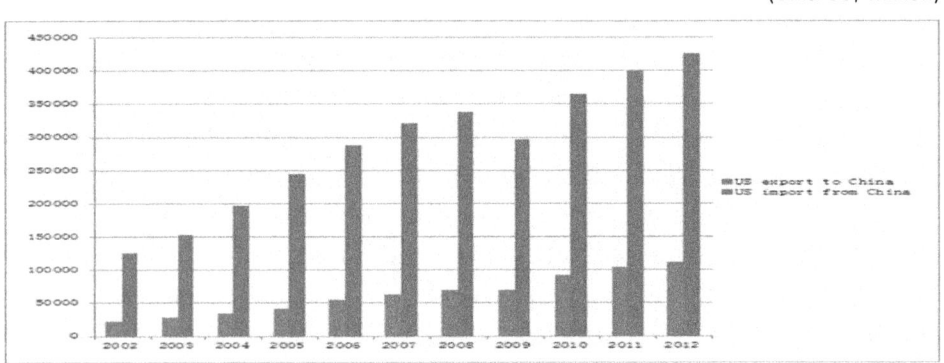

——Source: The United States Census Bureau.

---

[12] The statistics that China and the US provide In s1 and 2 vary because of the different tools used and factors considered.

Table 3. US-China services trade (US statistics)

(Unit: US$ million)

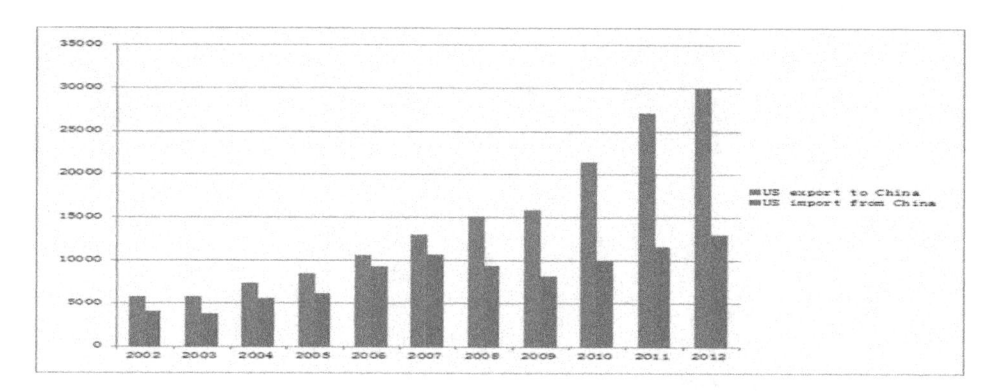

[Bar chart showing US export to China and US import from China, 2002–2012]

—— Source: US Department of Commerce, Bureau of Economic Analysis.

Table 4 Inter-dependence in visible trade between China and the US

(Unit: %)

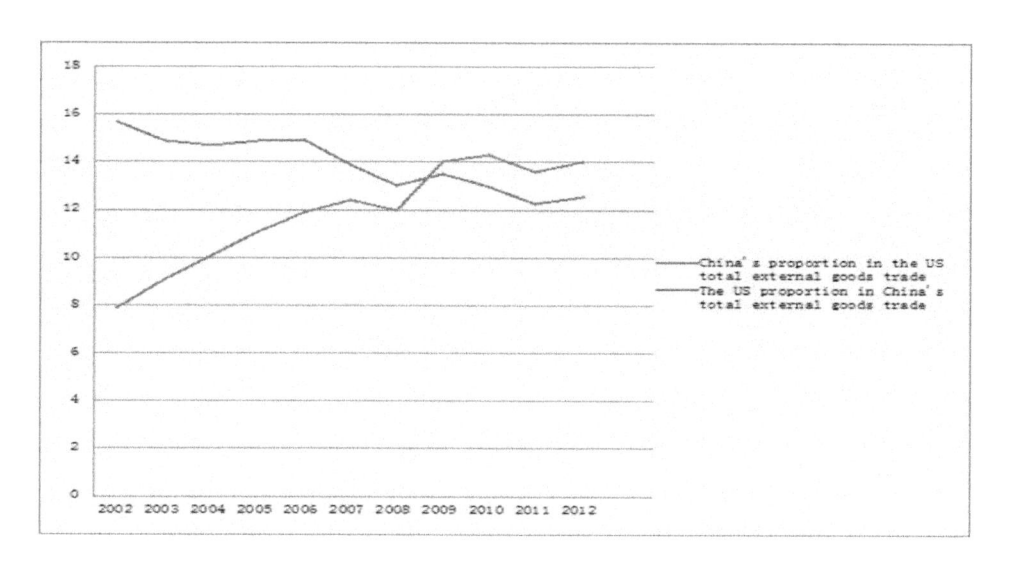

[Line chart showing China's proportion in the US total external goods trade and The US proportion in China's total external goods trade, 2002–2012]

—— Source: the US statistics cited from the US Census Bureau; China's statistics cited from China National Bureau of Statistics, annual data.

Second, with the rapid growth of Chinese foreign reserves, China has held more US Treasury securities (See Table 5). It has been the largest holder of US Treasury debt since it overtook Japan in 2008. China is, in fact, "regurgitation-feeding" the US economy through buying the US Treasury securities and other dollar assets.

Table 5 China's holdings of US Treasury securities

(Unit: %)

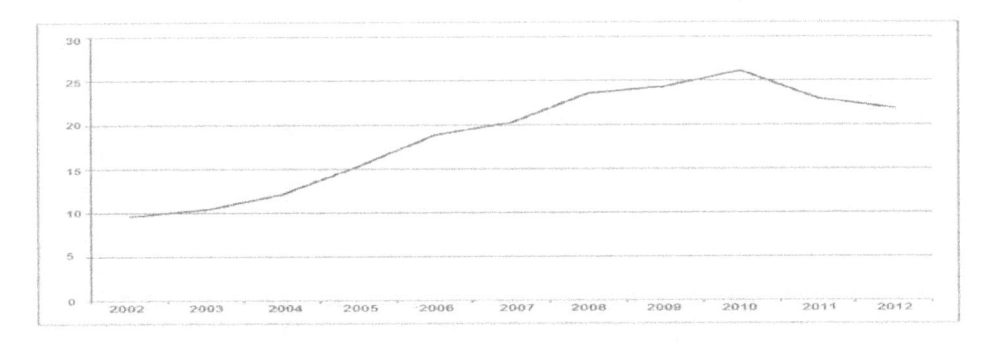

—— Source: US Department of the Treasury.

As can be seen from Table 6, China's foreign goods trade has witnessed rapid growth, matching the same proportion of the US after China's accession to the WTO. China, therefore, has become a new driving force stimulating world economic growth and enjoying a reputation as one of the "twin engines" of the world economy along with the US. This makes the role that China plays more crucial in world multilateral economic organisations.

Table 6 China and US proportions of world visible trade

(Unit: %)

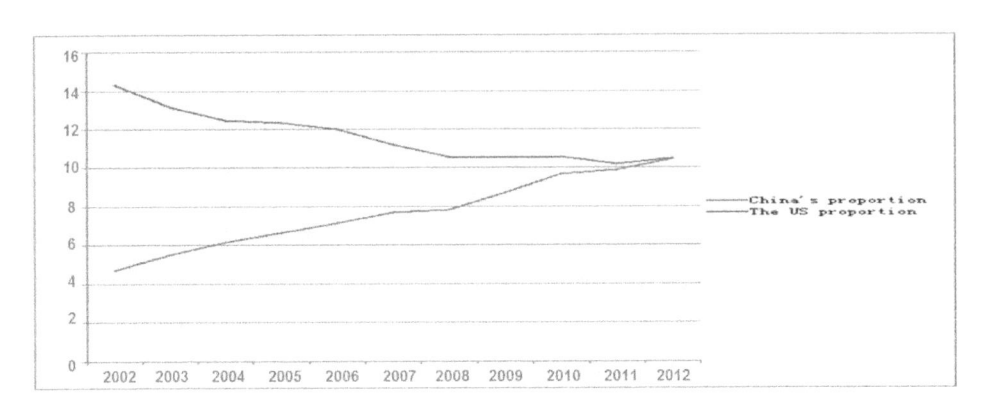

—— Source: WTO, statistics, databases

All these development trends add to China's influence with the US, and make the Sino-US relations more equal.

The trend towards globalisation has led to renegotiation between states and all other actors, which caused a "hollowing-out" of sovereignty and increased the influence of external factors upon domestic policies.[13] Therefore, this article will analyse Sino-US strategies of economic diplomacy with the state-market-society interactive model.

3. An analysis of US economic diplomacy strategies toward China

It is argued that there are three main objectives of US economic strategy in the Asia-Pacific: economic growth, rule-making and long-term presence.[14] This is true. Another perspective, focusing on domestic politics, can also help to understand US economic strategies toward China. The state-market-society interactive model, as already noted by a Chinese scholar, is relevant when analysing US economic diplomacy strategies for China.[15] The basic feature of US trade politics can be referred to as "conflictual politics"; the making of US policies of economy and trade for China is the result of bargaining among the US government, enterprises and social forces.

US domestic politics is, to a large extent, interest-group politics. Under this political system, interest groups make efforts to lobby Congress through in order to exert pressure upon government departments whose main duties are making and executing external economic policies. In order to protect their interests or to realise their anticipated profit, those interest groups benefiting or being damaged from open trade will play significant roles in the making of foreign economic and trading policies by any political activities. Congress is influential in economic and trading policy-making for China. Members of Congress are spokespersons of different groups and fields. In their actions against China, for instance, members of Congress are intensively lobbied by interest groups. The US government, on the other hand, has to seek a balance among these conflicts and discord.

Conflict and friction can be easily triggered among interest groups due to their different interest structures. Those groups whose interests may be impeded by imported goods, sometimes known as "import-competing groups", ask for government subsidies to reduce the impact of imported goods; "export-promoting groups", by contrast, hope to open overseas markets and seek support from government to create opportunities abroad. For example, US textile dealers' groups

---

[13] Shaun Breslin. International Relations, Area Studies, and International Political Economy: Rethinking the Study of China's International Relations. *World Economics and Politics*, 2003(3):64

[14] Matthew P. Goodman. US Economic Engagement in East Asia and the Pacific. *Statement before the US Senate Committee on Foreign Relations, Subcommittee on East Asian and Pacific Affairs.* 18 Dec. 2013. 446 Dirksen Senate Office Building

[15] Wang Yong. *The Political Economy of China-US Trade Relations*. Beijing: China Market Press, 2007

such as NCTO (National Council of Textile Organisations) and AMTAC (the American Manufacturing Trade Action Coalition) have been fighting to limit textile imports from China; on the other side of the fence are importers, retailers and consumers who would be beneficiaries from importing textiles from China. Domestic frictions can also be evoked in the US about the renminbi exchange rate. As for the US government, it would balance itself among conflicts like these. Meanwhile, the claims of import-competing groups have been frequently used by government as a bargaining chip in negotiations with China in requesting the latter to open its market further; by doing so, the export-promoting groups are satisfied at the same time. In this connection, it is never too difficult to understand some tactics adopted by the US government. Take its foreign trade negotiations, for instance. In the hope of allegedly resisting protectionism, the US government keeps reminding states that the government is suffering from pressure from domestic protectionism in the hope of securing an earlier compromise. Tactics and strategies like this have often proved effective for the US.

The chain of domestic interest groups from both sides has been extended since the US and China further opened their markets to one another. China-US common interests have overstepped the national boundary and "transnational" interest groups have consequently formed. Therefore, US economic diplomacy towards China is not only to be found at the level of "government-to-government", but also among Chinese domestic enterprises and even social actors. It is widely acknowledged that the US is enthusiastic in spreading concepts and ideas. It has been long expected to establish a "consensual", strategy to persuade Chinese economic participants in believing that a perfect market mechanism conforms to China's interests as well.

4. An analysis of China's economic diplomacy strategies towards the US

As a late-comer to the international economic system, China has been suffering great pressure from the US. Compared with US economic diplomacy strategies, Chinese counter-measures seem to be more passive, responding to US requirements at times.

One of China's most favoured tactics is to adjust its domestic institutions with the help of external pressure. Most obviously, China has speeded up the transition to a market economy after joining the WTO, improving the significance of its constitution and perfecting the laws and regulations of the market economy system.

Furthermore, to ease tensions resulting from the Sino-US trade imbalance, China took the initiative to restrict some export goods or sent purchasing delegations to the US. In 2005, for example, an agreement was reached between China and the US that China would make a concession to alleviate the impact of Chinese textile exports by restricting such exports. Besides, China has sent many purchasing delegations to the US since 2003. For instance, a Chinese economic and trade delegation made a purchase contract worth US$16.21bn with its US counterpart in 2006, of which US$4.6bn was spent on buying 80 Boeing 737s, making it the largest single purchase in Chinese history.[16]

After joining the WTO, China has come to realise that the existing multilateral economic mechanisms are also vital to its own economic improvement. China began to utilise these mechanisms to counter US threats of sanctions, and even proactively proposed sanctions towards the US within these mechanisms. For example, in April 2002, the Bush administration opened Section 201 Temporary Safeguard Measures to impose additional duties on steel imports from the EU, China and Japan. China, in coordination with other victim countries, took the US to the WTO dispute settlement mechanism, and the WTO judged that Washington had violated related its rules and the US was required to revoke the decision within a definite time. China's decisive action surprised the US side.[17]

5. A comparative analysis of China-US economic diplomacy

The differences in the economic strategies of China and the US reflect their domestic institutional differences. The US is a developed country whose political system guarantees and encourages its interest groups to play a part in both public policy and social activity. Therefore, interest groups have a substantial amount of freedom in tackling foreign policies and domestic issues. The Chinese government is more "independent" and focused when facing external economic issues. China's interest groups are in a comparatively weaker position. The US mobilises different interest groups to participate in the process of government decision-making. The combination of pressures from the US government, Congress, interest groups and the public often combine to force China to make a compromise in bilateral trade negotiations. By contrast, the Chinese government fails to apply domestic pressure as a bargaining chip because of the lack of support from powerful societal groups. Besides, industrial and educational circles have limited power in decision-making and the government is exclusively responsible for foreign affairs. The US makes best use of this circumstance and focuses its attention on the Chinese government to secure concessions. In other words, the US is utilising "society" to counteract the Chinese "government" and put China in a disadvantaged negotiating position.

---

[16] Wang Yong. *The Political Economy of China-US Trade Relations*. Beijing: China Market Press, 2007: 322

[17] Wang Yong. *The Political Economy of China-US Trade Relations*. Beijing: China Market Press, 2007: 402

Section 2 China's economic diplomacy towards the EU

After the sixth Sino-EU Summit in October 2003, both sides officially established a comprehensive strategic partnership. Since this time, and particularly after 2005, China began to consciously use its means of economic diplomacy to realise its national political and economic interests. A strategy for economic diplomacy was gradually under way, ranging from political leaders to specific charging government agencies, and used to guide the practice of economic diplomacy. The EU, one of China's most important trading partners, has enjoyed dynamic economic cooperation with China in recent years and accumulated extensive experience and trust in its interactions, pushing forward the Sino-EU bilateral strategic partnership to a new height. Since the onset of the global financial crisis, especially the sovereign debt crisis in certain EU countries, China has been faced with both opportunities and challenges. A summary of the achievements and problems in China's economic diplomacy towards the EU is conducive for us to have a good understanding of the new challenges and opportunities that confront China and the EU in their strategic partnership.

I. Political and economic situation of China

1. On the part of the EU, the Lisbon treaty officially came into effect in 2009. The EU's construction of a common diplomatic and security policy scored a new progress. Internationally, the EU strove to play a dominant role in issues such as climate change and reform of the financial system, and it actively took part in trying to solve hotspot issues and fight against Somali pirates. However, the European debt crisis threatened European integration and further institutionalisation. The crisis also set back the entire EU economy, foreign trade volumes dropped and the political situation became turbulent. Consequently, EU integration was beset with difficulties. To ease the crisis and boost the economy, the EU and its member states launched a series of financial bailout schemes and economic stimulus packages. The EU enhanced financial supervision by establishing new financial regulations, increased its support to the green low carbon economy by formulating long-term development planning. Since the EU's economic fundamentals are more solid than those of the US, it is less likely to cause a global crisis. China should have an accurate grasp of the crisis and economic situation in the EU. It should not be deceived by the calls of some to bail out Europe. Rather, China should engage in trade and investment in the EU in a prudent and scientific way.

2. There is a great disparity in national strengths among EU member states. They also differ from each other in industrial structure and post-crisis influence. Though Germany has good working relations with China, there are tremendous heterogeneity in both ideology and views between the two sides. As Germany's economic condition has no big problems, so it is the means for the EU to step out of the

crisis. Therefore, China should exert greater efforts in investment and cooperation with Germany, both in strength and range. On the one hand, this investment is somewhat risky. On the other hand, it may win a favourable impression and pave the way for cooperation. France still maintains its traditional hold on the EU. The French President François Hollande took the lead in visiting China after China's new leaders emerged, exploring ideas for in-depth cooperation in politics and the economy between the two sides. The UK, as a traditional ally of the US, has little scope to make any progress in political cooperation with China. However, Sino-UK cooperation in the establishment of the renminbi offshore market and financial diplomacy are very promising. Belgium is home to several institutions of the EU. Sino-Belgium economic and trade cooperation and political communication enjoy exceptional advantages. Both sides may have financial cooperation and learn from each other. Moreover, China should treat separately those countries "in crisis" and consideration should be taken into bilateral strategy on the basis of return on investment.

3. China will remain a developing country for quite a long time to come. Despite its rapid economic growth, China's structural transformation of its economy is under huge pressure, which has an immediate impact on the implementation of its strategy for economic diplomacy, including Sino-EU relations. The global financial crisis and economic recession have exerted a tremendous influence on the Chinese economy. Export growth has been sluggish, the ability to attract capital has been impaired and huge pressure has been placed on structural adjustment. The structural transformation of the Chinese economy will have a profound influence on Sino-EU economic and trade relations, and it will also impact China's foreign investment and opening its market wider to the outside world. China should use its market and capital capacity in a rational way and strive for long-term sustainable growth through systematic structural transformation and foreign strategy. This is in line with the strategic arrangement which serves the fundamental interests of China.

II. Cooperation and achievements of China's economic diplomacy towards the EU

1. Mechanisms and platforms of China-EU cooperation

A series of institutionalised economic and trade dialogues and exchange mechanisms have been set up between China and the EU, including bilateral and multilateral platforms. So far, more than 50 negotiation and dialogue mechanisms have been established covering politics, the economy, trade, science and technology, environmental protection and energy. Such an institutionalised cooperation network has laid a solid foundation for promoting bilateral economic and trade cooperation and resolving conflicts in the economy and trade.

Bilateral meetings of leaders from both sides are mostly involved in issues concerning economic cooperation and suggestions for developing bilateral economic and trade relations; a great number of economic and trade agreements and contracts have been concluded. After the financial crisis, most bilateral talks have covered topics such as enhancing coordination and cooperation to cope with the crisis, and solving problems that exist in bilateral trade and investment. Second, multilateral cooperation that focuses on mechanisms such as meetings of leaders of China and the EU and the Asia-Europe Meeting (established in 1996) has had a tremendous influence. For example, the Sino-European Industrial and Commercial Summit was set up in 2004. The Sino-European Vice-Premier Level High Level Economic and Trade Dialogue Mechanism was established in 2007, officially launching substantial negotiation on a partnership agreement. Together with prestigious international economic coordination and cooperation mechanisms such as the normalised Sino-European Economic and Trade Joint Committee and the G20, political negotiation and dialogue mechanisms at various levels between China and Europe have been constantly improved. In addition, friendly and pragmatic cooperation on the basis of mutual benefit in various fields keep deepening. These multilateral platforms played an irreplaceable coordinating role and helped both sides cope with the crisis.

2. China-EU trade relations

Trade and economic ties between China and the EU have flourished in recent times. The trade volume totalled US$546bn in 2012. However, influenced by the financial crisis and the adjustment of foreign trade policies between individual countries, bilateral economic and trade underwent adjustment and upheaval. As a result, the growth rate of foreign trade slowed down remarkably. China's overall trade situation took a sudden turn for the worse. Nevertheless, its efforts to change the growth mode of foreign trade have paid off and produced encouraging results. Currently, the EU is China's largest trade partner, the largest source of technical imports and an important investment source. Correspondingly, China is EU's largest source of imports and the second largest trade partner. Trade between the two sides has become huge and developed rapidly. Mechanical and electrical products, transportation equipment, base metals and base metal products are China's major imports from the EU, accounting for nearly 70% of the total. China's export commodities to the EU include mechanical and electrical products, textile, raw materials, furniture and toys. As the largest trade entity in the world, the EU takes the leading position in international service trade. An audit of the EU's trade policy by the WTO shows that, in terms of degree of openness, the EU's service in trade (especially basic telecommunications and finance), both internal and external, are more open than those of the WTO.

Notwithstanding their growing cooperation, China and the EU compete with each other in strategy for their trade areas (FTA). While the Doha round of trade talks under the WTO suffered a major setback, the EU, due to short-term needs, upheld mercantilism to push forward its FTA. However, in the long run, it has all along attached great importance to building its normative power and to formulating standards and rules on a global scale. In particular, the EU is committed to formulating trade rules and using them to push forward bilateral relations, including relations between the US and Europe, between the US and Japan, and between the US and China. In addition, the EU has launched a series of FTA negotiations and constructions, which are not only a manifestation of mercantilism but also the inevitability of developing its normative power. In particularly, the US and the EU are negotiating a Transatlantic Trade and Investment Partnership (TTIP), which will exert profound influence on standards and rules on global trade, and also on the trade partnership between China and the EU. After the Doha round negotiation stagnated, FTA strategy is another major strategic orientation of China's opening up and free trade. Though the EU has stressed on many occasions that its FTA strategy does not aim to contain China, it is negotiating on a series of FTA frameworks with neighbouring countries of China, which has posed high external pressure on China. In fact, China is exploring the possibility to launch FTA negotiations with the EU. Both sides have a similar stance on developing and reforming the multilateral trade system. China may think about the possibility to further cooperation with the EU in the environment where the global trade order is being remodelled.

3. Investment of China and the EU

International investors attach great importance to China's huge market, its market potential and investment and trade environment. The EU's investment in China has witnessed vigorous growth, rising 8% in 2004 and nearly 30% in 2005 (the UK and Germany's direct investment in China increased by over 40% and the average investment size also rose). In addition, large-scale merger and acquisition (M&A) projects also proliferated. Foreign-funded enterprises continue to be a driving force for China's export growth and structural upgrading. In 2006, newly-established enterprises under the investment of the 15 EU countries in China dropped by 7.98% and the actually utilised amount of foreign capital increased by 2.51% compared with the same period of the previous year. The EU has become China's third largest source of foreign investment. In 2006, China's non-financial FDI in the EU amounted to US$130m. Since the implementation of the Income Tax Law of the People's Republic of China on Enterprises with Foreign Investment and Foreign Enterprises in 2007, super-national treatment that foreign-funded enterprises had enjoyed in China for 20 years came to end. China's non-financial investment volume in the EU reached US$500m in 2007. After the start of the financial crisis in 2008, major investment institutions in the world held that China's stable market and high rate of return on investment brought about a rare opportunity of "Bringing In" and "Going Out" of China's market. In 2010, China actively invested in Europe, with investment volume increasing five-fold over the previous year. Several Chinese enterprises undertook large-scale project investments in Europe. In 2011, the EU's direct investment in China increased by 3.26% compared with that of the previous year. In 2012, the number of new enterprises established by EU companies in China totalled 1,698, a year-on-year decrease of 2.6%; paid-in overseas investment of US$6.107bnrepresented a year-on-year decrease of 3.8%. China utilises both "quality" and "quantity" of foreign investment, enhancing the introduction of advanced technology, managerial experience and highly-competent people. It also lays emphasis on balanced development of different regions, protecting the environment, making rational use of resources and integrating the utilisation of foreign investment with upgrading the domestic industrial structure and technical level. In this post-crisis period, China should further standardize foreign capital management and show more discretion in using its foreign investment.

Over the past 10 years, Chinese investment in foreign countries has grown strongly, and across an expanding range of investment fields. Forms of investment have included cross-border mergers and acquisitions, share right replacement, overseas listings, establishing R&D bases and industrial parks. China has ranked first among developing countries in terms of foreign direct investment (FDI). By June 2011, the stock of China's global FDI had reached US$330bn, a 10-fold increase over the figure in 2002. Chinese investment in the EU has been on the increase, totalling US$8.2bn in 2012. The gross stock of China's direct investment in 27 EU countries experienced rapid growth, amounting to US$24.4bn in 2012. However, China's investment is relatively small, and the restriction of its domestic and foreign rules and regulations limit its investment capability. In view of this, China should improve its policy on foreign investment promotion, supervision system and legal guarantee, strive for a breakthrough in key fields and projects and win-win result with collaborative agents.

4. Sino-EU financial dialogue

In recent years, China's financial markets have opened wider to the outside world, financial reform has quickened and its financial diplomacy has been very active. In 2006, China's financial market underwent all-round opening-up and entered into a stage of deeper reform. In addition, stock system reform and listing of state-owned banks, reform of the capital market and reform of the mechanism for setting the renminbi exchange rate, etc, have promoted the internationalisation and mercerisation of Chinese financial market. Financial laws and the law enforcement system have been reformed and improved. Enhancing international financial dialogue and cooperation will help China make better use of both domestic and overseas markets and resources. China should also strive to participate in the formulation of international rule-making to maximise its influence as a big power.

Progress has been made in financial cooperation between China and individual EU countries. China's Ministry of Finance visited its counterparts in the UK and France in 2003. Central banks of European countries, including France and Italy, accredited representatives to their embassies in China and maintained close contact with the People's Bank of China. In 2010, Premier Wen Jiabao and the Spanish and Greek prime ministers achieved a higher level financial diplomacy. In terms of the EU, China's Ministry of Finance and the European Investment Bank (EIB) exchanged views on future cooperation in October 2003. In February 2005, the Ministry of Finance and the Directorate-General for Economic and Financial Affairs (ECFIN) established a Sino-EU Financial Dialogue Mechanism, which is an important platform to conduct policy exchanges in macroeconomy and finance. The ministry has also held meetings with the World Bank on topics such as loan projects. In addition, China and the EU have made joint efforts to carry out reform of the global financial system and make macroeconomic predictions at such platforms as the G20, the Asia-Europe Finance Ministers' Meetings, the World Economic Forum (WEF), the China-EU High-level Economic and Trade Dialogue and the China-EU Industrial and Commercial Summit. The EU and China can promote bilateral trade and investment by financial and fiscal cooperation.

5. Technical and labour service cooperation between China and the EU

Sino-EU technical cooperation started in 1981. China took part in the European Galileo programme in 2003. In 2004, China renewed the China-EU Scientific and Technological Cooperation Agreement. In 2006, it introduced more than 23,000 technologies from the EU, accounting for nearly 40% of the total number of its technology import contracts in the year, with a contract value of nearly US$100bn. In 2009, both sides signed the China-EU Agreement for Scientific and Technological Cooperation, marking a new stage of Sino-EU cooperation in this area. Currently, the EU is China's largest source of technology. Germany, France, the Netherlands, Italy and the UK are China's major source countries of technology imports. Germany is China's third largest source country of technology imports, after only the US and Japan. China's introduction of Airbus planes and key projects such as Dayawan nuclear plant reflect the high level of technical cooperation on both sides. In recent years, China and the EU have cooperated in fields such as the international thermonuclear experimental reactor programme, hydrogen energy, fuel cells, biofuel, clean coal, energy efficiency and renewable energy sources. In 2009, both sides signed an agreement on environmental governance. Both sides have also cooperated in sustainable production and consumption, biodiversity, river governance, air pollution prevention, climate change and emergency responses to environmental pollution accidents.

The global economy recovered in 2005. Europe and the Asia-Pacific region became the core market of international project contracting. Large-scale European transnational construction enterprises held advantages in technology, management and capital, while those from developing countries including China were committed to improving their technical level and managerial expertise and strived to enter the international market. As international engineering projects became larger and more complicated, a system of industrial division of labour and cooperation gradually took shape between the two sides. Chinese engineering contractors energetically tapped the European market and large-scale projects grew rapidly. Owing to its specific technical standards, market access and labour policy, China is still faced with huge challenges in tapping the markets of Europe, North America and Oceania. We can see from a comparison between global 225 contractors that Chinese contractors, who are less competitive in Europe and the US. However, with the expansion of strength of China's contracted projects in other countries, these markets will surely score tremendous development.

As almost all countries have an increasing demand for high-level professionals and trade in services, international labour cooperation has become an important topic of economic diplomacy. Germany is China's largest target country for labour exports to the EU. Contractor workers are still mostly unskilled. China's Ministry of Commerce of China has formulated a series of documents concerning the management of foreign labour cooperation so as to pursue development China needs to support its export of labour services in areas such as taxation, information service and management with a view to cultivating professionals with the technical ability and quality to take part in international labour service cooperation. To facilitate the implementation of a "going global" strategy for Chinese enterprises, China's delegations all over the world use diplomatic resources to form a service network to provide Chinese enterprises with information and services concerning local policies, commerce, labour service and security so as to help them enter the local market, reduce international risks and strengthen the protection of overseas companies and citizens.

6. Energy and environmental cooperation

Energy cooperation between China and Europe started with the creation of an energy working team conference in 1997. In 2004, both sides signed an R&D cooperation agreement on the peaceful utilisation of nuclear energy. In 2005, they signed a Memorandum of Understanding for the Strategic Dialogue on Sino-Europe Energy Transport between China and Europe. Four years later marked the signing of the Sino-Europe Fiscal Compact on Clean Energy Center and the Sino-Europe Joint Declaration on Clean Energy Center. In recent years, China and Europe have cooperated in an international thermonuclear experimental reactor programme, hydrogen energy, fuel cells, biofuel, clean coal, energy efficiency and renewable energy sources. Denmark has taken a lead in Sino-Europe energy cooperation. In January 2006, Denmark's Ministry of Foreign Affairs and China's Ministry of Commerce signed an agreement on a three-year wind power generation project with total funds of about US$7m. However, since China and the EU are both net importers of energy, there are inevitable areas of conflict that are manifest in energy diplomacy. For example, the two sides have different energy diplomacy strategies towards oil-producing countries in Africa and the Middle-East.

For a long time, the EU has built up normative power and influence in the field of international environmental management, playing a leading role in rule-making, international negotiations and cooperation. China and the EU have huge potential for cooperation in fields such as sustainable production and consumption, biodiversity protection, river governance, air pollution, climate change and emergency responses to environmental pollution accidents.

III. Problems in economic diplomacy between China and the EU

1. Trade friction and trade imbalances

Though China's export volume accounts for less than one-tenth of the world's total, it is faced with 60% of trade protection measures. After the financial crisis, global trade competition has intensified. Such protection is not only defensive, but also strategically offensive and used as a tool to compete for overseas markets. Trade friction has emerged in new areas. For example, the number of intellectual property rights cases has increased; the focus has switched from primary commodities to consumer goods and higher-end technical products; developing countries have launched more protective cases against China; carbon tariffs has become a new trade protection measure; and trade protection has become more prevalent in services, finance, investment and employment.

Trade friction between China and the EU has focused on industrial and light industrial products, such as mechanical and electrical products, chemical products, textiles and shoes. These frictions are the result of various factors, all of which are underpinned by structural contradictions. The root cause of global trade friction is summed up by the phrase, "America and Europe consume, while China processes". Europe and the US depend on China's manufactured products and short-term equilibrium is unrealistic. The EU cites its huge trade deficit with China, the impact of Chinese products in the EU market and China's market access barriers for EU exports and investment. The EU's direct investment in China is an additional reason for the trade deficit. EU member states differ from each other in economic comparative advantages and most compete with China in trade. Due to the financial crisis, the EU was more inclined to take protective measures to ease the impact of the economic downturn and rising unemployment. The EU has often articulated its dissatisfaction by implementing anti-dumping and anti-subsidy protective measures. The trade structure imbalance was apparent in the textile dispute between China and the EU in 2005, the footwear and car components tariff dispute in 2006, an anti-dumping investigation of some iron and steel fasteners in 2007 and the more recent anti-dumping and anti-subsidy investigation over photovoltaic products and the communication industry. At the same time, the EU has all along advocated multilateral trade liberalisation and flexibly manoeuvred and used WTO rules, and made the best use of the clause of "exception principle" to protect its rights and interests. As a result, the EU launched many trade dispute settlement cases in the WTO. For example, in 2005, the EU, having signed a bilateral trade agreement on textiles with China, adopted a "voluntary export restriction". After the expiration of the bilateral agreement, the EU initiated a "dual control system" which meant its readiness for a new trade remedy.

China's economic strength and enhanced global prestige have imposed pressure on European society, as a result of which the EU decision-makers are inclined to make passive policy response. However, China should spare no efforts to solve the deep-seated structural problems in its manufacturing industry: China has an imbalanced internal economic structure and a great number of labour-intensive products are exported to Europe and America and China's market economy status is not recognised. Premier Wen Jiabao stressed that China has no intention to pursue a trade surplus, that its rapidly growing trade surplus has become one of its major economic challenges, and that the fundamental cause is the international industrial structure. To remove trade friction and imbalances, Chinese economic and ministerial leaders have conducted negotiations with EU institutions. In addition, Chinese enterprises and industrial associations have actively responded to lawsuits. The Chinese government has taken some measured responses and will seek to eradicate its balance of payments surplus as a priority of its economic diplomacy. After all, China is a big trade power but not a strong trade power. Chinese enterprises should have a better knowledge of international trade rules and enhance rule application.

Bilateral negotiations and regular consultations are the means to solving trade friction; they help to bridge an information gap and facilitate an in-depth exchange of views for a peaceful settlement of divergence dispute. China and the EU solve their disputes mainly through political diplomacy featuring negotiation, mediation and conciliation. This is a more stable and predictable route than legal redress. Despite containing some flaws, the dispute settlement mechanisms in the multilateral trading system of the WTO are important channels to effectively solve trade disputes between countries. In addition, non-governmental industrial associations and enterprises have close connections, and can play an important role in a variety of areas such as information distribution, policy publicity, organisation and coordination, litigation and responding to lawsuits. The coordination mechanism may be used as an important complement to the exchanges, communication and conflict resolution between non-governmental interest groups.

2. Market economy status

Faced with constant friction with its trade partners and discriminatory treatment, China's primary diplomatic goal is to win recognition of full market economy status from the outside world, which will provide external trade and foreign investments with an advantage. By May 2013, more than 50 countries (including Switzerland, Australia, New Zealand and South Korea) had recognised China's full market economy status. However, no consensus on this issue has been reached between China and Europe.

This issue falls into the field of common trading, featuring exclusive policy-making power. However, given the attitude of EU member countries, especially different standpoints of western and eastern European countries, this issue has more than just economic significance. Instead, it is a key intermediate variable in Sino-EU economic diplomacy. As a matter of fact, industrial interests and national interests which are in competition with those of China are negative forces for giving China's market economy status. This pattern will not change with the verbal declarations of the European Commission and individual state leaders. In practice, it will be almost impossible for China to win EU recognition of its market economy status before 2016. What is most unacceptable to China is that, in the face of the transitional period provided for in China's entry to the WTO, it is very likely that the EU will not recognise China's market economy status even after 2016. This will have a profound impact on China, which regards market economy status as a recognition and acceptance from the international community of China's 30-plus-years of reform and opening up. In fact, it is a key variable in solving trade frictions involving tens of billions of US dollars. Therefore, from both strategic and policy levels, China will never give up negotiations with the EU in this area.

3. High-tech product control and intellectual property rights protection

The EU, boasting a technical trade management system with more than 300 directives and 100,000 technical standards, is one of the major places in which technical trade barriers are in use. These barriers mainly involve the following aspects: various technical regulations and standards that have high requirements and are frequently revised; rigorous requirements for packaging, labelling and labour protection; green barriers; and efforts made to control China's participation in the formulation of international rules. Differences between China and the EU in product costs, control over high-tech products and intellectual property have lasted for a long time. Though the EU's technical barriers are not directed against China, its desire to be a maker of international rules does imply an element of trade protection. China requires the EU to relax export controls on high technology, including military technology. The EU, however, requires China to devote greater efforts to fighting piracy and protecting intellectual property rights (IPR).

Technical cooperation between China and the EU is closely related to their respective strategy of innovative development. As both sides have started to reform their economic models, cooperation is expected to expand from economy and trade to new areas such as high-tech trade, IPR, new energy, energy-saving technology and personnel training. These new directions require the EU to eradicate the following trade barriers: many technical regulations and standards with high requirements and subject to frequent revision; rigorous requirements for packaging, labelling and labour protection; green barriers; the suppression of China's participation in the formulation of international standards. Therefore, China needs to take advantage of its market to expedite the formulation and popularisation of its domestic technical standards; improve its system of intellectual property rights protection; make great efforts in fiscal and financial regulation; expand trade investment; support cooperation between small and medium-sized enterprises; promote technical innovation, propel the EU to transfer technology to China and make joint efforts to fight against trade protectionism.

4. Investment barriers and market access

The institutional arrangement for bilateral investment between China and the EU can be found in the Agreement on China-EU Economic and Trade Cooperation in 1985 and the China-EU Partnership and Cooperation Agreement, on which both sides began negotiating in 2007. However, there is no unified legal norm that is equally binding upon both parties. Because of this, the EU and China accuse each other of creating barriers that hold back the sound development of bilateral trade and investment. To adapt to the new situation of Sino-EU economic diplomacy, both sides should negotiate in the following areas: investment liberalisation, investment protection, sustainable development and an appropriate dispute settlement mechanism (DSB). China faces challenges such as free mobility of the renminbi capital fund account, the renewal of laws and regulations and the modernisation of labour protection standards. The greatest challenge that the EU faces is the further coordination in power of investment negotiations between EU institutions and its member states.

There is much room for cooperation in fields such as bilateral investment agreement between China and the EU. After the Treaty of Lisbon took effect, the EU has exclusive authority in investment, which is both an opportunity and a challenge for Sino-EU cooperation that begins with China's launching negotiations on the bilateral investment agreement. A unified EU has raised its standard for negotiations on investment in foreign countries. It has also won the right to set the agenda on investment negotiations with the US. On the other hand, China has begun negotiations on unified EU standards and the results are widely anticipated. The European sovereign debt crisis and China's economic transformation have brought about a once-in-a-century opportunity for China's foreign investment. Deciding how best to build up a coordinated strategy at national level to invest in America, Europe, Africa and Southeast Asia is one of China's top priorities. China should not only strive for mutually beneficial cooperation, but also attach great importance to the mode of joint capital and avoid various national risks. It is likely that the next Sino-EU summit meeting will be a starting point of negotiations on a bilateral investment agreement, which would be a positive step for the development of Sino-EU relations. The agenda itself is of vital significance for China to enhance its abilities and acquire a good understanding of international rules. In a broader sense, the advancement of Sino-EU investment and market access will greatly push forward the reform of the multilateral trading system.

IV. A summary and evaluation of Sino-EU economic diplomacy

Sino-EU relations, based on multifaceted cooperation and competition, covers a great number of issues under discussion including trade, investment, fiscal and financial cooperation, international aid, technical cooperation in labour services, energy and the environment. So far, both sides have established more than 50 institutionalised economic and trade dialogue and exchange mechanisms, in areas such as politics, the economy, trade, science and technology, environmental protection and energy. Furthermore, bilateral meetings and multilateral dialogue have created a broad platform for Sino-EU cooperation. The institutionalised cooperation network between China and the EU lays an institutional basis for promoting bilateral economic and trade cooperation and resolve economic and trade friction. In trying to summarise the achievements and problems in Sino-EU economic diplomacy, we need to answer the following questions: What is so special about Sino-EU economic and diplomatic relations compared with China's other bilateral relations concerning economic diplomacy? How will China cope after the EU has established a unified foreign policy to make overall arrangements for its economy and diplomacy? Have Sino-EU relations concerning economic diplomacy reached the goal of strategic partnership that both sides originally expected?

First of all, we should have a clear idea about the specialness of Sino-EU strategy for economic diplomacy and its unique features. With its strong economic strength in trade and political normative rights, the EU stands out among China's numerous bilateral partners. Therefore, the EU and China have a broad prospect for trans-regional cooperation in fields such as global economic management and transformation, formulation of multilateral trade rules, bilateral investment and market opening, R&D of high-technology and new energy development, regional security, social structural reform, ecological protection and the green economy, legal construction and human rights protection. We should examine Sino-EU relations in terms of numerous bilateral and multilateral platforms. In particular, we should develop Sino-EU relations through platforms such as the WTO and G20, so as to enable the EU and European countries to play a bigger role in the implementation of China's global strategy.

Second, more than 10 years have passed since China entered into the WTO. In this period, China has assimilated rules in areas such as freedom, opening up, the rule of law and the market economy, which help the country to restore its confidence in interacting with the international community. In addition, China has become more active in its foreign economic policy and greater efforts have been made in investment, aid, energy and technical cooperation as well as participation in the reform of the international economic system. In the past decade, China's diplomatic goal has given priority to the economy rather than politics and diplomacy has become a tool to expand economic benefits. Economic diplomacy between China and the EU has recently encompassed government procurement and business contracts. The EU remains China's largest trading partner, which is the result of the smooth development of the Sino-EU partnership. However, as China's economic diplomacy is still in its infancy, its deficiencies and limitations have begun to appear. Problems in industrial structure, imbalanced development between urban and rural areas, pressure of environmental protection, scientific and technological innovation capacity and international social responsibilities have become more obvious which has become a disadvantage of China's foreign policy. For the foreseeable future, China should actively set up topics for its economic diplomacy and influence the formulation of international rules through multilateral mechanisms so as to push forward a new international political economic order that is conducive to China's national strategy on the basis of win-win cooperation.

Third, though more than 10 years have passed since the establishment of the overall strategic partnership between China and Europe, both sides have different interpretations for the basic concept of "strategy". China lays emphasis on guidance and control over policies, while the EU stresses coordination and internal negotiation in different policy domains. The EU thinks that strategic relations may help both sides to solve bilateral problems through consultation, while China holds that strategic relations may cope with some core interests and major concerns. All this gives rise to another problem: how to determine China's core interests and strategic concerns? The author holds that the current diplomatic issues under discussion are not necessarily China's core interests. Topics such as "market economy status" and "lift a ban on arms sale" are often mentioned as tasks that seem impossible to complete. The former is caused by the rigorous trade decision-making mechanism within the EU, while the latter by the EU's lack of a unified foreign policy and of political leadership with actual decision-making capacity. Diplomatically, there must be a declaration of vital interests in an appropriate manner. However, it should be conducive to pursuing actual economic benefits. Those issues under discussion that contribute to China's economic structural transformation and social stability and development are more important. At the 11th summit meeting between China and the EU in 2009, Premier Wen Jiabao stated: "The core of Sino-EU relations is its strategic importance, its connotation is its comprehensiveness and its key is its advancing with the times. Therefore, both sides should enhance mutual understanding, take into account the concerns of the other side and promote in-depth and sustainable development of bilateral relations." In 2013, Li Keqiang paid chose Germany as a destination on his first overseas tour since coming into office as Premier of the State Council. This indicates China's new administration attaches great importance to Sino-EU relations. China has all along viewed Europe from a strategic perspective and supported European integration. 2014 was the 10th anniversary of the establishment of an all-round partnership between China and the EU. Looking forward, there are many new opportunities. Both sides should grasp overall cooperation, seek a proper settlement of disputes and differences to facilitate progress in the comprehensive strategic partnership between the two sides. Against the dual backdrops of the EU sovereign debt crisis and the structural transformation of the Chinese economy, China should make better use of its economic means (investment, finance, procurement, etc) to enter a European market that is in need of capital. In addition, China should attach great importance to the high-tech field. It should be far-sighted and have risk awareness in political and economic interactions with its partners in Europe.

V. Future strategic choice of Sino-EU economic diplomacy

As both China and the EU have reached the stage of mutually readjusting their economic development modes, future bilateral cooperation is expected to be deepened and expanded, in areas such as high-tech trade cooperation, bilateral investment agreements, consumer goods safety, energy-saving technology, mobility of talented personnel, opposing trade protectionism, enhancing fiscal and financial supervision, expanding trade investment, supporting small and medium-sized enterprises, promoting scientific and technological cooperation, coping with climate change and enhancing coordination in macro-economic policy. Given the financial crisis, in terms of Sino-EU economic diplomacy, research should be conducted on how to cooperate and develop in specific fields and how to make Chinese enterprises "go global". In addition, studies should be conducted on overseas investment and risk aversion of the Chinese government and its enterprises, and reform of Chinese manufacturers under the EU carbon tax system.

China and the EU are more economically interdependent with each passing day, which does not necessarily lead to coordination in politics or diplomacy. Instead, economic friction and stagnation have damaged political trust and strategic foundations. Therefore, China and the EU should keep up with the times, and renew their strategic thinking and relevant policy documents. Both sides should play a guiding role in coordinating economic and diplomatic policies. After all, reform is the only way to turn external challenges into external opportunities. As a matter of fact, it is through reform that China and the EU have developed themselves. China, advocating the establishment of a community of common destiny, hopes to develop its national strength and realise its national interests in the new international relations featuring equilibrium and mutual benefit. Though the win-win strategy is currently counter-balanced by various forces and the zero-sum game in world politics, such dialectical concept reflects traditional Chinese culture and contributes to world politics. It is precisely because of the zero-sum phenomenon as represented by the trade disputes between China and the EU that win-win strategy is essential for the development of the Sino-EU strategic partnership. In the course of the formulation and practice of Sino-EU strategy for economic diplomacy, China should grasp this period of strategic opportunity, build up and maintain the dynamic process of its competitive edge through strategic management so that it can take advantage of its huge economic strength and turn it into effective diplomatic resources to safeguard the development of Sino-EU relations and peaceful development.

Section 3 China's economic diplomacy towards Japan

Thanks to China's sustained economic growth, Sino-Japanese relations have been constantly deepening. Economic and trade cooperation has become an important pillar of relations between the two countries.

Since 1980, owing to China's adoption of its reform and opening-up policy and a change in Japan's industrial formation, Japanese enterprises have begun investing in China on a massive scale. In recent years, this has been matched by a trend for Chinese enterprises to invest in Japan. Meanwhile, the governments of both countries have increased purchases of the other's national debt. Social exchanges have also been rising, most notably in the number of Chinese holidaymakers going to Japan.

Chinese-made products are everywhere, from department stores to supermarkets. Since the second half of the 1980s, a great number of cheap and consumer-oriented Chinese products have swept the world. By the end of the 1990s, as the added value of Chinese manufacturing products gradually increased, Chinese domestic enterprises had become stronger and inward investment levels had soared. China was known as "the workshop of the world". However, many Chinese people, especially the more affluent, still prefer Japanese-made household appliances, watches, cars, cosmetics and food items.

I. Adjustment of economic structure

However, all this has changed with the occurrence of the nuclear accident caused by the earthquake in Japan. In contrast, China has witnessed great development. In recent years, owing to economic structural adjustment, China has gradually reduced the export ratio of products with low economic returns in favour of those with high economic returns. As Chinese and Japanese economic structures start to converge, competition and rivalry has increased.

II. Evolution of China's economic and political status

China has integrated into the world economy and now influences the world economic system through its opening to the outside world. China has been a major recipient of foreign capital for a number of years, which has promoted the domestic economy and lowered the global cost of production of transnational companies. On a global level, this has changed production patterns and stimulated capital and trade flows. China has become a stronger, more prosperous nation, while Japan experienced a "lost decade". Japan's trade deficit with China has increased, causing apprehensiveness among the Japanese people that is sometimes construed as a "China Threat".

III. Emergence of energy and resources competition

China's energy demand has soared in line with the development of its economy and the upgrading of its industrial structure. As both Japan and China are characterised by relatively small natural resources, contradictions between the two sides have gradually intensified. The main manifestations include: Japan begins to compete with China in the pricing power of iron ore; Japan stirs up disputes over China's gas fields in the East China Sea; Japan makes thoughtless comments on China's rare earth exports, etc. Meanwhile, Japan has intensified its research on rare earth alternatives and proposed theories such as "urban mineral resources". Outwardly, Japan has begun to vie for important industrial mineral resources in areas such as South America and Oceania to stockpile resources for future development. In addition, Japan has adopted a policy to impose pressure on China in economy, trade and advanced technology with a view to compelling the latter to make concession in its rare earth policy.

IV. China-Japan-South Korea Free Trade Agreement (FTA)

If the China-Japan-South Korea Free Trade Agreement materialises, it will greatly influence Sino-Japanese economic relations and benefit bilateral diplomatic relations. Under the influence of the FTA, China and Japan will expand mutual benefits through economic relations and have more people-to-people exchanges, which should make a contribution to building up mutual trust.

The China-Japan-South Korea Free Trade Agreement was proposed as a political idea in 2002. According to *Nikkei News*: "East Asia boasts three large economies, with a population of approximately 1.5bn. Their gross GDP accounts for nearly 70% of Asia's. If trade barriers are broken thoroughly in this region, the economic and social benefits generated will be inestimable."

If China, Japan and South Korea can establish the FTA, it will greatly facilitate to the establishment of an East Asian community. At the ASEAN 10+3 Summit in 2001, Japanese Prime Minister Koizumi put forward the establishment of an East Asian Community. After the Democratic Party of Japan took office, Japanese Prime Minister Yukio Hatoyama brought up the idea of the framework of "East Asian Community" at the ASEAN summit in October 2009, hoping to consolidate Japan's political and economic status through regional unity and peace and to bailout its declining economy. However, "East Asian Community" is riddled with internal contradictions. It is sometimes associated with the Great East Asia Co-prosperity Sphere, the term Japan gave to its wartime empire under the guise of pan-Asian liberation. Some Japanese scholars even argue that an East Asian Community is supposed to exist under Japan's leadership. As is well-known, the East Asian "10+3" system boasts two major players, China and Japan. If this argument is extended, it will inevitably cause political and economic friction. Satoshi Amako, a professor from the Institute of Asia-Pacific Research of the Graduate School of Waseda University, holds that non-economic factors in cooperation in East Asia have four main strands. First, inter-governmental relations; mutual trust in people-to-people relations; historical problems, China Threat, competitive relations between China and Japan, etc. Second, market completion and a widening gap between rich and poor. Third, North Korea nuclear issue; influence brought about by the issue of the Korean peninsula. Fourth, lessons from the Asian financial crisis and the return of the US to Asia.

V. Yoshihiko Noda regime and Chinese and Japanese economies

On 9 September2012, an APEC economic leader's meeting was held in Haishenwai, where President Hu Jintao held an informal meeting with Japanese Prime Minister Noda Yoshihiko. However, the next day, the Japanese government made the decision through its cabinet council to nationalise the Diaoyu Islands (known in Japan as the Senkaku Islands). This move infuriated the Chinese people, resulting in massive anti-Japanese demonstrations throughout China. This was the lowest point in the 40 years since China and Japan normalised diplomatic relations in 1972. Consequently, Japanese enterprises suffered great losses as a result of boycotts of Japanese goods in China and the forced closure of several Japanese enterprises.

During the Koizumi administration from 2001 to 2005, China strongly opposed Koizumi's visit to the Yasukuni shrine, which commemorates anyone who has died in the service of the Japanese empire. As a result, bilateral political relations were brought to a deadlock for a long time. Nevertheless, Japanese enterprises continued to invest in China. This period was called "cold politics and warm economy" in Sino-Japan relations. Up until recently, Sino-Japanese relations have been close, resulting in an interdependence between the two countries. On the one hand, Japanese enterprises wanted to expand into the huge Chinese market, while China was eager to obtain Japan's high-technology and managerial experience. If we consider the current situation of Sino-Japanese economic relations, deteriorating political relations will inevitably harm bilateral economic relations. Nevertheless, the tendency of close Sino-Japanese relations will continue. It is necessary for both sides to use diplomatic wisdom to surpass the "cold politics and warm economy" prevalent in the period of the Koizumi administration. However, as Yoshihiko Noda regime took its own course, economic cooperation between China and Japan is faced with the risk of "putting the clock back". "Trade deficit exceeds Yne3,200bn, the highest record of the comparable figures since 1979" -- this was the trade performance report for the first half (from April to September) of 2012 issued on October 22 by Japan's Ministry of Finance. In spite of numerous factors, the public views the Diaoyu Islands dispute between China and Japan as an important cause of Japan's declining exports. Figures also show that Japan's export volume to China slumped sharply to 14.1% in September 2012, with the month's deficit reaching a historical new high over the past 30-plus years. "China risk" is a term coined by the Japanese media and is used to stress the insecurity of investment in China. A trade report by Japan External Trade Organisation stated that, in the first half of 2012, Japan's deficit with China was 2.6 times higher than that of the same period of the previous year, totalling Yen1,401bn. Gross export volumes to China decreased by 5.7% on a year-on-year basis. The primary cause of the growing trade deficit was that Japan's exports of iron and steel and machinery products to China decreased for the first time since 2009. The above-mentioned figures seem to prove that Sino-Japanese relations have entered an era of "cold politics and warm economy".

VI. Conclusion

Though Sino-Japanese diplomacy has encountered problems and difficulties due to the Diaoyu Islands dispute, we should not forget the common interests of both sides, of which economic relations are the most important. Furthering economic development in China and Japan is in the common interests of both countries. Enhancing regional cooperation is another common interest. If the overall economy in East Asia with China and Japan as the core is prosperous and stable, the economies of both sides will be more prosperous and mutual trust will follow. Third, the concept of the East Asian Community, created by joint action that is based on respecting the diversity of history, culture, and nationalities and traditions of the region. It is a community for common prosperity, peace and mutual trust. As a matter of fact, China and Japan should become a powerful driving force for this community. As economic globalisation deepens, the basic task in East Asia for China's economic diplomacy is for further cooperation and to contribute to the stability and prosperity of the region.

Section 4 China's economic diplomacy towards BRICS

Jim O'Neal, the former chairman of Goldman Sachs Asset Management, coined the term BRIC in 2001 to encapsulate the four emerging market countries of Brazil, Russia, India and China. Ten years later, South Africa joined the group to turn BRIC into BRICS.

However, it was not until 2009 that the first official BRIC summit was held. In 2010, the original four countries created the BRIC Cooperation Mechanism. The global financial crisis played an important role in bringing these countries together and persuading them to talk with a common voice. The coming together of these rejuvenated emerging countries might suggest a challenge to the US dollar's hegemony in the global financial system, while others think the concept is likely to fade over time as conditions and priorities change. Whatever happens, this cooperation mechanism indicates China's economic diplomacy attaches great importance to cooperation with emerging countries as it attempts to reduce its reliance on developed countries in Europe and North America.

I. A political and economic survey of the BRICS group

As an organic whole, the five BRICS countries account for 43% of the world's population and 16% of economic output. Its trade volume is 15% of the global figure, while its overall economic growth rate exceeds 8%, far higher than the 2.6% growth rate of developed countries and 4.1% growth rate of the world. Calculated by purchasing power parity (PPT), BRICS' economic growth contributes to more than 60% of the world economic growth. Given the rising power of these nations, some scholars regard the BRICS mechanism as a platform for a possible shared government between the North and the South, meaning that the future global economic system could be jointly managed by developing countries, with the BRICS as the core.

The relatively strong performance of the BRICS countries since the start of the financial crisis, in terms of capital formation, exports, bulk commodity consumption and foreign exchange reserves, shows that BRICS countries have truly become a force to shape the global economic pattern. In terms of contributing to global economic growth, it has already surpassed developed countries. After the financial crisis, emerging economics such as China have achieved economic recovery while developed countries in Europe and America have mostly stalled. Under these circumstances, the outstanding status of BRICS in the global economy is expected to be maintained and enhanced. It also indicates that the global economic pattern is undergoing a transformation that will bring about profound change in the global political system.

As the prestige of BRICS has been enhanced, their leaders have tried to speak as "representatives" of developing countries advocating more participation in global governance, the construction of a new world order and pushing forward reform of the international financial system. However, owing to the fact that developed countries in Europe and America enjoy deep-rooted status in international affairs and boast powerful comprehensive national strength, there is still a great gap between them and emerging countries. Therefore, BRICS need to undergo a period of accumulation before they can shape the international order.

It is undeniable that China, playing a crucial leading role in the BRICS, has a great influence on the other four. Its sheer scale and the size of its economy are much greater than the other four BRICS countries. In addition, China's rapid economic growth has stimulated an increasing demand for bulk commodities, which has promoted sustained economic growth in Russia and Brazil, which abound in resources. Therefore, whether China is minded to deepen the political role of "BRICS", and what plans it has for the grouping will determine the future of this cooperation mechanism.

II. Political and economic situations of each BRICS country

Though the BRICS countries are emerging economies with rapid economic growth rates, each one has followed its own development path, with some highly dependent on energy exports and others dependent on stimulating growth through high investment and exports and others having a more advanced services sector. Different development paths bring about both opportunities and challenges to the BRICS countries. And while all BRICS countries dream of developing themselves into big powers, they have a great deal of divergence.

1. With its huge economy and high economic growth rate, China has been called a "pacemaker" by the BRICS countries. However, China is also caught up in many problems. Domestically, it needs to conduct in-depth reform of its economic structure; it is experiencing a rapidly ageing population; its development is inhibited by environmental problems and a lack of energy resources. China is not immune from the influence of adverse external factors such as global economic recession and growing protectionism in developed countries brought about by

the financial crisis. As a consequence, China needs to slow down its economic growth rate. It has pursued domestic reform that does not threaten economic development momentum and it has enhanced cooperation with developing countries to reduce its reliance on Europe and the US. Therefore, China's cooperation with the BRICS may be viewed as an attempt by the Chinese government to spur domestic reform through external forces. As it deepens cooperation with similar developing countries, China must optimise its economic structure, reform its market mechanism and exploit its advantages. While cooperating with the other four BRICS countries, China should give priority to economic cooperation, sparing no effort in pushing forward reform of the international financial system and reducing its reliance on the US dollar. It should also pursue renminbi settlement within the BRICS as part of its goal to internationalise the currency.

2. Having gone through "10 lost years" when it was mired in debt and suffering rampant inflation, Brazil's economy has begun rejuvenation since 1994. Its reform plan in the 1990s laid a solid foundation for the country to become the world's sixth largest economy in 2011. Like Russia, Brazil is endowed with natural resources, a large population and vast territorial area, which makes possible its dream of rising as a great power. It has benefited considerably from the rise in international demand for commodities. Though it has suffered from debt and the impact of the financial crisis, Brazil has been able to build momentum in economic development. More than just a major supplier of minerals and agricultural produce, Brazil is currently the world's ninth largest steel producer and fourth largest automobile manufacturer. Furthermore, its technology levels are close to those of developed countries, while democracy has matured quickly and a large middle class has been established. These strengths will benefit Brazil in its cooperation and trade contacts with the BRICS. In addition, under the administration of President Cardozo, Brazil's diplomacy has begun to attach more importance to cooperation with other Latin American countries and South-South cooperation, which foreshadows its priority to cooperating with BRICS countries. Its participation in the BRICS Cooperation Mechanism conforms to Brazil's need to share opportunities in economic development, and enhance multilateral cooperation and prestige in the international arena. However, its debt problem, the huge disparity between rich and poor, and high costs have resulted in a decrease in domestic investment and a recent decline in economic growth.

3. Russia is endowed with abundant natural resources and a developed manufacturing industry, which sets it apart from all other BRICS. As the world's largest exporter of natural gas and the second largest of oil, Russia enjoyed fast economic growth during the period of high oil prices. Though the country managed to ride out the global financial crisis, it was under pressure to reform its economic structure. The sudden sharp fall in oil prices in 2008 imposed a huge pressure on the

economic transformation of the country. In 2011, Russia successfully joined the WTO, which has brought about new opportunities for it to open its markets, enhance external economic exchange and promote domestic economic reform, as well as consolidate cooperation with the other BRICS. However, Russia's economic policy has wavered in the past 10 years, particularly over whether it should follow the Western model. When he was president of the country, Dmitry Medvedev adopted a pro-European and pro-American foreign economic policy. However, when Vladimir Putin became head of state once again in May 2012, Russia has adopted a more hardline stance against the West and a greater focus on South-South cooperation and the BRICS in particular. Russia has a high expectation of the BRICS cooperation mechanism both politically and economically. Its ministry of foreign affairs regards the BRICS mechanism as an "important element in forming a new world order and a tool for its member countries to conduct strategic cooperation".

4. Since the 1990s, India began to carry out economic reform oriented to an open economy, privatisation, market reform and globalisation. In recent times, it has maintained steady economic growth. New and high-tech industries have emerged, bringing India a great advantage in cooperation among the BRICS. Moreover, the solid foundations of agriculture and manufacturing industry and a powerful and prosperous tertiary industry have laid a solid foundation for its trade contacts with the other BRICS counties. After the financial crisis, India's economic growth became sluggish and its inflation rate approached 5%. This has dented investor confidence in India. India prioritises foreign trade, describing it as the "engine" for stimulating economic growth. In this sense, it is easy to understand India's enthusiasm for the BRICS Cooperation Mechanism in that it aims to share the opportunities and benefits brought about by the fast economic growth of emerging countries. This, however, does not mean that India has no intention to expand the political prestige of BRICS. Indeed, India has shown great interest in adding its weight in global governance and the construction of a new world order by taking advantage of being a BRICS country. However, this enthusiasm is tempered by India concerns over China's rise.

5. South Africa is the largest economy in Africa. Its entry into BRICS has added a new driving force for economic development, and it also makes the grouping more representative. South Africa abounds in mineral and agricultural resources, which help it gain an advantage in its economic exchanges with the other BRICS countries. However, due to its reliance on foreign investment and the external market, the global financial crisis struck a heavy blow on the economy. In 2012, South Africa's economic growth rate was only 2.5%, while inflation approached 6% and unemployment reached 25%. In addition, the economic downturn has caused social unrest. This new member of BRICS obliviously needs to prove itself by rejuvenating its economy. It also needs to help itself through economic coop-

eration with the other BRICS countries. Due to the fact that its economy is smaller than other member countries, and its economic growth rate is lower than the world average, South Africa's entry into the BRICS can be seen as being driven by political considerations. South Africa intends to enhance its international prestige in Africa and even the world at large by joining the group. For their part, the original BRIC nations wanted the grouping to be more representative of developing countries in the international arena. South Africa has high expectation for the political and economic cooperation with the BRICS mechanism.

III. The foundation and divergence of cooperation between China and the other BRICS countries

The foundation for cooperation between China and the other BRICS countries is based on their common economic and political interests. The five members are all developing countries with huge potential, each dreaming of being a big power. These common features help them share many common interests. However, disagreements are inevitable. As the strength of each member country grows, the "gold brick" would be disintegrated if no efforts were made to deepen mutual trust and to build up an effective mechanism for close cooperation and dispute settlement.

1. Common interests and divergence in economic development

The BRICS have strong complementarities in international trade. Each member state has its own distinctive mix of advantages such as market size, resources, labour services, science and technology. China's manufacturing industry, Brazil's abundant raw materials and developed animal husbandry, Russia's rich oil resources, India's information industry and South Africa's mineral industry, are highly complementary to one other, and constitute a booming market between the BRICS countries. China is a major importer of iron ore, soybeans, gold and gems from these countries, while it exports garments, shoes and hats, plastic products, chemicals, transportation equipment and machinery. This represents a highly complementary arrangement for economic cooperation between the BRICS countries. In 2010, China's bilateral trade with Brazil, Russia, India and South Africa increased by 56.2%, 37.6%, 35.3% and 49.6%, respectively, all of which were higher than China's global trade growth rate that year of 34.7%. Today, China is the largest trade partner of Brazil, Russia and South Africa, and the second largest trade partner of India. It is the largest export market of Brazil and South Africa and the third largest export market of India and the sixth largest export market of Russia. The BRICS market is playing a more and more important role in China's foreign trade. On the other hand, China's prestige in the market of BRICS countries is rising with each passing year. This lays a foundation for further economic cooperation.

However, we should be aware that BRICS is confronted by challenges such as an excessive reliance on the market of developed countries and intensifying trade friction. It should be remembered that, although the trade growth rate between the BRICS countries has increased rapidly, their mutual trade accounts for only 3% of the world total. In addition, mutual trade volume accounts for a low proportion in the total foreign trade of each member country. In 2011, exports and imports between Brazil and China took up 17.3% and 14.5% respectively of the gross exports and imports of each side. The export and import volume between India and China took up 6.2% and 11.9% of the gross export and import volume of each side respectively; the corresponding figures for trade between China and Russia were 7.1% and 16.3%, and for China and South Africa were 12.1% and 14.1% respectively. Moreover, with increasing exchange between China and the other BRICS countries, trade friction has been on the rise. For example, from 2002 to 2010, 188 cases of trade friction occurred between China and the other BRICS countries, accounting for 23.1% of China-related trade frictions. Nearly 80% of cases were anti-dumping. Furthermore, the imbalance of bilateral trade structures and the convergence of industrial structures and issues concerning the renminbi exchange rate have all given rise to trade friction between China and the other BRICS countries. These are serious concerns that need to be addressed by China and the other BRICS member countries in the coming economic reform.

Investment levels between the BRICS countries are very low. All member states have invested most in developed countries, though the BRICS countries are becoming richer and more attractive investment destinations. China's investment stock in Brazil, Russia, India and South Africa is still surprisingly low.

Reasons for the dearth of investment include the barriers that exist between the BRICS countries, similarities in industrial structure, imbalanced bilateral trade, a mismatch of resources and demand, and even cultural differences. The main factor, however, is the natural complementarity between the BRICS countries which can no longer satisfy the need for further economic cooperation. Therefore, member countries must make in-depth adjustment to their industrial structure and enhance coordination. If investment levels cannot be boosted, ties between the BRICS countries will continue to loosen and mutual trust will be eroded. Besides, their reliance on developed countries reveals a fundamental weakness despite their calls for a reform of the international system. To tackle this problem, China should work together with the other four member countries to reform their domestic economic structures and enhance exchange and coordination, establish specialised agencies such as trade and investment dispute settlement mechanisms and deepen cooperation and mutual trust.

2. Common interests and divergences in politics

In contrast with the great achievements in economic development, BRICS political cooperation in the political arena may be described as "prudent" and "ambitious".

The concept of "BRICS" was proposed as early as in 2001. However, it was not until in 2009 that the four countries, Brazil, Russia, India and China held the first summit meeting. Actually, no substantive promise was found in the Joint Communiqué issued at the meeting. Rather, it just appealed to implement the consensus reached at the London G20 Financial Summit - improve the international trade and investment environment, promise to push forward the reform of international financial institutions, and increase the representation of emerging and developing countries in international financial institutions. Face to the challenge of financial crisis, BRICS came together after eight years of talks. However, at the second summit meeting in 2010, the four member countries came to an agreement on "specific measures for cooperation and coordination" through consultation; the BRIC cooperative mechanism took initial shape and South Africa became a new member. At the Sanya summit meeting in 2011, the five countries established their status as the representative of developing countries with more confidence and used it to advocate reform of the international financial currency system, and "common and differential liability" on climate change and environmental issues. Such a contradiction precisely explains the urgent need for cooperation between the member countries.

As developing economies, the BRICS countries have gradually found that they have a common concern: only by reforming international institutions, enhancing their prestige and right to speak these institutions and reducing their reliance on the US dollar can they further develop their economies. However, they are aware that such a crucial reform cannot be achieved by the effort of a single member country. Take the IMF as an example. It stipulates that key decisions cannot be approved unless they receive 85% of all votes. Therefore, a country with 15% of the voting rights has veto power. As the EU countries have 32% of the voting rights and the US has 17%, the BRICS' road to reform is blocked by these developed countries. However, if all BRICS member countries cooperate, they perhaps may account for more than 15% of the voting rights to pave the way for the reform of the international financial system. In this respect, China, a leading country in the mechanism, should shoulder its responsibility and take the actions needed to propel and guide the other members to participate in reform. For example, they may establish a common "BRICS" financial institution for local currency settlement in trade between the member countries. This is also a route of the internationalisation of the renminbi.

To realise the dream of becoming big powers, the five developing BRICS countries will be confronted by many barriers set up by established developed countries. The topic of climate change and the environment is one of these barriers. In this respect, the BRICS fashion themselves into an image of developing countries and stand out for "common and differential liability", which conforms not only to their own interests, but also to the common interests in political cooperation between the BRICS.

With the expansion of national strength and powers of the BRICS states, their concerns and cooperation scope are also expanding. They have achieved economic benefits that have overflowed to the political arena such as cooperation in energy safety and anti-terrorism. In addition, "BRICS" is a platform that provides its member countries with a channel to express their opinions. For example, at the Sanya summit meeting, BRICS expressed their support of Russia's entry into the WTO. We can foresee that the BRICS summit will gradually develop into an important meeting deserving worldwide attention, which can influence international affairs of vital significance.

However, we should also foresee that, with the rise of BRICS, their divergent interests and frictions will also materialise. Let us not go into questions such as historic conflicts and power struggle between member countries. As a matter of fact, such issues should be addressed in the BRICS cooperation mechanism in future: how to coordinate the internal contradictions and potential conflicts between the members, how to resolve disputes between the rising powers, how to encourage benign competition instead of protectionism and how to increase strategic mutual trust. These issues also determine the depth of cooperation between the member countries. It is of vital importance for China, as a "pacemaker", to position itself in the BRICS mechanism to promote cooperation with member countries. Therefore, this is not only a policy of economic diplomacy but one that also involves the intricate situation of domestic reform.

IV. Development prospects for China's economic diplomacy towards the BRICS countries

China and the other BRICS countries have a solid foundation for cooperation, ranging from economic and political fields and to non-traditional areas of security. These emerging economies, which are at a similar development stage, have much in common and share considerable scope for complementarities. However, in terms of relations concerning China's economic diplomacy towards the other member countries, conflicts and friction between both sides are even more than those between China and developed countries. Moreover, both sides have a weak strategic mutual trust and substantive cooperation has yet to be achieved. Compounded by the financial crisis and following financial turbulence in recent years, a shadow has come over the BRICS concept, especially for Brazil and India.

In contrast with the suspicions of outsiders, leaders of the five member countries have expressed confidence. At the fifth summit meeting of BRICS in 2013, Chinese President Xi Jinping responded to the claim that the BIRCS were fading by quoting the phrase, "Like-minded people get on well in spite of being oceans apart". From the Durban Declaration released at this meeting, one may see that the five member states have begun substantive financial cooperation, established a development bank and made emergency storage arrangements. These actions should not be regarded as anti-Western, but rather as an attempt to deepen the cooperation mechanism and reduce their reliance on the West. Furthermore, compared with the declarations released at the previous two summit meetings, the Durban Declaration reflected more explicitly the common appeal in international affairs and attitude of the five member countries towards active participation in global governance.

Evaluating the development prospects for China's economic diplomacy both towards the BRICS mechanism and towards each of the other four member countries, we should first evaluate the influence of the financial crisis. The crisis was a double-edged sword, making the BRICS appreciate the practical significance of cooperation, while also exposing them to huge pressure of reform. Currently, all BRICS are under pressure from inflation and face challenges in economic structure. All the BRICS countries are vulnerable to these challenges, even China, whose economy is the strongest. Nevertheless, no one can afford to ignore the potential of sustained economic growth. As the markets of developed countries are sluggish, an emerging market is expected to be formed through the cooperation mechanism between China and the other member countries so as to stimulate economic growth and reduce reliance on developed economies. In view of the current situation, the focus of cooperation between China and the other member countries will still be in international finance. Particularly, after the financial crisis, priority has been given to the reform of international institutions, urging the developed countries to fulfil their responsibilities and to reform the international financial supervision system, etc.

The convergence of these five countries will exert huge influence. The nature of this cooperation between the BRICS countries and the pace at which cooperation proceeds will depend on the position of China, a core member of the BRICS, and the determination of the other member countries. In view of this, China should attach great importance to the BRICS platform so that it can facilitate China's participation in global governance, establish a new world order and enhance its international prestige. Moreover, China should take the initiative to make use of its pre-eminence in the BRICS, and actively guide the development orientation of the BRICS cooperation mechanism. While engaging in adjusting its domestic economic structure, China should enhance economic and trade cooperation and mutual trust through foreign investment and promote understanding and inclusiveness to the member countries.

Section 5 China's economic diplomacy towards Central Asian states

I. Introduction

Over the past decade, China's relations with Central Asia states have reached unprecedented levels of economic cooperation. For the last 20 years, trade turnover between China and five Central Asian countries has grown 100-fold. In 1992, trade turnover between the countries amounted to US$460m, rising by the end of 2012 to almost US$46bn.[18] Trade and economic relations should continue to grow rapidly in coming years, especially considering Chinese President Xi Jinping's visit to four Central Asian countries (excluding Tajikistan) from 3 to 13 September 2013. Xi made his first official visit to Turkmenistan, Kazakhstan, Uzbekistan and Kyrgyzstan as president of China, bringing investments worth a total of US$48bn. He hoped the visit could "signal the opening of a new silk road connecting the Eurasian landmass with East Asia through China, ushering in a new economic and political era".[19]

His grand tour of central Asia started with Turkmenistan. Ashgabat is a key partner of Beijing in the petroleum sector and the largest exporter of natural gas to China. As a matter of fact, Turkmenistan has the world's fourth or fifth large reserves of natural gas. On 4 September, Xi Jinping and Turkmen President Gurbanguly Berdymuhamedov put into operation the first line from the "Galkynysh gas field, which has been developed with the direct involvement of China National Petroleum Corporation (CNPC).[20] The project includes the construction of several gas processing plants, which in addition to 30bn cubic metres of natural gas, should ensure the supply of about 2m tons of sulphur and 210 tons of gas condensate. The total project cost is about US$10bn, of which US$8bn was provided by China in the form of loans. Moreover, according to other signed agreements, Turkmenistan will increase its gas supply to China from the current 40bn cubic metres a year to 65bn cubic metres by 2015.[21]

In Kazakhstan, CNPC acquired an 8% stake in a project to develop the promising Kashagan oil field. The two sides also signed an agreement to increase the supply

---

[18] "China and Central Asia trade increased by 100 times," ИА «Казинформ», May 28, 2012

[19] "Central Asia's new silk road, paved by China," *East Asia Forum*, October 26, 2013

[20] Mathieu Boulogne, Xi Jinping's Grand Tour of Central Asia: Asserting China's Growing Economic Clout (Washington: The George Washington University, 2013), 2

[21] Ibid., 2

of oil from Kazakhstan to China through the Atasu-Alashankou pipeline, transporting up to 20m tons a year. Kashagan is the largest oil and gas field in Kazakhstan. Located in the northern part of the Caspian Sea, its reserves are estimated at 4.8bn tons of oil and more than 1,000bn cubic metres of natural gas.[22] Development of the field is carried out by a consortium of the world's leading oil and gas companies including Eni, Total, Royal Dutch Shell, ExxonMobil and Inpex. By joining these shareholders, China has gained access to the largest oil field in the region.

Meanwhile, China has signed 31 agreements with Uzbekistan and investment deals worth US$15bn. Much of the investment concerned the establishment of new production facilities in Uzbekistan. For instance, Uzbekistan Reconstruction and Development Fund and China Development Bank signed an agreement on joint financing of prioritised investment projects worth a total of US$11.6bn. However, the most anticipated project concerned discussions for expanding the Central Asia-China pipeline. Actually, Uzbekistan is not only a country through which the Turkmen gas will be transported, but it has its own gas reserves that are exported to China. Since Xi Jinping's visit to Turkmenistan, it was decided to accelerate the launch of a third gas pipeline and construct a fourth one, but this issue had to be agreed with Uzbekistan. As a result, negotiations were successful, without triggering any objection from Uzbekistan.[23]

In Bishkek, capital of the Kyrgyz Republic, Xi Jinping and Kyrgyz President Almazbek Atambayev signed a joint declaration on 11 September announcing a strategic partnership between the two nations. China is mainly interested in Kyrgyzstan's transport and communications capabilities. Perhaps the main purpose of the visit was to agree on the route of the fourth Turkmenistan-China pipeline, which unlike the previous three must pass through the territory of Kyrgyzstan. China also agreed to provide cash-strapped Kyrgyzstan with some US$3bn in credits for energy and infrastructure projects, with US$1.4 of that going to build the pipeline extension through Kyrgyzstan to China.[24]

It is also worth noting Xi Jinping's speech at Nazarbayev University in Astana, Kazakhstan, where he proposed that China and Central Asian countries build an "economic belt along the Silk Road", a trans-Eurasian project spanning from the Pacific Ocean to the Baltic Sea. This proposed economic belt is inhabited by "close to 3bn people and represents the biggest market in the world with unparalleled potential". [25]

---

[22] "Central Asia: China Flexes Political and Economic Muscle," *Eurasianet, September* 12, 2013

[23] "Xi Jinping signs deals worth US$15b in Uzbekistan," *South China Morning Post*, 10 September 2013

[24] "Central Asia: China Flexes Political and Economic Muscle," *Eurasianet*, September 12, 2013

[25] "Xi proposes a "new Silk Road" with Central Asia," *China Daily*, September 8, 2013

In the sphere of economic and cultural exchanges Xi Jinping's visit has brought fruitful results. The leaders of China and four Central Asian countries have been unanimous about the need to establish long-term and stable cooperation in the energy field. At the same time, the signed deals clearly indicate Kazakhstan and Turkmenistan energy attractiveness for China, and the importance of the transit potential of Kyrgyzstan and Uzbekistan.

Yet it remains unclear what are the actual goals of China's diplomacy in Central Asia. What is hidden under the guise of "mutually profitable relations"? Does China attempt to dominate and seek to replace Russia as the leading regional power and supersede other global powers? Are regional and internal security concerns the key factors of an active economic policy? Some believe these issues are particularly relevant in light of the fact that China issued several multi-billion dollar loans to Central Asian states and that, by doing so, these states got into debt dependency.

This section attempts to explain the content and objectives of China's economic diplomacy in Central Asia. In order to better understand the specifics, it is important to start with an overall historical background of bilateral relations, then elaborate on the central question of the paper and finally come up with a conclusion.

II. Historical background

The relationship between China and Central Asia has a long history in which politics and economics are closely intertwined. Traditionally, Central Asia has been one of the key priorities of China's economic policy. In the heyday of the Silk Road (until the mid-2nd century AD) the territory of modern Central Asia served as a transport bridge between China and Europe. That was when China was an external driving force of economic development in the region as well as the main source of scientific knowledge and technology. However, the development of maritime transport in the Age of Discovery (16th Century AD) caused a reorientation of world trade overland routes (which was the basis of the Silk Road) to the sea. The essential cheapness of sea transport led to the economic and geographic isolation of Central Asia.

In the second half of the 19th century, Central Asia was part of the Russian Empire and consequently the region's economic ties were mainly with Russia. As a result, this region broke out of economic and geographic isolation and obtained a substantial intensification of economic ties. After the fall of the Russian Empire, a new stage of Russian-Central Asian economic relations took place. Until the collapse of the Soviet Union, Russia had been a powerhouse of economic development in Central Asia, having a decisive influence on the formation of the region's modern economic character. During this time, economic ties between China and Central Asia were almost suspended.

The collapse of the Soviet Union in 1991 and the sovereignty gained by Central Asian countries was a starting point of the revival of active bilateral relations. Of course, Central Asian countries have also been the focus of major powers since 1991. There was the so-called "geopolitical pluralism" characterised by the presence of global actors in Central Asian regional politics, pursuing their own goals and interests. It is not surprising that China, which has long borders with Central Asian states, has become one of the most active players in this game. Beijing implemented a new economic policy in Central Asia, as part of an overall strategy that reflected China's transformation into a centre of the global economy and world politics.

Nonetheless, the first half of the 1990s was characterised by cautious behaviour. In that period, China kept an eye on the newly-emerged independent states. It established trade contacts, mostly in the form of "shuttle trade", a practice where traders shuttle back and forth across borders to buy and sell goods. The development of full economic relations at the time was not prominent on the agenda of the PRC's policy in Central Asia and was regarded by Beijing as an opportunity to stimulate the economy of Xinjiang Uighur autonomous region, which borders Central Asia, rather than any as a bigger priority for the country as a whole. This was largely due to the uncertainty of China's long-term interests in the region and the limited capacity economic, political and diplomatic capacity of the PRC.

But from the mid-90s, China has begun to take more focused and practical steps in economic influence in the region. Moreover, the discovery of significant oil and gas reserves in Central Asia at that time, along with other natural resources and a potentially large market (with a population of about 55m people) has been regarded by Beijing in the context of the developing inland areas of China.

Because of economic, geographic and other factors, one of the main tasks in this strategy has been Xinjiang's development. Using the geographical proximity of Central Asia, Beijing hoped to tap the region's potential for the rapid industrialisation of Xinjiang and also to promote Chinese products through Xinjiang directly to the markets of Central Asia and in turn stimulate economic growth in its bordering territories. Therefore, a significant impetus was given to the development of economic relations along with the intensification of cooperation in the field of security (including the framework of the "Shanghai Five") in the second half of the 1990s. This has been reflected in the PRC's investment activities in Central Asia (mainly oil and gas) and the dramatic increase in trade cooperation.

It is also believed that the intensification of bilateral trade relations was largely facilitated by the financial and economic crisis in Russia in 1998[26], which led to a sharp decrease in the scale of Russian-Central Asian economic relations. At the time, countries in the region began to show increasing interest in imports of Chinese products, mainly consumer goods and engineering products. Xinjiang, in turn, has started to act as a marketplace, accumulating 60-70% of Sino-Central Asian trade.

Since the beginning of the 21st century, China has intensified its economic relations with Central Asia largely due to the strengthened US presence in and around the region. Chinese policy-makers sought to prevent the scenario in which they could find themselves at a disadvantage and at the same time ensuring unimpeded access to the resource-rich region. Beijing has identified economic activities (exports, imports, investment and loans) as a core element of its economic diplomacy in Central Asia. Meanwhile, China laid emphasis on a fundamental strengthening of its position by increasing the volume of trade, and intensifying investment and financing activities, especially in terms of granting a wide range of credits to Central Asian states.

III. China's economic diplomacy towards Central Asia

1. Content

The content of China's economic diplomacy covers a range of economic tools implemented by China in Central Asia, and in particular the importance of energy.

Since the emergence of five independent states in Central Asia, their hydrocarbon resources acted like a magnet to various states. The most active in the region have been Russia, the US, the EU and China. Huge interest was expressed by American and European oil companies. Most attention was focused on Turkmenistan, with its significant gas reserves, and Kazakhstan, which has the largest oil deposits in this region.

Numerous international consortiums hurried to stake out a position in the potentially rich oil and gas deposits. Oil and gas company investments have played a key role in the development of hydrocarbon deposits, allowing Central Asian countries to achieve economic recovery and stabilise the political situation. China, however, was steady in developing its energy priorities for the region. With the increasing needs of the Chinese economy for hydrocarbon resources, Beijing raised interest in expanding access to oil and gas in Central Asia. Therefore, in the past decade, China has increased its share in the energy sector.

---

[26] David M. Kotz, *Russia's Financial Crisis: The Failure of Neoliberalism*? (University of Massachusetts, 1998), 35

China's participation in Kazakhstan is defined by the existence of oil companies such as CNPC and Sinopec. In fact, the Kazakhstan-China oil pipeline is China's first direct oil import pipeline allowing oil imports from Central Asia. It runs from Kazakhstan's Caspian shore to Xinjiang in China. The pipeline is owned by CNPC and the Kazakh oil company KazMunayGas. By 2008, its capacity amounted to 17.2m tons a year. Nevertheless, Kazak and Chinese officials stated that the existing Kazakhstan-China oil pipeline capacity would be expanded to 20m tons of oil by the following year.[27] In addition to this, China and Kazakhstan signed an official agreement on CNPC's acquisition of an 8.33% share in the Kashagan offshore oil project for US$5bn. Regarding Turkmenistan, energy cooperation is centred upon the Turkmenistan-China gas pipeline, which was put into operation in 2007 when Gurbanguly Berdymukhamedov and Hu Jintao signed an agreement to build a gas pipeline.[28] China and Uzbekistan are tied to the joint exploration and development of the Mingbulak gas field and the PRC is also involved in hydropower resource projects in Kyrgyzstan.

The intensification of trade and economic relations with Central Asia allows Beijing to use reciprocal economic and resource potential to develop its western territories. At present, the volume of trade between Xinjiang and Central Asian countries is more than 80% of total bilateral trade. But still economic relationships with Central Asia are deeply imbalanced. With the exception of Kazakhstan, the volume of trade with the other republics remains insignificant.[29] Bilateral economic relations between China and Kazakhstan are considered the strongest in the region. At present, China is the largest trading partner of Kazakhstan. Sino-Kazakh bilateral trade turnover amounted to US$25.6bn in 2012. This figure totalled US$13.57bn in the first six months of 2013, increasing by 23% compared with the same period of 2012. It is expected the volume of the trade turnover will exceed US$30bn in 2013.[30]

Granting credit and finance is one of China's most efficient tools in economic diplomacy. In the first decade of the 21st century, Beijing has begun to actively use the practice of granting targeted loans to Central Asian states on relatively favourable terms to the latter. The volume of financial resources was around US$25bn by 2010. But Xi Jinping's recent "Grand Tour" to the region has brought a new

---

[27] "Нефтепровод Казахстан-Китай будет расширен до 20 млн тонн нефти," *Kursivkz*, 8 October 2013

[28] "Central Asia-China Gas Pipeline To Start Service Next Year," *Asiaport Daily* News (Downstream Today), 7 July 2008

[29] Mathieu Boulogne, Xi Jinping's Grand Tour of Central Asia: Asserting China's Growing Economic Clout (Washington: The George Washington University, 2013), 3

[30] "China's trade with Kazakhstan to top US$30bn in 2013 – envoy," *Azernews*, 7 September 2013

package of investment and loans worth around US$48bn.[31] At the end of the 1990s, China's financial resources in Central Asia accounted for less than US$1bn (provided in the form of investment only to the oil and gas industry in Kazakhstan), yet during the first 10 years of the 21st century, the total volume increased by more than 20 times.

Thus, China's economic diplomacy has been built on three fundamental pillars: securing increasing demand for energy; active trade policy expressed in trade turnover expansion; and an investment policy providing multi-billion dollar loans.

2. Objectives

The second objective is to diversify import sources. Central Asian oil and gas fields constitute a reserve required by the PRC against the background of instability in the Middle East and North Africa from which it receives almost 80% of all imported energy supplies. In particular, the loss of Chinese companies in Libya during the civil war was substantial. The threat of disruption to supplies from these regions is one reason for the PRC's revitalised interest in Central Asia. In this case, attention is drawn to the fact that Uzbekistan is a leading recipient of Chinese investment. Most likely, this is due to the fact that the US provides massive financial aid to Tashkent, coupled with the active participation in the construction of railway lines to Afghanistan. In turn, Beijing does not want to lose its leadership position in the Uzbek economy. At the same time, Kazakhstan and Kyrgyzstan have a pro-Russian foreign policy, which is consistent with China's current interests considering Russia is an ally in a number of international issues.

Another reason for China's interest in Central Asia is the slowdown in China's exports. The central government in Beijing has cited stimulating domestic demand as a key economic policy priority. In this regard, the development of its western provinces will contribute to the growth of domestic demand, and to a more stable security situation in western provinces. The steady development of Xinjiang is very important for China in terms of internal security. That is why the economic factor is considered as one of the most significant in stabilising the situation in Xinjiang. In addition, uncertainty after 2014 associated with the reduction of Western troops in Afghanistan could lead to issues of regional security and stability, especially as both the PRC and Central Asia have borders with Afghanistan. Therefore, the intention of the Chinese leadership to establish new long-term partnership agreements with Central Asian countries seems to be reasonable.

---

[31] Mathieu Boulogne, Xi Jinping's Grand Tour of Central Asia: Asserting China's Growing Economic Clout (Washington: The George Washington University, 2013), 3

Given the size of the Chinese economy and the rapid development of almost all its industries, the main engine of economic development in the "China-Russia-Central Asia" context is seemingly that China could convert its economic success into political dividends. This raises the question of how Russia, as the main military and political force in the region, will respond to China's increased economic influence in Central Asia. Actually, the Kremlin is trying to include former Soviet republics to its regional Customs Union block, which so far includes Belarus and Kazakhstan. Besides, Moscow hopes to gain control over the supply of Kazakh oil to the EU so that the oil is being pumped through Russian pipelines instead of alternatives to the south. With regards to China's economic diplomacy, Russia has not officially expressed any great concern. Alexey Maslov, who is the head of the Higher Economic School of Oriental Studies in Moscow, notes that China's recent policy is an "encroachment on traditional sphere of Russian interests."[32] But all this is to be expected because China's presence in Central Asia was observed in 2008-09 during the economic crisis. "At the same time, by providing large loans to Kazakhstan, Uzbekistan and Tajikistan, China supplied their economies. It seems to me, these loans turned into a canal linking Central Asia with China. Yet China tends to use another important thesis. China is trying to confirm the thesis of a common historical destiny with Central Asia. This initiative comes from both China and Russia. This suggests that in the international arena, China arguably coordinated with Russian initiatives and therefore Russia turned a blind eye on the activity of China in Central Asia." Alexander Rahr is an expert at the German-Russian Forum on relations between Russia and Central Asia. He says: "It was not easy. But the choice was made. Because Putin is unable to simultaneously struggle with NATO and the West, on the one hand, and China for influence in Central Asia, on the other hand. However, the growing influence of China in Central Asia appeared to be comforting for Russia because of the lack of serious ideological differences between Beijing and Moscow. In other words, it is diplomatic wisdom. But still I have a firmly held view that Beijing pursues political objectives in Central Asia."[33]

Nonetheless, it is clear for the Central Asian leadership that economic cooperation with the PRC is based on mutual political trust and China has always understood the mental and cultural identity of Central Asia. Unlike the US or the EU, it shows respect for the political and economic course chosen by Central Asian states. During his tour of the region, Xi Jinping reaffirmed that China would never interfere in the internal affairs of Central Asia countries and never seek a dominant role in the region or foster its sphere of influence.

---

[32] "Китай - Центральная Азия: отношения перешли в "золотую эпоху"?, Gezitter, 30 September 2013

[33] Ibid

3. Conclusion

Since 2001, the economic component came to the fore of China's regional policy in Central Asia. One of the most important indicators of this component is the massive increase in Chinese financial resources allocated to the region.

Currently, China's economic policy there is to secure the most favourable external conditions to achieve a breakthrough in terms of future sustainable growth and subsequent transformation into one of the global economic centres. Trying to get closer to solving these tasks, China has decided to more actively involve Central Asia in its policy by making a choice in favour of strengthening positions in the national economies of Central Asia via the intensification of project and investment activity and an increase loans to these countries.

The growing economic cooperation between China and Central Asian countries is mutually beneficial. However, there are questions about the long-term impact of China's economic diplomacy the region. Particularly in Kazakhstan, some experts perceive the growing presence of Chinese national companies and the influx of Chinese labour as a demographic threat to the population. Obviously, the reasonable alternative to wide-ranging negative perceptions could be to put in place an integrated and mutually beneficial multilateral cooperation including China, Russia and Central Asia. In this regard, it is necessary to exploit the potential of the Shanghai Cooperation Organisation, to transform it into a powerful economic bloc. As a result, the development of mutually beneficial interstate economic cooperation between China and Central Asian countries requires consolidation of the political will of all these countries in terms of the most effective use of SCO potential for the joint development and implementation of strategic initiatives within the organisation.

Section 6 Southeast Asia

I. Guiding concept and goals of China's economic diplomacy towards Southeast Asia

China sticks to the diplomatic guideline of being a good partner to its neighbours and the diplomatic policy of fostering an amicable, secure and prosperous neighbourly environment. From the perspective of economic development, with the advancement of globalisation and economic integration, China should depend on both the domestic market and resources and overseas markets and resources to develop its economy. At the 10th meeting of diplomatic envoys in August 2004, Chinese President Hu Jintao pointed out: "We should enhance economic and cultural exchanges and push forward the implementation of the strategy of open-door to the outside world by integrating "bringing in" and "going out". Southeast

Asian countries are important neighbours of China. Whether from the perspective of neighbouring diplomacy or from an economic perspective, Southeast Asia has been a priority of China's diplomacy. China's economic diplomacy during the era of Hu Jintao was accomplished under the guidance of the "going global" strategy.

The main objectives of China's economic diplomacy towards Southeast Asia are: first: deepening bilateral economic and trade relations for mutual benefit and implementing the foreign policy of "prospering neighbours"; second: playing down regional conflicts and enhancing political and security mutual trust; third: upgrading cooperation between China and the ASEAN.

II. Practice of China's economic diplomacy towards Southeast Asia

In the period of Hu Jintao, China's economic diplomacy towards Southeast Asia was accomplished jointly by the central government, local government, Chinese embassies and consulates in the ASEAN countries, agencies of commercial counsellors and China's transnational companies. The main forms included: building up regional cooperation platforms; pressing ahead foreign trade and investment; providing economic aid.

1. Building regional cooperation platforms

The China-ASEAN Free Trade Area (CAFTA) is an important institutional arrangement of China's economic diplomacy towards the ASEAN. The establishment of CAFTA was a tremendous success and a major manifestation of China's economic diplomacy towards Southeast Asia during the presidency of Hu Jintao. The concept of establishing CAFTA was first put forward by China in 2000. After the approval of China and the ASEAN Senior Officials Conference and Economic Ministers Meeting, the proposal was officially announced at the fifth 10+1 summit (ASEAN plus China) in 2001. In 2002, both sides signed the Framework Agreement on China-ASEAN Comprehensive Economic Cooperation and decided to establish CAFTA in 2010 and officially launched the construction of the free trade area. The scope of cooperation between the two sides involves fields such as cargo and service trade and investment. In January 2004, China began to implement the "Early Harvest Package", providing tariff concessions to cargo from ASEAN countries. In November 2004, both sides signed the Goods Trade Agreement and Agreement on Dispute Settlement Mechanism. According to this agreement, China cut tariffs for 3,408 kinds of products and its average import tariff to ASEAN decreased from 9.9% to 8.1% since July 2005. In 2007, China made another tariff cut for 5,375 kinds of products and the average tariff decreased to 5.8%. Also, both sides signed a Service Trade Agreement in January 2007. Two years later, an investment agreement was signed between the two sides. In January 2010, CAFTA was established as scheduled, signalling a breakthrough in China's economic diplomacy towards ASEAN.

China also attaches great importance to economic diplomacy towards the sub-regions of Southeast Asia. For example, economic cooperation in the Greater Mekong Sub-region (GMS) is one of the manifestations of China's economic diplomacy towards Southeast Asia. It is a mechanism in which the ADB took the lead in 1992 and six countries (China, Vietnam, Laos, Cambodia, Burma and Thailand) along the Lancang-Mekong River jointly participate. China attaches importance to economic cooperation in the GMS and actively pushes forward the improvement of the regional cooperation mechanism. Since the second GMS summit meeting in 2005, the Chinese government has spared no effort in cooperating with the GMS in the following nine fields: transportation, energy, telecommunications, the environment, agriculture, human resources, tourism, trade and investment and played an active role in various coordination mechanisms. Furthermore, China is committed to encouraging the local governments to establish trans-boundary economic cooperation areas with neighbouring countries such as Burma and Vietnam through the likes of the China Ruili-Burma Muse, China Boten-Laos Borten, and the China Red River -Vietnam Lao Cai. The construction of the three economic cooperation areas is well under way. It is noteworthy that Ruili Pilot Site bordering Burma has become one of the major development zones of the NDRC. These trans-boundary economic cooperation areas are also important manifestations of China's economic diplomacy towards Southeast Asia.

2. Foreign trade

In China's economic diplomacy towards the ASEAN, the Chinese government has built up a platform for economic and trade exchanges through commercial and trade negotiations and dialogue with ASEAN's top leadership. In October 2003, Premier Wen Jiabao attended the seventh China-ASEAN Summit Meeting at which he officially proposed that, from 2004, the China-ASEAN Expo be held in Nanning, Guangxi Zhuang autonomous region. This proposal received widespread support from all leaders of the 10 ASEAN countries. Since the establishment of the China-ASEAN Expo, it has yielded substantial results, promoting economic cooperation and mutual visits between the two sides.

For a long time, ASEAN has been one of China's important trade partners. Except for a few years, bilateral trade volume has maintained a rapid growth rate. Construction of China-ASEAN has furthered the bilateral economic and trade relationship. In 2002, the total volume of trade between China and ASEAN amounted to USS$54.767bn; ASEAN was China's fifth largest trade partner; and China was ASEAN's third largest trade partner. In 2003, the total volume of trade between the two sides totalled USS$78.22bn. In 2004, the figure reached US$100bn. In 2007, it registered US$200bn, fulfilling the set goal. By 2012, the bilateral trade volume had amounted to US$400bn, with an average growth rate of 22%, 7.3

times that of the 2002 total. By 2013, China had become ASEAN's largest trade partner and ASEAN was the third largest trade partner of China. Meanwhile, it remained China's fourth largest export market and the second largest source of imports. In addition, great achievements were made in the opening of and exchanges in service trade.

Figure 4.2: Trade between China and ASEAN (2002-12)

Unit: US$100bn

Year	Import& Export	Exports	Imports	Balance of trade	Year-on-year growth rate of imports and exports (%)
2002	54.767	23.569	31.198	-7.629	31.6
2003	78.26	30.93	47.33	-16.4	42.9
2004	105.88	42.902	62.978	-20.076	35.29
2005	130.37	55.371	74.999	-19.628	23.3
2006	160.84	71.314	89.526	-18.212	23.37
2007	202.508	94.139	108.369	-14.23	25.9
2008	231.117	114.142	116.974	-2.832	14
2009	213.011	106.297	106.714	-0.417	-7.8
2010	292.776	138.207	154.569	-16.362	37.5
2011	362.854	170.083	192.771	-22.688	23.9
2012	400.093	204.272	195.821	8.451	10.3

Data source: Department of Asian Affairs of China's Ministry of Commerce http://yzs.mofcom.gov.cn/

Trade volumes between China and Malaysia, China and Singapore and China and Thailand have been the fastest-growing. Trade between China and Southeast Asian countries has maintained rapid growth. In particular, trade between China and Laos and trade between China and Vietnam are most noteworthy.

Figure: Import and export volume between China and Southeast Asian countries

Unit: US$m

	2002	2005	2009	2012	Growth rate (2012:2002)
Malaysia	1,427	3,070	5,197	9,483	564.5%
Singapore	1,403	3,315	4,786	6,927	393.7%
Thailand	856	2,181	3,819	6,975	715.1%
Indonesia	793	1,679	2,839	6,623	734.7%
Vietnam	326	820	2,105	5,044	1,445.2%
The Philippines	526	1,756	2,054	3,638	591.6%

Figure *(continued)*

	2002	2005	2009	2012	Growth rate (2012:2002)
Burma	86	121	290	697	709.1%
Cambodia	28	56	94	292	958.8%
Laos	6	13	75	172	2,590.4%
Brunei	26	26	42	163	518.5%

Data source: National Bureau of Statistics (NBS) http://www.stats.gov.cn/tjsj/

3. Foreign investment

As Southeast Asia and China are close neighbours with similar cultural backgrounds, it is natural that there has been considerable foreign investment. At the end of 2003, China's direct investment in ASEAN countries amounted to US$587m. At the end of 2005, the figure reached a new high of US$1.256bn. By the end of 2010, it had amounted to US$14.35bn, a 50% increase compared with that of 2009. The investment scale expanded drastically. China's direct investment in ASEAN increased in 2008 by nearly 2.57 times compared with that of 2007. Due to the financial crisis in 2009, the growth rate of China's investment in ASEAN slowed down but investment volume still increased by 8.6% over that of 2008. In 2010, China's investment in ASEAN resumed to rapid growth, increasing by 63% compared with that of 2009 (refer to the figure below). By the end of June 2013, the cumulative amount of Chinese investment in ASEAN countries was nearly US$30bn, about 5.1% of China's FDI. ASEAN has become the fourth largest economy in terms of China's FDI. Moreover, the relative ranking of Chinese investment in ASEAN is on the rise. In 2000, China's FDI in ASEAN ranked 11th in terms of ASEAN'S absorption of FDI. In 2009, China climbed up to fifth place. By 2010, China had become the largest investor in Burma, Laos and Cambodia. The status of China's investment in other ASEAN countries is also on the rise.

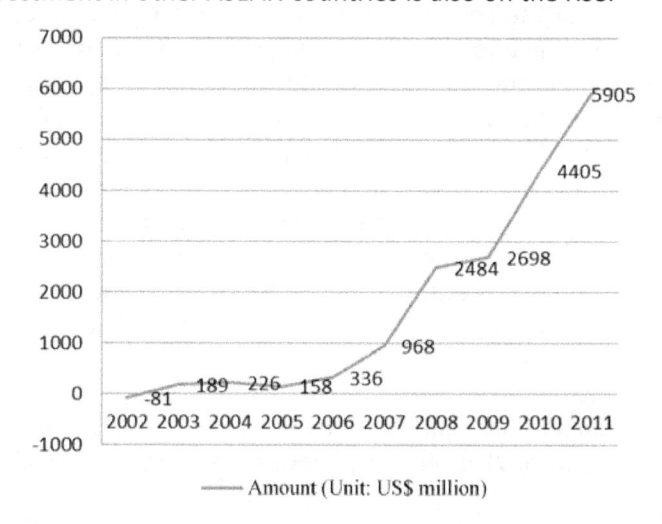

Amount (Unit: US$ million)

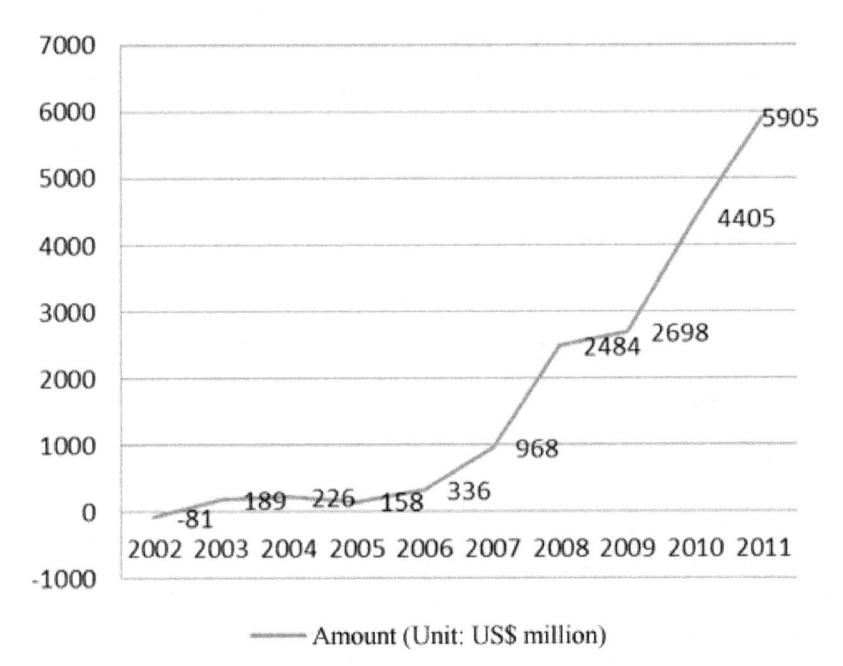

Figure: Flow of China's FDI in ASEAN (2002-11)

Data source: Statistics Bulletin on China's Foreign Direct Investment

China's investment in ASEAN is accomplished through Chinese enterprises' "going global", with the Chinese government playing a leading role. With the further development of investment, Chinese enterprises, which used to focus on contract engineering, have shifted to fields such as infrastructure construction, electric power, energy, telecommunications, mining and manufacturing.

As energy is one of the key projects of its investment in Southeast Asia, China has made unremitting efforts to ensure its energy safety. Burma is a key energy supplier to China and transpiration corridor. In March 2006, the governments of China and Burma signed an official agreement on constructing oil pipelines at Nay Pyi Taw. In March 2009, both sides signed a government agreement on building a crude oil and natural gas pipeline. In June 2010, Chinese Premier Wen Jiabao and Burmese Prime Minister Thein Sein announced the official construction of the oil and gas pipeline. China-Burma Crude Oil Pipeline will start from Maday Island, passing through Pakhine state, Magway division, Mandalay and Shan state, and enter Ruili, Yunnan province, before passing through Dali, Chuxiong and ending in Kunming.

In addition, as China's high-speed rail technology becomes more mature, many heads of state, political VIPs and delegations speak highly of China's railway modernisation. Southeast Asia was the first chosen destination for China's high-speed railway. So far, China has negotiated with countries such as Laos, Cambodia, Thailand, Malaysia, Singapore and Burma on high-speed railway cooperation projects and has made achievements in countries on the Indo-China peninsula. Since President Xi Jinping took office, China has sped up its steps in "high-speed railway" diplomacy.

4. Financial aid

Financial aid is another important means of China's economic diplomacy. Southeast Asian countries are one of the important regions where China provides financial aid.

China renders financial aid to Southeast Asia in the following ways: humanitarian aid, reducing and cancelling debts and concessional loans.

In terms of humanitarian aid, many countries in Southeast Asia were affected by the Indian Ocean Tsunami in December 2004, causing heavy casualties and property losses. The Chinese government provided goods and materials valued at Rmb21.63m without delay and sent an international rescue team to the affected countries. Later, it added to the amount of assistance, raising the total to Rmb690m. At the end of 2006, the Philippines was lashed by a typhoon. The Chinese government provided goods and materials of Rmb5m and spot exchange of US$200,000. In 2008, Burma was hit by a tropical storm. China offered US$500,000 of spot exchange and US$500,000 of material aid. Later, China provided a supplementary aid of Rmb30m to the country.

In addition, China has reduced and cancelled debts owed to China. Since 2002, China began to implement the Asian Debt Reduction Plan. For example, it reduced and exempted all due debts that Cambodia owed China in 2002. China reduced and exempted three sums of interest-free loans that Laos owed to China in 2003 and interest-free loans that the Laos government owed to China in 2004. In 2003, China exempted Burma's two sums of interest-free loans owed to China. In 2010, China exempted a debt of more than US$200mthat Cambodia owed to China.

China has also provided concessional loans to Southeast Asian countries and improved their infrastructure construction through project cooperation. In 2012, the Chinese government provided concessional loans of US$302m to Cambodia for the country's highway and water conservancy projects. In addition, it provided concessional loans of US$112m to the Philippines in aid of its water supply in Ungar and a second-phase project of pipeline renovation.

To promote cooperation in economic development, trade and investment between China and ASEAN, to break away from traditional aid featuring unilateral capital or goods and material output without pursuing economic returns and to explore a new-type and long-lasting aid mechanism, the Chinese government has decided to render its support to infrastructure construction in ASEAN countries. This is also a reflection of China's economic diplomacy towards Southeast Asia against the backdrop of the financial crisis.

In 2009, Premiere Wen Jiabao declared at Boao Forum for Asia that China would establish the "China-ASEAN Investment Cooperation Fund" totalling US$10bn to support regional infrastructure construction in fields such as bilateral infrastructure, energy resources and information communication. Chinese Foreign Minister Yang Jiechi said that China would provide ASEAN countries with credit and loans worth US$15bn, including concessional loans of US$1.7bn within the coming three or five years. In 2010, the China-ASEAN Investment Cooperation Fund officially went into operation, which made China the third largest capital source of ASEAN countries after the IMF and the ADB.

Section 7 Caribbean-China economic relations: what are the implications?

I. Introduction

Traditionally, the Caribbean's closest economic relations were with the US, Canada and Europe, and it is only in recent times that the islands have diversified their relations to include other partners. Ties with North America were informed primarily by geostrategic considerations, the US, and Canada to a lesser extent, seeing the Caribbean as having significance particularly in the context of the Cold War due to its geographical location. Ties with Europe were based on a historical colonial relationship. Traditional economic relations with China were established from the Chinese migrants who came to work in the Caribbean after the abolition of African slavery. Current geopolitical considerations and changes in the global economy have led the Caribbean to engage in a new type of relationship with China. This engagement has several implications for Caribbean development as well as for the Caribbean's foreign relations with other partners.

II. China's growth in the world economy

In 2003, a Goldman Sachs study projected that China's economy would be larger than that of the US by 2041 and the second largest economy by 2016; it was projected to overtake Germany by 2007 and Japan by 2015. In terms of per capita income it was projected that China's could match developed economies by 2050 (about US$30,000 per capita at the 2003 level). In terms of currency movements, China's renminbi could be worth twice as much by 2013 if growth was sustained and the exchange rate was allowed to float freely. In terms of growth patterns, it was projected that while there would be a slowdown, high investment rates, a large labour force and "steady convergence" would allow China to become the largest economy by 2041 (Wilson and Purushothaman 2003). On average, China has experienced close to double-digit annual growth rates for the last 30 years. In 2009, the Chinese economy grew by 8.7% while that of the US and the EU went into recession. China will therefore be the main driver of global growth, creating opportunities for a market for Latin American and Caribbean exports. Chinese overseas investment grew from less than US$1bnbefore 2001 to more than US$60bn in 2010 (Chen 2011). The phenomenal rise of China provides an attractive option for the Caribbean. The specific factors driving the Caribbean's interest in China are outlined below.

III. The Caribbean's interest in China

Caribbean states are drawn to the prospect of China contributing to their economic and social development. More specifically, China is able to provide development assistance, investment and an opportunity to diversify the Caribbean's trade and economic relations. The Caribbean views China as an important source of development aid, foreign direct investment (FDI) and trade for generating long-term growth and development in the region. Therefore, China's membership of the Caribbean Development Bank and the Inter-American Development Bank is important for deeper financial and economic cooperation (China Daily 2010).

Second, the Caribbean sees China as a voice for Southern countries and an intermediary between the Caribbean and developed countries in multilateral forums. In essence, China is seen to be able to bridge the gap between developed and developing countries, in particular, small and vulnerable ones.

Further, the Caribbean wishes to align with China, because of the potential that China holds for transforming the global economic order.

Third, China presents an alternative to aid and development assistance from the US and EU. The Caribbean has decreased in importance to both the EU and the US. The African, Caribbean and Pacific Group of States (ACP)is no longer considered to be a relevant framework to the EU. Additionally, among the three regions in the ACP, Africa has stolen the spotlight and the Caribbean and the Pacific have been marginalised. The Caribbean saw declining US interest, aid and assistance from the beginning of the 1990s. Caribbean countries are particularly attracted by the Chinese policy of neutrality, non interference and ease of access to Chinese loans. Along with other emerging players in the Caribbean, China therefore represents a counterweight to the economic and political influence of the EU and the US.

We now turn to the Caribbean's interest in China and examine the reasons why it has embraced China as a partner.

IV. China's interest in the Caribbean

First, the "One China Policy" plays a major role in defining China's economic relations with the Caribbean. Historically, China's interest in the region were driven by its ambitions to usurp Caribbean diplomatic support for Taiwan. Taiwan needs support as it continues to seek recognition at the UN and in other multilateral forums and has been courting leaders with aid for infrastructural and development projects. China, too, is very generous to countries supporting the "One China Policy". Both the People's Republic of China and Taiwan continue to battle in the Caribbean using aid and grants as weapons as they vie for supremacy.

Second, and more recently, the motivation for China's actions in the region has evolved from the narrow One China Policy and is now also being driven by larger, global geostrategic interests. China's foreign policy position towards the Caribbean is a reflection of its broader foreign policy objectives in an increasingly globalised economy. Starting from the late 1970s, China undertook economic and diplomatic reform driving it to seek and receive foreign investment, technology and expertise. Since then, the People's Republic has emerged as a major global exporter, increased its membership and participation in international organisations (Dumbaugh 2008) and extended its tentacles to various parts of the globe, including the Caribbean. Current relations between the Caribbean and China must therefore be seen in the context of the forces of economic globalisation that have created opportunities for the rise of China as a global player, fuelling the need for new markets, investment opportunities and new sources of raw materials to sustain its economic growth.

Third, China is also interested in the Caribbean as part of its objectives to attain food and energy security and sustain its rapid economic growth. China's growth is happening at a phenomenal rate and so are its energy needs. China therefore wants to get its hands on oil reserves wherever they exist, and the Caribbean is one such place. The Caribbean is a rich source of minerals: asphalt and gas in Trinidad and Tobago; bauxite in Jamaica and Guyana; and timber and minerals in Guyana. The Caribbean also has vast amounts of maritime resources and Guyana, Belize and Suriname have land for agricultural production (Bernal 2010).

Fourth, the Caribbean provides an attractive market for Chinese products and investment. The Caribbean, including Cuba and the Dominican Republic and the Overseas Countries and Territories (OCTs), has a combined population of about 40m, offering a market for Chinese products. Additionally, the Caribbean can be an entry point for Chinese products to the US, Canada and EU. CARICOM countries provide a 'production platform' due to preferential arrangements provided by the Caribbean Basin Economic Recovery Act (CBERA), the Caribbean-Canada Trade Agreement (CARIBCAN) and the CARIFORUM-EU EPA. The Caribbean also provides investment and business openings for Chinese firms and employment of Chinese labour (Bernal 2010).

Fifth, China's presence in the Caribbean is part of its strategy towards acquiring big power status. China's behaviour is indicative of its ambitions towards having a global reach and exerting influence across various regions of the globe. China is doing this on several fronts, and can be seen in the spread of Chinese firms and investments beyond traditional regions such as the Americas and its efforts to influence the agenda of entire regions. China has been trying to do this through its participation in regional institutions such as the Inter-American Development Bank and the Caribbean Development Bank. Its desire to participate in regional and multilateral forums in the Caribbean and Latin America was stated in a 2008 policy document towards this region.

The next section examines how these mutual interests are manifested in economic relations between the two parties.

V. Caribbean-China economic relations

Trade, investment and development cooperation

China's economic relations with the Caribbean are largely bilateral in nature although the China Caribbean Economic and Trade Cooperation forum represents a pseudo regional approach. The Third Trade and Economic Forum in September 2011 points to a deepening of China-Caribbean relations. At the forum, China promised US$1bn in preferential loans for Caribbean economic development; US$1bn from the China Development Bank for special commercial loans towards infrastructural development; a donation of US$1m to the CARICOM Development Fund; approximately 2,500 training opportunities and 30 opportunities for studying master's degrees in China; support and training for natural disaster mitigation and prevention, and support for increasing and diversification of exports (Wang 2011). Below we undertake a brief analysis of China's trade with CARICOM.

Figure 1 - Value of CARICOM trade with China 2001-2010

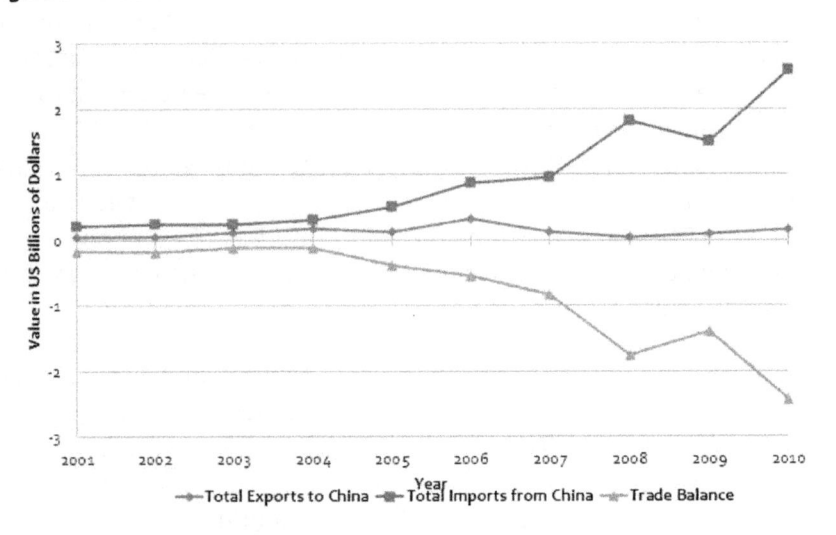

Source: Based on International Trade Centre calculations

Figure 1 indicates that CARICOM trade with China is on the increase; however it is overwhelmingly in China's favour. Except for 2009, imports from China have grown steadily in between 2001and 2010. CARICOM exports to China have not seen a similar pattern, increasing only slightly up to 2004, and fluctuating between 2005 and 2010, with the highest increase in 2006. Therefore the trade deficit is getting progressively larger except in 2009 but there was a widening of this deficit again in 2010.

Table 1: Value of CARICOM's top 10 Exports to China, 2001-10 (US$ thousands)

Product label	Total value(US$), 2001-10
All products	1,262,001
Inorganic chemicals, precious metal compound, isotopes	711,037
Iron and steel	173.679
Mineral fuels, oils, distillation products, etc	95,145
Wood and articles of wood, wood charcoal	94,531
Organic chemicals	61,076
Ores, slag and ash	41,254
Copper and articles thereof	18,636
Aluminium and articles thereof	17,054
Articles of iron or steel	11,542
Electrical, electronic equipment	10,503

Source: Based on International Trade Centre calculations

Table 2: Value of CARICOM's top 10 Imports from China, 2001-10 (US$ thousands)

Product label	Total value(US$), 2001-10
All products	9,484,332
Ships, boats and other floating structures	2,417,264
Electrical, electronic equipment	7,870,13
Machinery, nuclear reactors, boilers, etc	7,120,12
Articles of iron or steel	5,220,17
Iron and steel	3,493,14
Plastics and articles thereof	3,307,82
Vehicles other than railway, tramway	3,145,13
Articles of apparel, accessories, not knit or crochet	2,921,78
Furniture, lighting, signs, prefabricated buildings	2,879,00
Footwear, gaiters and the lilie, parts thereof	2,829,33

Source: Based on International Trade Centre calculations

Tables 1 and 2 show that China's top 10 products are finished manufactured products while CARICOM's top 10 exports are raw materials. This indicates that there may be existing opportunities in the Chinese market that are underexploited by CARICOM entrepreneurs, such as plants and cut flowers, meat, dairy products and eggs. Chinese products may also be competing with local businesses, farmers and craftsmen in product areas such as ceramics, beverages and vegetables.

Figure 2: Exports from CARICOM to China, US and the EU, 2001-10

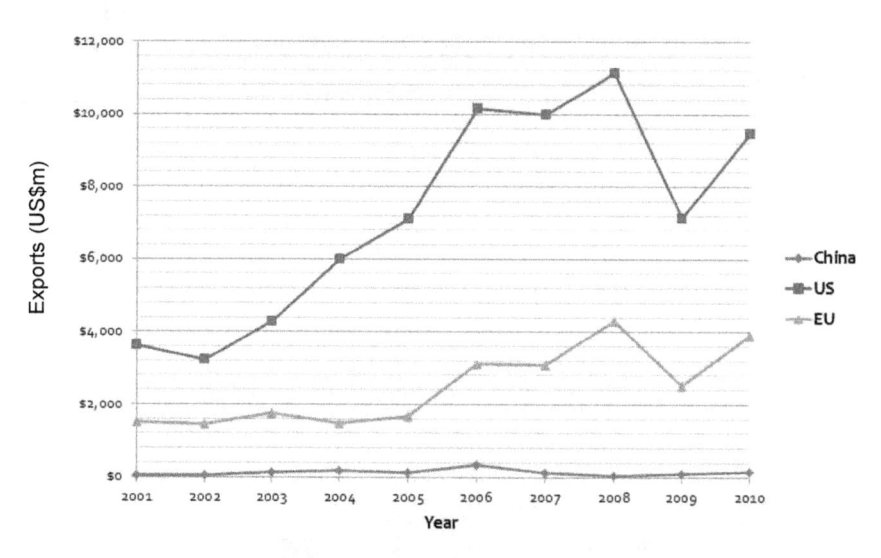

Source: Based on International Trade Centre calculations

China's Economic Diplomacy

Figure 2 illustrates that exports to China have fluctuated over the 10-year period. Additionally, China is a very small export market vis-à-vis the US and the EU for the 10-year period.

Figure 3: Imports to CARICOM from China, US and the EU, 2001-10

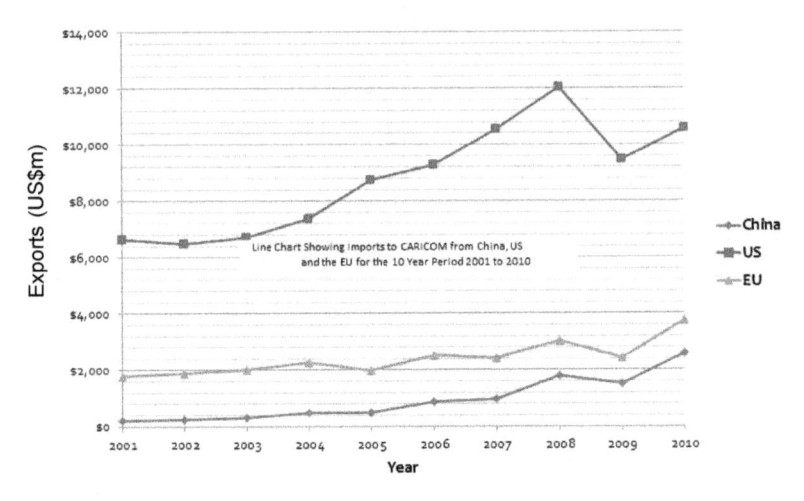

Source: Based on International Trade Centre calculations

Figure 3 shows that, unlike the exports market from 2001-10, China has become an increasingly significant import market compared with traditional partners, the US and the EU. However, as imports from China have increased, imports from the US and the EU have not been not decreasing. Chinese imports, therefore, do not seem to be displacing those from the US and the EU, but total imports are increasing with China in the equation.

Trade balance between CARICOM and China, US and the EU, 2001-10

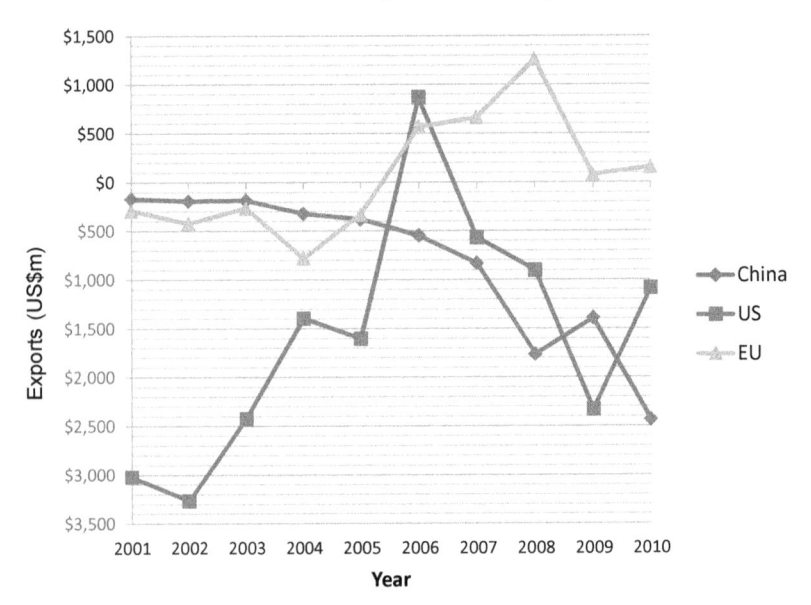

Source: Based on International Trade Centre calculations

Figure 4 shows that whereas there have been periods of surplus in trade with the US and the EU, there has consistently been a trade deficit with China for the ten year period.

Having looked at developments in the trade arena, we now examine recent examples of development projects with select Caribbean countries. In September 2011, Jamaica signed grant agreements totalling US$8m with China. China has in the past assisted with several major projects, including one in the tourism sector that involved the construction of Montego Bay Convention Centre in 2011. China signed a loan agreement with the government of Jamaica in 2011 valued at US$400m for infrastructural work. The US$65.3m Palisadoes Peninsula project is being financed by a loan from China EXIM Bank (Jamaica Information Service 2011). Trinidad and Tobago received Rmb40m in grant funding from the Chinese government during the Third China Caribbean Trade and Economic Forum. In 2009, the National Academy of the Performing Arts (NAPA) was completed through a concessional loan by China (Government of the Republic of Trinidad and Tobago 2009) and in March 2011, Trinidad and Tobago and China signed a concessional loan agreement valued at Rmb210m for the completion of infrastructural work on NAPA (Tach 2011). China and the Bahamas signed a technical and cooperation agreement ahead of the Third China Caribbean Trade and Economic Forum, which provides grant funding for infrastructural and other projects. This agreement brings the total Chinese investment in the Bahamas to an estimated US$2.66bn (Thompson 2011). In June 2011, China agreed to provide Barbados with a grant of just over US$3m for various small-scale development projects (Greene 2011). In 2011, Chinese grant funding built four scoreboards for the Widley Gymnasium in Barbados valued at US$1.7m (Austin 2011). At the Third China Caribbean Trade and Economic Forum, Guyana and China signed an agreement for a Rmb30m grant for funding several projects (Stabroek News 2011). Over a 40-year period, China helped fund about 40 projects in the form of grants, and interest-free and concessional loans to Guyana and wrote off nine mature debts (Kaiteur News 2011). Upon establishing diplomatic relations with Dominica, the Chinese promised to undertake infrastructure development on four projects in the island totalling more than US$100m (Saunders 2011). Dominica has received approximately ECD$7.2m from China, having signed an agreement on technical and economic cooperation. China agreed in 2007 to provide grant aid of USD$100,000 for disaster relief (Government of Dominica 2007). It has assisted Antigua and Barbuda in various areas, including a street lighting programme, concessionary loans and grants for the Sir Vivian Richards Cricket Stadium, an airport terminal and a secondary school in Five Islands (Caribarena News 2011). In 2010, China provided 86% of the cost of rehabilitating the St. Paul's Sports, Cultural and Development Organisation in Grenada (Government of Grenada 2011). In Suriname, China has designed and built the Foreign Ministry building and provided aid in the following areas: military assistance, construction of low-income housing, help with shrimp farming and an upgrade of the national television network (Simone 2011).

While there may be benefits to be derived from this type of engagement, there are concerns about the balance of the benefits. One of the distinct features of development cooperation in the area of infrastructure projects in the Caribbean is the dominance of Chinese labour. In the case of Trinidad and Tobago, between 2008 and 2011, out of 2,996 Chinese who obtained permits to work, approximately 2,731 were for the construction sector (Ministry of National Security). This means that nearly 3,000 Chinese workers held jobs that would otherwise have gone to Trinidadians. In Guyana, Chinese investments in the metal and manufacturing sectors totalled US$1bn between 2003 and 2008 (Kiateur News 2011). In Jamaica, the Chinese company COMPLANT acquired assets of Jamaica's sugar industry, and in August 2011 China announced plans to invest approximately US$156m to renovate three sugar factories and adjoining land (Douglas 2011). In August 2011, China Investment Corporation (CIC) announced plans to acquire a 10% stake from French firm GDF Suez in Atlantic LNG in Trinidad and Tobago. CIC will also acquire 30% of GDF Suez's Exploration and Production division (Bagoo 2011). Chinese foreign direct investment in the Caribbean reached US$72bn from the end of 2001 to 2005. However, this investment has been concentrated in manufacturing and has not been matched by investments in the services sector (CRNM 2007). This limits the extent to which CARICOM businesses are able to pursue linkages with their Chinese counterparts.

The above developments have implications for Caribbean development, regional integration and Caribbean foreign policy relations. This is the subject of the concluding section.

V. Implications and the way forward

The huge and increasing trade deficit that exists between CARICOM and China is very unhealthy and unsustainable for long-term development. Increasing amounts of cheaper Chinese imports may also be replacing local products. CARICOM countries need to balance their efforts at boosting exports to China against promoting infrastructural development. Additionally, there is need to undertake and evaluate the effectiveness of infrastructural projects to assess their impact on social and economic development.

Second, the trade relationship between China and the Caribbean is largely based on the importation of manufactured products from China and the exportation of raw materials from the Caribbean. Scholars have already observed that the nature of the trade relationship with China holds the danger of replicating that of the Caribbean with its traditional partners (Girvan 2011). Additionally, the nature of Chinese investment employing mainly Chinese labour does not promote technology transfer. Many would have hoped that the relationship with China, a fellow developing country, would have been different from that of traditional partners and would have encouraged innovation and creativity, but this is not the case up to this point.

Third, CARICOM has not engaged with China in a manner that promotes regional integration. This is reflected in the predominantly bilateral nature of the relationship which may lead to competition among Caribbean States for assistance from China. If this trend continues, it poses the danger of further hindering the cohesion of CARICOM and the integration process. Regional integration should be the foundational pillar for informing the nature of engagement with China.

Fourth, the increasingly comfortable relationship that the Caribbean has now developed with China means that the latter has greater confidence in its foreign policy relations with other partners. China is now seen as a favoured partner, which may result in a divergence from traditional partners, especially for development cooperation. The fact that China is seen by the Caribbean as a fellow developing country may further contribute to the shift. China comes with advantages, among them the fact that they it was never a coloniser and is not perceived as having been in an exploitative relationship with the Caribbean in the past. There is therefore a greater feeling of camaraderie and partnership that makes relations with the emerging players more comfortable even if it is not necessarily always more beneficial.

In this context, the Caribbean may be able to use the opportunity to take advantage of competition among emerging and traditional players for their benefit in negotiations and other areas of engagement. This has already sparked renewed interest in the Caribbean (and Africa) by the EU, for example. The EU's interest in seeking Caribbean support in multilateral forums through the Joint Caribbean-EU Strategy (JCEUS) is a manifestation of this interest. The JCEUS is in part informed by the EU's recognition that its position and influence in the region is being challenged. This scenario also has implications for US foreign policy towards the region. Although the Caribbean has declined in geo-political/strategic importance, there is now cause for concern regarding the US's security for example. This concern stems from China's investments in oil and gas in Venezuela and the wider hemisphere.

Fifth, China's policy of non-interference in the governance of countries and claims of no conditions attached to development assistance have a special appeal to Caribbean countries. This is because of complaints about cumbersome and tied assistance related to aid and development assistance from traditional partners. For instance, EU trade and development cooperation and assistance are dependent on partners' ability to adhere to particular normative principles. The Caribbean is therefore drawn to China because it is easier to secure loans and access development assistance.

Although China has denied that it is pursuing a particular model of development, there are some key elements that are common in its engagement with third countries: China has indicated that each country should choose a development path that is suited to its peculiar needs; China claims that non-interference is at the centre of its policy of engagement and claims not to get involved in a country's internal affairs; China's development strategy is not driven by ideological considerations and it does not insist on values such as good governance, democracy and human rights as a prerequisite for engagement on trade and development cooperation. While it is true that China is not concerned with governance, human rights and the rule of law, there are other types of conditions, for example in the use of Chinese labour, design and technology associated with Chinese aid and investment. Additionally, a lack of emphasis on human rights, the rule of law and good governance may be detrimental for the long-term social and economic development of the Caribbean Region.

In conclusion, the critical value of any type of engagement with new or traditional players is the extent to which the relationship strengthens regional integration, an important prerequisite for Caribbean development. Development projects and programmes should be part of a broad, long-term strategic plan for strengthening regional integration. A more coordinated regional approach is therefore necessary in directing Chinese aid and development assistance towards Caribbean integration. Perhaps one way this can be fostered is through greater coordination among Caribbean air and sea ports, and through telecoms networks and innovation relating to ease of travel among CARICOM countries. In this vein, it is important for CARICOM, like China did in 2008, to produce a joint policy paper towards China as well as towards other emerging and traditional partners.

Chapter 6

Prospects for China's economic diplomacy in the new century

Since China's entry into the WTO in 2001, its interaction with the world economy has entered the fast lane. In the 10 years since its accession, China's economic diplomacy has developed into an important part of its overall diplomacy. In 2004, President Hu Jintao and Premier Wen Jiabao stressed the importance of economic diplomacy at the ninth Diplomatic Envoys Meeting and at the Working Conference on China's Economic Diplomacy Towards Developing Countries. The two leaders also put forward a guiding principle for China's economic diplomacy: "mutual respect, equal treatment, promoting economic development through political mutual trust, integrating politics and economic development, reciprocating and mutual benefit, common development, diversified forms, and focusing on actual effects".

In 2005, Premier Wen introduced the concept of "economic diplomacy" in a government work report for the first time. The report at 17th Party Congress stated that, "as an important constituent part of the nation's overall diplomacy, economic diplomacy should make a difference". The financial crisis in 2008 was a turning point, resulting in tremendous change to the international political and economic order, which has benefited developing countries. In addition, the crisis pushed forward the transformation of the system of international economic governance. China's status and role in this transformation has experienced change, shifting from "keeping a low profile" in the past to "doing something". During the National People's Congress and Chinese Political Conference in 2009, foreign minister Yang Jiechi summarised the key tasks of China's economic diplomacy, which had stepped out of the initial stage and headed steadily for the fast lane.

Peace and development remain the current themes. To inject vigour and vitality into the Chinese economy and raise its competitiveness is the main content of China's economic reform as well as a prerequisite for and guarantee of economic exchanges with foreign countries. In the past decade, especially after the economic crisis, China's economic diplomacy has been confronted by complex internal and external environments.

From the perspective of the internal environment, China, given its special national conditions and stage of development, is faced with a series of challenges and obstacles. First, it is a large developing country with uneven regional economic development whose economic development has been inhibited by a lack of energy and other resources. Second, China has a huge population and its human resource and scientific and cultural levels are still on the low side. Third, its foreign trade and economic cooperation feature a high degree of dependence, while its export-oriented economy lacks growth potential and employment pressures are emerging. Fourth, its financial market system is characterised by low efficiency; financial security and the supervision system are far from perfect and reform of the financial system lags behind. Fifth, the risk of a huge quantity of foreign exchange reserves and pressure of external debt servicing has gradually built up. Sixth, China's reform in the currency and finance markets has focused primarily on national security issues. Seventh, a traditional planned economic system inhibits Chinese economy's integration with the world economy. Eighth, public policy and service system is far from perfect and people's livelihoods need to be improved. Ninth, China has adhered to the socialist road, which has met with hostility and suppression. Last but not the least, owing to historic tradition, China's foreign policy tends to be politically conservative and unitary, as a result of which it cannot satisfy the actual needs of the country's foreign contacts.

On the other hand, China's economic development and social progress have provided advantageous conditions for the transformation of its economic diplomacy. For one thing, through decades of development, China's economy has become the second largest in the world. Now, China is the largest exporting country, the second largest importing country, the third largest importer of services and the fourth largest exporter, making the country a world economic giant and laying a solid foundation for the future expansion of foreign relations. For another, China boasts a huge domestic market with increasing business potential and appeal; the strength of the market has enhanced China's right to speak in the post-economic-crisis era. Furthermore, China has considerable late-mover advantages. Therefore, while exploring the development road with its own characteristics, China represents the interests of developing countries and participates in formulating international rules. What's more, Chinese state-owned enterprises, with their great strength, have an advantage in international competition. Private enterprises are very aggressive and have gained a good momentum in internationalisation, becoming the main force of China's economic diplomacy. Besides, China is able to pool efforts to accomplish major undertakings. China boasts a strong social cohesion which guarantees the implementation of the nation's economic and external strategy. China follows a peaceful development path that is chosen by its people and implements a strategy of opening-up and cooperation under the guidance of the Scientific Outlook on Development, which are a solid foundation for economic diplomacy.

From the perspective of the external environment, China's economic diplomacy is faced with a series of new situations and challenges. As the international financial crisis has a far-reaching influence, global problems emerge all the time. Unbalanced global development has continued and global industry is undergoing a restructuring. The comprehensive recovery of the world economy is faced with a series of uncertainties. Rising trade protectionism makes China the largest target country of global trade remedy measures. Issues concerning trade friction are increasingly serious, expanding from the traditional manufacturing industry to emerging industries. What's more, technical barriers, green barriers, and trade friction with emerging countries have multiplied. Therefore, China has a hidden worry about "falling into the trap of the international division of labour". America's Rebalance Strategy in the Asia-Pacific has brought about an adjustment of the order in the region. As a result, destabilising factors around China threatens the country's traditional security. China is faced with an unfavourable geopolitical situation, with territorial disputes and regional problems emerging all the time. With the rise of emerging big powers, international political and economic patterns have undergone significant changes. Developed countries and emerging countries, to safeguard their own development benefits, take advantage of international rules and their own strengths to marginalise China or cause international competition. Apart from this, faced with mounting pressure in the area of climate change and environmental protection, China is required to fulfil international obligations as a responsible big power.

Second, the world power pattern and international economic order is expected to be reconstructed, which provides China's economic diplomacy with an important strategic opportunity. The Report of the 18th National Congress of the CPC pointed out: "With the in-depth development of world multi-polarisation and economic globalisation, cultural diversity and social informationalisation have witnessed steady advancement; scientific and technical revolution heralds new breakthroughs; global cooperation expands in a multi-layered and comprehensive manner. As the overall national strength of emerging market countries and developing countries is growing, international balance of power develops in a direction conducive to safeguarding world peace. As a result, more favourable conditions are available to maintain the overall stability of the international situation". The frustration of globalisation highlights the importance of economic diplomacy. Multi-polarity expands the operational space of economic diplomacy. Process of regionalisation provides multiple platforms for economic diplomacy. An open economy featuring mutual benefit lays a foundation for economic diplomacy to have a positive impact. The US carries forward its Asia Pacific rebalancing strategy, which, from the short term, seems to contain China. However, in the long run, it is likely to provide an external opportunity for China and other countries in the Asia-Pacific region to cooperate in economic diplomacy concerning economic development, trade and security, urging China to attach importance to East Asia and Southeast Asia from the strategic level. In addition, the new technological and energy revolutions make it possible for China to participate in international competition and formulate international rules.

During the 10 years when Hu Jintao and Wen Jiabao headed the administration, no significant changes occurred in the orientation of China's economic diplomacy. Thinking and strategy of China's economic diplomacy entered a period of relative stability. First, the opening strategy for mutual benefit; second, adhering to the principle of integrating independence and participating in economic globalisation; third, a new proposal for enhancing cooperation of the international community. However, the past decade has witnessed some changes, which are mainly involved in the strategy and modes of economic diplomacy. By shifting its attention from "promoting diplomacy through economic exchange" to "promoting economic development through diplomacy, China has attached greater importance to integrating itself into the international economic governance system and using the rules to bring about greater influence of its economic diplomacy. In addition, China has gradually disentangled itself from a condition that meant it was inhibited by the external environment. Now, it has become more confident in safeguarding its core economic interests and has had more methods to use.

Over the past decade, China has made tremendous progress in its economic diplomacy in areas such as foreign trade, investment, international finance, foreign aid, international energy cooperation and international environmental pollution reduction and control. It has also has scored remarkable achievements in developing an export-oriented economy and has become a strategic asset influencing the whole world. China has become the second largest economy and the largest exporting country in the world. In 2012, China's foreign trade volume amounted to nearly US$4,000bn, ranking second in the world; state foreign exchange reserves exceeded US$3,000bn; FDI reached US$77.2bn, rising to third place in the world. Furthermore, China has accelerated issues such as renminbi internationalisation, free trade zone construction and regional cooperation mechanisms. What's more, China's right to speak and decision-making power have increased in multilateral economic diplomatic platforms such as the UN, WTO, IMF and the World Bank. While China is deepening its institutional reform in a comprehensive way and developing its open economy, economic diplomacy, which is a powerful tool to coordinate domestic reform and open up to the outside world, will exert its influence in a wider range of fields and at more levels.

Over the past 10 years, China has played a more and more important role in the construction of international mechanisms. For example, China has spurred institutional cooperation between the BRICS countries; twice pushed forward reform of the IMF's voting rights; and actively participated in G20 summits. At regional level, China is committed to building up ASEAN 10+N, SCO, the China-Japan-South Korea Free Trade Area and Ministerial Conference of the Forum on China-Africa Cooperation. The 17th Congress of the CPC proposed the "implementation of a strategy of free trade zones" and stated that "supporting and improving international trade and financial institutions, promoting liberalisation of trade and investment that are of vital importance to the realisation of the development goal in the new era. None of them can be neglected". By 2015, a Regional Comprehensive Economic Partnership will have been established involving ASEAN plus China, Japan, South Korea, India, Australia and New Zealand, which has emerged from the Trans-Pacific Partnership Agreement (TPP). From ASEAN 10+3 to 10+6, a strategic consensus was reached at the summits of Southeast Asian leaders held in Phnom Penh, Cambodia. If the RCEP is established, it will be the largest free trade area in the world with a population of 3bn, and a total GDP of US$20,000bn. This is, in essence, a rudimentary "Asian Community".

Sino-US, Sino-EU and Sino-Africa cooperation have also made a breakthrough. China and the US have launched four rounds of strategic economic dialogue. China and the EU have issued documents on bilateral relations and established a comprehensive strategic partnership. Economic and trade ties between China and the EU have entered a honeymoon period, featuring high-speed development. In 2006, on the occasion of the 50th anniversary of the establishment of diplomatic relations between China and Egypt, the China-Africa Cooperation Forum Summit was convened in Beijing. This was a huge international gathering at the highest level and involved the greatest number of participants of state leaders in the history of Chinese diplomacy. It has become a milestone in the history of Sino-Africa relations.

Over the past 10 years, China has showcased its innovativeness and made breakthroughs in many fields. First, it has gradually attached importance to learning from and transforming international rules. Instead of continuing to passively follow international codes of practice, it is committed to influencing international economic rules under the current system framework. China sticks to its dual identity as both an "obligation undertaker" and a "progressive reformist". Second, China used to be a net recipient of foreign capital but now it has redoubled its efforts to invest abroad. With a favourable balance of trade in the early years of the 21st century, China has amassed huge foreign exchange reserves and stockpiled great wealth. Influenced by the financial crisis, China has a desperate need to transfer its surplus industrial capacity and capital through foreign investment abroad. As China is gradually becoming a new force of investment in the international market, it is up to the outside world to facilitate this investment and protect China's interests. This transformation is of vital significance to the interaction between China and the outside world. Third, China is implementing a national energy strategy, encouraging oil enterprises to "go global" to seek and expand oil resources, strengthen safety management of the oil and gas pipelines of central Asia and Russia to ensure the stability of energy supply and energy environmental safety. Fourth, China is accelerating the opening of the financial industry and enhancing financial security. It actively participates in international coordination and cooperation in coping with the international financial crisis, presses ahead with renminbi internationalisation, takes the initiative to promote convertibility of the currency, and reforms and improves domestic financial institutions so as to facilitate sustainable economic and social development. Fifth, China has redoubled its efforts to protect its overseas interests. In support of the "going global" strategy of Chinese enterprises, 230 Chinese embassies and consulates stationed throughout the world integrate its diplomatic resources into a service network. Several evacuations of Chinese nationals, for example from the Solomon Islands in 2006, from the Philippines in 2012 and from Libya in 2011, show China's national strength and determination to safeguard its overseas interests.

However, during the past 10 years, China has been confronted by many severe challenges. First, as trade protectionism in almost all countries has tended to rise, China's external economic environment is not optimistic. Second, the US's shift of its strategic focus to the Asia-Pacific region and some countries' interpretation of the "China Threat" will influence China's economic development. The global economy faces risks, coupled with frequent occurrences of trade friction, upward pressure on renminbi appreciation, and mounting pressure brought about by the rapid expansion of China's economic status. Third, China's huge trade volume has made the Chinese economy excessively dependent on foreign markets; steady economic growth is based on the production of commodities with low added-value, as a result of which a large number of energy and other resources have been damaged and consumed. Besides, it easily leads to trade sanctions from the outside world, which will deteriorate the trade environment. Fourth, China's rapid rises has caused the international community to look upon it with concern. Public opinion in the West sometimes asks "whether China will rule the world". On the other hand, these same countries are busy doing business with China and vying for the Chinese market.

Inevitably, there exist some problems and obstacles in China's economic diplomacy. First, the transition between China's economic strength and its political influence is not satisfactory. Though China's economic strength has grown, it has not brought about a dominant position in its foreign relations. Instead, it is faced with mounting pressure in international politics. "Growing strength" and "worsening conditions" have become an acute contradiction in China's economic diplomacy. The reason lies in the fact that China's economic strength has not been fully utilised. Nor has it been translated into actual influence in foreign relations. Economic resources flow among different governmental departments and become eliminated by bureaucracy. Only by pinpointing national interests, comprehensively implementing a grand strategy and enhancing internal coordination and the construction of an external strategic mechanism can China's economic strength be effectively put into use.

Second, China is faced with severe trade friction, involving issues such as product quality, standards, intellectual property, trade surplus, price standards, a high degree of foreign trade dependence and gloomy prospects for the sustainable development of foreign trade. So far, China's market economy status has not been fully recognised. Products involved in trade defence cases have shifted to consumer goods and middle and high-end products. Anti-dumping investigations against China launched by other emerging countries are on the rise.

Third, China's strategy for economic diplomacy still needs to be upgraded. Currently, China's economic diplomacy mostly involves addressing specific economic affairs and lacks a clear strategic goal and orientation, China finds it cannot handle many international economic issues. In view of this, China should establish a concept of economic diplomacy in a broad sense and pinpoint its foreign economic relations so that it can have a definite objective.

Fourth, China's economic diplomacy mechanism is far from perfect and coordination and cooperation between different units are insufficient. Though the Department of International Economic Affairs of the Ministry of Foreign Affairs, the Department of Outward Investment and Economic Cooperation of the Ministry of Commerce, the Department of International Affairs of the Ministry of Finance, the central bank and the institutions in charge of international finance have made joint efforts to build up a government-level network for a functional organisation of economic diplomacy, coordination between these agencies is far from mature. Sometimes, they contradict and hinder each other so that they fail to face up the challenges that are brought about by globalisation. Therefore, China should establish a high-level cross-department coordination mechanism and an advisory body in the core decision-making layer so as to enhance the top state leader's ability to manage its diplomatic activities and to form a macro strategy for economic diplomacy that transcends departmental interests.

Fifth, China lacks research and talented personnel in economic diplomacy. From 2003 to 2012, there were about 1,000 items with "economic diplomacy" as the key words concerning academic achievements. Among them, doctoral dissertations and Master's theses took up one-quarter. Major research and teaching units included the Research Center of Economic Diplomacy of Tsinghua University (2005), the Centre for Economic Diplomacy Studies of China Foreign Affairs University (2009), the China Center for International Economic Exchanges (2009), the Centre for Economic Diplomacy Studies of University of International Business and Economics (2010) and Wuhan University Center of Economic Diplomacy (2012). Generally speaking, there are just a few institutions and researchers in this regard. Besides, studies on economic diplomacy are still at the initial stage. Since its entry into the WTO, China has cultivated talent who are proficient in international economic negotiations, but they cannot satisfy the need of this economic power. Therefore, the level of decision-making and art of its implementation need to be improved.

The Chinese economy has entered a new development stage. Economic diplomacy will be one of China's diplomatic priorities in the following 10 years. During this period, the international economy will resume growth in its adjustment and economic globalisation will continue to forge ahead. Therefore, China needs to make a breakthrough in its economic diplomacy on the basis of its previous achievements so as to adapt to its domestic reform and opening up. According to its foreign minister Wang Yi, China will blaze new trails and forge ahead in its economic diplomacy. First of all, it will make great efforts in constructing the Silk Road Economic Belt which was put forward first by China and the 21st Century Silk Road on the Sea. This will be the focus of China's economic diplomacy. The Ministry of Commerce will push forward the construction of "one belt and one road", quicken the construction of free trade areas along the belt and the road, and collaborate with countries to study and carry out the cooperation measures.

Second, China will speed up the implementation of the strategy of multilateral and bilateral free trade areas and view various regional and cross-regional free trade proposals such as the Trans-Pacific Partnership Agreement (TPP) with an open mind. Actually, China's strategy for free trade areas has undergone a remarkable change, in that it pushes forward domestic economic reform by honouring its international commitments through free trade areas. This reform process focuses on high added-value industrial upgrading and innovation, as China quickened its opening up and integration into the world economic system through its entry into the WTO. With the stagnation of the WTO and the Doha round in recent years, China has had to assess the key role of free trade areas in its domestic economic reform.

Third, actively participating in reforming international economic governance system and continuously enhancing China's rule-formulating right and right to speak will become the key goal of China's economic diplomacy. Vice-Premier Wang Yang once said that, as competition in rules and standards are the highest level of competition, we should be more active, confident and responsible in participating in the transformation of the international system and the formulation of international rules and in handling global issues so as to enhance China's influence and to create a fairer and more rational international economic order.

The aim of economic diplomacy is to create a favourable external condition and stable international environment for the realisation of strategic targets. In the future, China must strive for mutual benefit through the dynamic process of establishing and maintaining its competitive edge. At the 18th National Congress of the CPC in 2012, "Scientific Outlook on Development" was established as the guiding ideology that the ruling party must follow for a long time to come. It will not only influence China's domestic economic development but also determine the strategy and orientation of the country's diplomacy. "We should take promoting economic and social development as the be-all and end-all in implementing the Scientific Outlook on Development"; "we should take people-first as the core standpoint of the in-depth implementation of the Scientific Outlook on Development"; "we should take implementing a complete, coordinated and sustained development as the basis for the in-depth implementation of the Scientific Outlook on Development; and "we should take overall planning and all-round consideration as the fundamental method of the in-depth implementation of the Scientific Outlook on Development".

China should deepen economic restructuring in a comprehensive way, speed up a fundamental shift of its economic growth mode, push forward the strategic restructuring of the economy and the integrated development of urban and rural areas so as to realise a harmonious development. The Scientific Outlook on Development, facilitating the close integration of "promoting social and economic development" with "people first", stresses that we should implement the strategy of building up the country's strength with talented people and build an innovation-oriented country with a view to realising "comprehensive, balanced and sustainable development". In addition, China should adjust its economic structure, expand domestic demand and employment, and redouble its efforts in protecting IPR protection so as to prepare well for further international competition.

Moreover, China should play its due role in reforming the existing international rule system and make great efforts to formulate new international systems and rules so as to become a rule-maker. China should take the initiative to undertake international obligations that are suited to its national strength, provide more international public goods, and build up more "interest communities" by pushing forward the reform of the UN and of global economic governance of the G20. Furthermore, China should press ahead with the integration of its cultural features and values in the construction of new systems and rules so as to make it fit the characteristics of developing countries and oriental culture. The coming new technological revolution featuring the integration of the internet and new energy involves fields such as information, new energy, new materials, biology, space and the oceans. This is the only way for China to strengthen its comprehensive national strength and competitive forces by innovative development strategy, increasing investment in developing science and technology, striving for the commanding heights of scientific, technical and economic competition.

The Scientific Outlook on Development points out the importance of "overall planning and all-round consideration" and "comprehensive, balanced and sustainable development". It makes positive comments on the favourable policies it has followed towards neighbouring countries, and also shows clearly the vital significance of its diplomacy towards its neighbours to China's peaceful development under the new security environment. In the course of the world's centre shifting to the Asia-Pacific region and the US putting forward an Asia-Pacific Rebalance Strategy, China's surrounding environment is more complex. As a result, it has become the most important external factor of China's diplomatic strategy and security strategy. How to control America's eastward strategic move and China's rising strategic strength, how to create an order for the Asian-Pacific region featuring mutual trust and mutual benefits are of vital significance to promote China's economic and social reform and to safeguard regional stability. China has proposed a new pattern of relationship between the great powers; followed the guiding principle of good-neighbourliness and implementing favourable policies to its neighbouring countries; expanded cooperation scope; taken full advantage of existing multilateral mechanisms; created new multilateral mechanisms; appropriately handled territorial disputes and various crises; enhanced close ties and mutual approval through cultural and public diplomacy.

China should strive to develop a low-carbon and green economy. In international climate negotiations, it should steadfastly represent the interests of developing countries. China should not only coordinate the stances of the developed and developing economies on climate policies and environmental exchange, but also safeguard the basic rights and special interests of backward countries so as to make overall plans and strive for a leading role in the negotiation on global climate rules. Apart from this, it should cultivate a comprehensive security concept, putting network security, sea safety, energy security, space security and other non-traditional securities into a grand security strategy so as to create a favourable external environment for China's economic development and transformation.

The international financial crisis still impacts the existing international economic and financial system and economic governance structure. To adapt itself to the new situation caused by economic globalisation, China should make all-round improvements in its open economy and push forward the establishment of a fairer and more rational international political and economic new order. The 18th National Congress of the CPC developed China's foreign strategy of "peace", "development" and "cooperation" into "win-win", thus forming a complete logical system, which is conducive to establishing a "more equal and balanced partnership for global development" so that all sides in the same position can help each other and share the rights and liabilities together for the common interests of human beings. "Cooperation for win-win" means advocating the consciousness of a community of common destiny; while pursuing its own interests, the country should give consideration to the rational concerns of other countries. All countries should, while pursuing their own development, promote the common development of all countries. Efforts should be made to establish a more equal and balanced partnership for global development so that all countries may pull together in times of trouble and shoulder rights and responsibilities for common interests".

Greater diversity has become an important element of China's diplomatic strategy, which is reflected in diversifications of objectives, participating roles, modes of diplomacy and diplomatic strategies. The overall arrangement of China's economic diplomacy should strive for a grand strategic pattern with big powers as the key, neighbouring countries as its priority, developing countries as the basis, multilateral mode as an important stage, a great number of bilateral strategic partnerships as the support, active participation in international organisations such as the UN and G20 as the platform, economic and trade exchanges featuring equal emphasis on "going global" and "bringing in" as the main contents and regional cooperation mechanisms such as free trade areas as an important strategic measure. The arrangement should serve to make overall plans and take all factors into consideration and play a positive role in safeguarding current comprehensive national interests and lasting peace and in building up a harmonious world featuring mutual benefit.

In terms of China's strategy for economic diplomacy, efforts should be made to do a better job in handling the contradictions between various strategies, starting with development and security. As China is still a developing country, development is a number one priority for the country. China should not surpass development for the sake of absolute security. The second area is development and ecological environment. China must overcome constraints in development and the ecological environment, make overall plans for these areas so as to strike a balance and strive for more development opportunities and larger development space. The third area is development and reform. For a long time, China's institutional reform has fallen behind reform of the substantial economy. Therefore, it should further its reform to expand its development space and potential. Reform is the path to development, and also a prerequisite for translating external challenges into external opportunities. Fourth: development and win-win. China advocates establishing a community of common destiny, hoping to develop itself and realise its national interests in a new type of international relations featuring equilibrium and mutual benefit. Such a development concept is a concentrated reflection of traditional Chinese culture and also an outstanding contribution of China's diplomatic strategy to world politics.

To transform its economic development mode and establish an all-around affluent society, China should seize the period of strategic opportunity in its economic diplomacy. First of all, it should safeguard its peaceful development through scientific strategic management and take advantage of its expanding economic strength and translating it into diplomatic resources which may be effectively put into use. Second, while conducting its economic diplomacy, China should, under the guidance of Scientific Outlook on Development, promote economic and social development and build a new type of international system and rules by implementing the development strategy, reform strategy and innovation strategy so as to upgrade its core competitiveness in the revolution of new science and technology and new energy. Third, it should deepen ties with neighbouring countries and emerging market countries by implementing a peripheral strategy, security strategy and ecological strategy so as to establish a comprehensive security system for peripheral security. China should actively participate in negotiations on global climate and play its role as a responsible big power to join hands with other countries to deal with global challenges. Fourth, China should endeavour to open up a new dimension for its economic diplomacy by further implementing the open economy strategy, taking mutual benefit, cooperation and win-win as the principal line and an overall strategy featuring overall planning and all-round consideration and multi-elements.

About the authors

Dr Zhang Xiaotong, executive director of Wuhan University Center of Economic Diplomacy, executive director of Wuhan University-University of the West Indies Caribbean Studies Center, associate professor of the Department of International Studies of the School of Political Science and Public Administration, Wuhan University. Dr Zhang has been a visiting scholar at the School of Advanced International Studies of The Johns Hopkins University, in the US since September 2014. He studied at Shanghai International Studies University, China Foreign Affairs University, The College of Europe and VUB-Vrije Universiteit Brussel (ULB), where he obtained his doctoral degree of politics and social sciences. In addition, he was in charge of economic and trade affairs towards America and Europe at China's Ministry of Commerce. From 2004 to 2010 he worked for China's diplomatic corps in the EU. From 2011 to 2012, he worked for the Office of American Affairs under the Department of American and Oceanic Affairs at China's Ministry of Commerce (Mofcom). He participated in multilateral (WTO, APEC), bilateral (Sino-EU, Sino-US) and regional trade negotiations. His research focuses are economic diplomacy, Sino-US and Sino-EU economic and trade relations. He is one of the co-founders of Economic Diplomacy, an electronic academic journal. He published his monograph Brussels Diary and many theses in domestic and overseas journals such as China International Studies, Foreign Affairs Review, Chinese Journal of European Studies, International Trade, Northeast Asia Forum and Journal of World Trade (SSCI). He was invited to deliver keynote speeches and lectures at institutions including the Organisation for Economic Co-operation and Development (OECD), the European Parliament, Chatham House and The London School of Economics and Political Science.

Dr Hongyu Wang holds a BA in politics, an MA in administration and a PhD in Political Science from Vrije Universiteit Brussel (VUB), Belgium, together with a PhD in International Relations from Renmin University of China (RUC). Currently, Dr Wang is an associate professor, MA students' supervisor and executive director of the Centre for Economic Diplomacy at the School of International Relations (SIR) at the University of International Business and Economics (UIBE) in Beijing. Dr. Wang also affiliates with the Institute for European Studies (IES) at VUB as a senior associate researcher. He has published dozens of books, book chapters and articles on China's economic diplomacy and EU politics. He has led several research programmes funded by the Chinese government and his university. His research fields include European studies, international political economy, policy networks, EU-China relations and Chinese economic diplomacy. His email address: wanghongyu@uibe.edu.cn

Zhou Yongsheng, born in April 1963, professor of the Institute of International Relations at China Foreign Affairs University, Ph.D.; Director of Programme of Japan Policy Studies at The International Relations Institute, China Foreign Affairs University. His research focuses include: international relations in the Asia-Pacific, Japanese diplomacy and economic diplomacy. He has published more than 360 academic articles on international issues. His works of academic research include: Economic Diplomacy (published by China Youth Publishing House in February 2004) and Sino-Japanese Reconciliation: Road to Common Prosperity (Japanese version), first edition published by The Duan Press in December 2005.

Li Wei is an associate professor of International Political Economy (IPE) at the School of International Studies, Renmin University of China, Beijing. He serves as the vice dean of the Department of International Politics at the School. Before that he was a postdoctoral research fellow at the Institute of International Studies, Tsinghua University, Beijing. He earned his Ph.D at Fudan University in Shanghai. His areas of expertise are international relations theory and international political economy and his current research focuses on the politics of renminbi internationalisation and the reform of the international monetary system. Li Wei was a visiting scholar at the US Asia-Pacific Center for Security Studies (APCSS) based in Hawaii. He is the author of Institutional Changes and US International Economic Polices (Shanghai People's Publishing House, 2010, Chinese) and Balance Against the US Dollar (forthcoming, Chinese) as well as a number of articles on international monetary politics in leading Chinese IR Journals. He has translated Jonathan D. Kirshner's Currency and Coercion and David Kang's Crony Capitalism into Chinese. His e-mail address: Liwei09@ruc.edu.cn

Su Liang is a doctor of international relations. He studied at Renmin University of China and the College of Europe. His doctorate research subject was security and defence policies of Europe. His major academic interests include: European integration, EU-China relations and diplomatic studies. At present, he works as a journalist for a news agency.

Wu Junyi, is a research assistant to the Research Center for Economic Diplomacy of the University of International Business and Economics (UIBE). She majors in international politics (specialising in economic diplomacy) at UIBE's School of International Relations. Her research interests include: relations between major countries, relations between China and its neighbouring countries, politics and the economy of the Middle East .

Li Jing, associate professor of the Department of International Studies, post graduate supervisor, is vice-chairman of the Etiquettes Society of Hubei, member of Hubei Association for International Studies; executive vice-director and secretary-general of the Organising Committee of the First Hubei Etiquette Contest & Etiquette Image Ambassador, director of the Committee of Experts (Judging Panel). From 1996 to 2001, his masters' degree programme was European Political Science and his doctoral degree was International Studies at the VUB-Vrije Universiteit Brussel. In China, he was engaged in teaching and research on diplomatic studies, the comity of nations, and the Taiwan question. In recent years, he has published theses for prestigious core journals and at international conferences. He wrote Contemporary Etiquettes Series, which is a prescribed textbook for undergraduates and postgraduates in many domestic colleges and universities including Wuhan University, and is also on the reading list of many prestigious Chinese colleges and universities. It has been published for Communist Party members and cadres of government agencies (the book can be found in major bookstores and websites) of Zhejiang, Hunan, Guangdong, Inner Mongolia and other areas of China.

Liu Xing was born in Wuhan in 1989. She teaches at Wuhan New Oriental School, having studied at the School of Political Science and Public Administration, Wuhan University since 2011. In 2013, she obtained a masters' degree in international relations from Wuhan University. Her research focuses on China's economic diplomacy, energy diplomacy and the Taiwan Question. Her masters' thesis is entitled "A Study of the Roles of China's State-owned Oil Enterprises in National Oil Diplomacy".

Yan Zhanyu, a research assistant at the Research Center for Economic Diplomacy of University of International Business and Economics (UIBE), majors in international politics (specialising in economic diplomacy) at UIBE's School of International Relations. His research focuses on economic diplomacy between major countries and theories of international relations. He has published many articles, including Buddhism in International Relations, Structural Construction of Power: Trade of Scarce Resources and Act of States, and A Comparison between Structuralism and Reductionism under Counterfactual Reasoning.

Du Xiaona majors in international politics (specialising in economic diplomacy) at the School of International Relations of the University of International Business and Economics (UIBE). Her research interests focus on relations between major countries, relations between China and its neighbouring countries, and the politics and economy of the Middle East.

Chai Xiaolin serves as China's Deputy Permanent Representative to the United Nations Industrial Development Organisation. Before that, she headed the Department of WTO Affairs as Director General. A long-time practitioner in international development cooperation and a senior official for multilateral trade negotiations, Chai has also devoted 10 years to working for the United Nations Children's Fund (UNICEF). A graduate of Beijing Foreign Trade Institute in 1983, she received a Master in Public Administration at Harvard in 2001 with an honour for excellence in studies by the Mason Fellow Programme at the Kennedy School. Chai is also a frequent contributor on the issue of the multilateral trading system to prominent publications and is interviewed by the media in China.

Yuan Miao is a research assistant to the Research Center for Economic Diplomacy of the University of International Business and Economics (UIBE). She majors in international politics (specialising in economic diplomacy) at UIBE's School of International Relations. She took part in scientific research projects such as Correlation Index of the International Strategies of the World's Major Countries, a special project by the School of International Relations, in which she was in charge of data collection, compilation and analysis.

Liu Danyang is a masters' degree candidate of diplomatic studies at the School of International Relations of the University of International Business and Economics (UIBE). She is a research assistant to UIBE's Research Center for Economic Diplomacy. Her research focuses on currency and financial diplomacy, regional economy and diplomacy.

Zhou Wenxing is from the School of Political Science and Public Administration at Wuhan University. His research interests include studies on Taiwan and Chinese diplomacy.

Zhang Chengxin is from the School of Political Science and Public Administration at Wuhan University. His research interests include Chinese peripheral diplomacy after the Cold War and the diplomacy of Southeast Asian countries towards China.

Li Hongjia is a graduate from VUB-Vrije Universiteit Brussel. At present, she is a doctoral candidate specialising in the world economy at the China Institute for WTO Studies at the University of International Business and Economics and works as a research assistant to the Research Center for Economic Diplomacy at the University of International Business and Economics. Her research orientations include: transnational corporations and national trade strategies, international game-playing on environmental issues, Sino-EU relations in economic diplomacy. She took part in key research projects including the National Social Sciences Foundation and has published many articles in periodicals such as Computer Engineering and Designand China's Business Administration.

About the Authors

Ge Jianting is a lecturer at the School of Political Science and Public Administration, Wuhan University. From September 2002 to July 2006 he studied international relations at the Department of Policy Studies at Kyorin University and obtained a bachelors degree in policy studies. From April 2007 to March 2009, he studied international relations at the Department of Sociology at the Graduate School of Letters at Soka University in Japan and obtained a masters degree in sociology. From April 2009 to March 2012, he studied international relations at the Department of Sociology at the Graduate School of Letters at Soka University and obtained a PhD in sociology.

Li Yiheng is a research assistant to the Research Center for Economic Diplomacy at the University of International Business and Economics (UIBE). She specialised in economic diplomacy at UIBE's School of International Relations. Her research focuses on economic diplomacy.

Marlen Belgibayev is a research associate at Wuhan University Research Centre for Economic Diplomacy. He received his B.A. from Kazakh Ablai Khan University of International Relations and World Languages in 2013. In 2011-12, he was an exchange student at Kyung Hee University in South Korea, majoring in International Affairs. From 2011 to 2013, he worked as a leading researcher at the Institute for Economic Development and Economic Affairs (IDEA), a think tank located in Kazakhstan where he did analytical research related to public policy, the rule of law, private property and entrepreneurship development. In 2013, he was invited to the School for Public Policy Research Methods in India where, together with researchers from 16 countries, took part in a workshop on statistical analysis and how to apply it in public policy research. His articles have been published on several internet sites and in business magazines. In addition to his scholarly activity, he received the military rank of lieutenant in the reserve of the Armed Forces of Kazakhstan in 2014.

Tan Xiangning works at the Center for China & Globalisation where she specialises in the study on talents. She has participated in the study of many government research subjects. She obtained a bachelors' degree in economics from South-Central University for Nationalities and a masters' degree in international relations from Wuhan University.

Annita Montoute has been a lecturer at the Institute of International Relations at the University of the West Indies since July 2010. She lectures on International organisations, global governance and multilateralism at the Post Graduate Diploma and Msc. levels. She was a Research Fellow at the European Centre for Development Policy Management (ECDPM) in 2012.